The Sierra Club Family Outdoors Guide

The Sierra Club Outdoors Activities Guides

BACKCOUNTRY SKIING: *The Sierra Club Guide to Skiing off the Beaten Track*, by Lito Tejada-Flores

BIKE TOURING: *The Sierra Club Guide to Outings on Wheels*, by Raymond Bridge

CAVING: *The Sierra Club Guide to Spelunking*, by Lane Larson and Peggy Larson

THE COMPLETE BICYCLE COMMUTER: *The Sierra Club Guide to Wheeling to Work*, by Hal Zina Bennett

EXPLORING UNDERWATER: *The Sierra Club Guide to Scuba and Snorkeling*, by John L. Culliney and Edward S. Crockett

LAND NAVIGATION HANDBOOK: *The Sierra Club Guide to Map and Compass*, by W. S. Kals

SIMPLE FOODS FOR THE PACK: *The Sierra Club Guide to Delicious, Natural Foods for the Trail*, revised and updated, by Claudia Axcell, Diana Cooke and Vikki Kinmont

THE SIERRA CLUB FAMILY OUTDOORS GUIDE: *Hiking, Backpacking, Camping, Bicycling, Water Sports, and Winter Activities with Children*, by Marlyn Doan

WALKING SOFTLY IN THE WILDERNESS: *The Sierra Club Guide to Backpacking*, revised and updated, by John Hart

WEATHERING THE WILDERNESS: *The Sierra Club Guide to Practical Navigation*, by William E. Reifsnyder

WILDWATER: *The Sierra Club Guide to Kayaking and Whitewater Boating*, by Lito Tejada-Flores

The Sierra Club Family Outdoors Guide

HIKING, BACKPACKING, CAMPING,
BICYCLING, WATER SPORTS, AND
WINTER ACTIVITIES WITH CHILDREN

Marlyn Doan

SIERRA CLUB BOOKS

SAN FRANCISCO

The Sierra Club, founded in 1892 by John Muir, has devoted itself to the study and protection of the earth's scenic and eco-logical resources—mountains, wetlands, woodlands, wild shores and rivers, deserts and plains. The publishing program of the Sierra Club offers books to the public as a nonprofit edu-cational service in the hope that they may enlarge the public's understanding of the Club's basic concerns. The point of view expressed in each book, however, does not necessarily represent that of the Club. The Sierra Club has some sixty chapters coast to coast, in Canada, Hawaii, and Alaska. For information about how you may participate in its programs to preserve wilderness and the quality of life, please address inquiries to Sierra Club, 730 Polk Street, San Francisco, CA 94109.

Library of Congress Cataloging-in-Publication Data
Doan, Marlyn, 1936–
    The Sierra Club family outdoors guide / by Marlyn Doan.
      p. cm.
    Rev. ed. of: Starting small in the wilderness. c1979.
    Includes bibliographical references and index.
    ISBN 0-87156-442-4
    1. Family recreation. I. Doan, Marlyn, 1936– Starting small in the wilderness. II. Sierra Club. III. Title.
    GV182.8.D53 1995
    790—dc20
                                94-35087
                                      CIP

We gratefully acknowledge Frederick H. Kahn, M.D., and Bar-bara R. Visscher, M.D., for permission to reprint material from "Water Disinfectant in the Wilderness, A Simple, Effective Method of Iodination," *The Western Journal of Medicine*, 122: 450–453.

Production by Robin Rockey • Cover design by Big Fish • Book design by Amy Evans • Illustrations by Linda Wagoner and Stephane Krieshok • Composition by Wilsted & Taylor

Printed on acid-free paper containing a minimum of 50% re-covered waste paper of which at least 10% of the fiber content is post-consumer waste.

10 9 8 7 6 5 4 3 2 1

Contents

Acknowledgments

In writing this book, I owe special thanks to innumerable people. I am particularly grateful to the many families who shared the results of their own outdoor experiences with me. I want to express special appreciation to the people who have over the years inspired our family to go into the wilderness with children.

Without the help of my own children, the ideas in this book would have been untried theories. My special thanks to David, Amy, and Laura. They have been outdoor companions and gear testers without equal. Finally, my appreciation goes to my husband, Allen, who has shared with me the responsibility, work, and fun of taking children into the outdoors. These family times in the outdoors will always represent the very best memories of our past experiences together.

My deepest appreciation goes to Zola Ross who, with positive encouragement, taught me to write and teach. She also had the patience and kindness to read the entire rough draft of the original manuscript. This revised edition is dedicated to her memory.

WE'RE NOT THE ONLY ONES WHO THINK POLLUTION STINKS.

Photo by Art Wolfe

Pollution is in the air we breathe, the water we drink and the food we eat. It's destroying irreplaceable wildlife habitat, endangering thousands of species of plants and animals.

But you can help stop this senseless destruction by joining the Sierra Club. Together, we can sniff out a solution. Please join today.

M E M B E R S H I P   FO

☐ **Yes,** *I want to find a solution to pollution!*

NEW MEMBER NAME

ADDRESS

CITY/STATE   ZIP

☐ **Gift Membership:** A gift announcement card will be sent for your use.
Enter *your* name and address below.

DONOR NAME

ADDRESS

CITY/STATE   ZIP

Membership Categories (CHECK ONE)

	Individual	Joint
REGULAR *INTRODUCTORY OFFER*	☐ ~~$35~~ $25	☐ **$43**
SUPPORTING	☐ $50	☐ $58
CONTRIBUTING	☐ $100	☐ $108
STUDENT	☐ $15	☐ $23
SENIOR	☐ $15	☐ $23
LIMITED INCOME	☐ $15	☐ $23
LIFE	☐ $750	☐ $1000

Dues are not tax-deductible. Annual dues include subscription
to *Sierra* magazine ($7.50) and chapter publications ($1).

Enclose check or money order and mail to:

Sierra Club   J94GOINS1

P.O. Box 52968, Boulder, CO 80321

Residents of Canada, please remit in Canadian funds to:
Suite 303, 517 College Street, Toronto, Ontario MG6 4A2 (Eastern Canada);
P.O. Box 8202, Victoria, British Columbia, V8W 3R8 (Western Canada).

Recycled Paper ♺

1

Before You Begin

TO A CHILD, a mile is 5,280 interesting little things
to see. Taking youngsters into the outdoors is a slow,
one-step-at-a-time process, but when adults tune in to the
wilderness world as a child perceives it, their own experiences become rich and full. Last summer, I hiked into alpine high country with a group of adults. In a single day
we climbed 10 steep and tiring miles, stopping only for rest
and sustenance. The setting was a green blur. Until I
reached the top, which was my goal, I essentially saw
nothing.

Outdoor travel with children is not like that, and I am
glad. When we go into the backcountry with youngsters,
we never "make time." Although we cover very little
ground, we see everything—every centipede, moth, and
butterfly, every mushroom and fungus, every tadpole and
frog, every mica-speckled rock, every tidepool, anemone,
and hermit crab. We see patterns in the bark of the trees
and find porcupine quills underfoot. We discover salaman-
ders in ponds. In the high branches of trees we sight bird
nests of multiple sizes and shapes. We admire wildflower
colors and dewdrops on leaves. In one place we watch a
slithering snake, its black body emblazoned with yellow
and red, and in another spot we are mesmerized by a

ground squirrel stuffing in food till its storage pouches bulge comically.

Sounds echo in the quiet—the hollow thump of a woodpecker, the hum of bees, the shrill buzz of cicada—and we listen because we have the time. We are in no hurry. The children are along.

As a family in the outdoors, we have fun, we enjoy. We bring back memories that are special and sustaining to us as a family unit. At home we talk about past trips and long to return to favorite places. In a world where even youngsters are programmed into busy, separate-from-the-family routines, these outdoor times are our special shared experiences.

In the outdoors we are not separated by a way of living that delegates certain concerns to adults and others to children. We are a little like pioneers. In order to survive we have to work together, share, and cooperate. We meet the elements without such modern conveniences as houses, cars, and central heating to shield and insulate us. If cold and snow strike in midsummer, we all must cope with this unexpected turn of events. If a torrential rain falls, we must deal with that too. On each wilderness excursion we learn more about ourselves; even the very little ones do. We discover how far we can travel without mechanization, how well we can improvise when carefully laid plans do not work, and how cheerful and levelheaded we can be in adversity.

Taking children into the outdoors is a rewarding family experience, but it is not easy. It requires careful planning and demands organization. For the adult novice, it means learning very adequate outdoor skills before the children go along. In some ways, families in the wilderness are the same as families at home. Siblings still quibble over nothing. Youngsters who are picky eaters or poor sleepers bring these traits with them. But in many other ways these outdoor times are not at all like home. Throughout a trip, family members are physically close to one another. They play, work, and explore together from the beginning of each day until night, and at nighttime they crowd together in the tent's limited space. There are no interruptions—no television, no freeway noise, no rock music, no neighbors dropping in, no schedule of sports or classes to attend. Family life becomes simple, uncomplicated, and very close knit.

Activities that Take You into the Wilderness

There are many ways to experience the backcountry. In the summer you can day hike or you can backpack. You can canoe or kayak or find backcountry roads and bicycle. During the winter you can ski cross-country or snowshoe into the wildlands and even snow camp there overnight.

What you do with children in the outdoors depends on personal preference. Day hiking is the easiest activity to manage, and a child any age can go along. A nonwalker can travel in a carrier on an adult's back. The logistics for a day's hike are fairly simple.

When you backpack with youngsters, the plans and the trip become more complex. The younger the child, the greater the complexity. The more youngsters in the family, the more difficult the trip's logistics. However, because backpacking allows you to spend more time in the backcountry, it is potentially more enjoyable. Some families start taking infants backpacking as soon as the mother recovers from childbirth, while others wait until a youngster can walk well and carry a pack. The timing is a personal choice to be made by the individual family.

Backcountry bicycling can begin as soon after childbirth as the mother is ready to pedal. A young baby can be put in a child carrier; when older, the youngster can ride in a safe child seat on the back of the parent's bike.

Many families prefer a trailer or cart for transporting children behind the bike. With some special arrangements for managing gear, young children can be transported for

Figure 1. Trailer for bicycle trips with children

overnight camping trips. Large child trailers provide ample space even for the necessities and gear babies require. When youngsters ride their own two-wheelers, trip lengths diminish and the pace slows down considerably.

To participate in water sports, children should be good and fearless swimmers and be provided with life preservers that fit well and support the child's weight. Then, on easy day trips, they can be passengers in a canoe or double kayak or a raft on calm water. When day trips begin to work well, youngsters are ready to go along on overnight boat camping excursions.

In the winter, parents can ski cross-country or snow-shoe with young children tucked into carriers on their backs. A flat sled with a seat for a child and a waist harness that attaches to the skiing parent, the Norwegian-style *Fjellpulken,* also can allow families to bring young children along for a day of skiing. When youngsters walk well, they are ready to try out cross-country skis. The very young skier covers only yards, not miles, before stopping. On cross-country skis, youngsters glide and skate; they slide downhill. Some families prefer snowshoeing, which is more like walking. Parents who have plenty of experience with snow camping can share winter overnights with their children.

Learning, Then Teaching, Low-Impact Camping

The personal satisfaction any family derives from backcountry travel is, however, only a small part of the total wilderness experience. An equally important consideration is the responsibility of each family member, from the youngest to the oldest, to help lessen the impact of people on the wilderness lands that still exist throughout our country.

When only a few people visited wilderness areas, there were old ways of use that seemed perfectly acceptable. Traditionally, people hewed, cut, and carved their temporary shelters. They lashed together tables, cut boughs for sleeping cushions, and dug elaborate ditches to filter away rainwater. They used pack animals to haul in canned food, cast-iron frying pans, grills, and tarps and left much behind for another time. They buried the refuse from what they brought with them. When these visitors departed, small pockets of crude civilization remained. Since only a few, if any, isolated travelers ever passed through these areas, their intrusions on the natural shape of the wilderness did not seem to matter.

Today, however, all that has changed. Truly isolated wilderness lands are becoming more and more difficult to find. The backcountry boom is on, and the wildlands are experiencing unprecedented people pressure. As a result, traditional, high-impact camping has become intolerable. Practices that seemed reasonable for the few are impractical, unreasonable, and downright destructive in these times of heavy use. New ways, soft ways, careful ways of going into and using the backcountry have become an absolute necessity. For those who have gone heavy-handedly into the backcountry in the past, this is a time for breaking old habits and establishing new, low-impact ways of enjoying the wilderness. For newcomers to the backcountry, the task at hand is merely to learn from the beginning the best ways to come and go in the wild country without damaging what is there.

Children accompanying their families into the out-of-doors for the first time have no inappropriate habits to break. They know only the camping techniques that their parents are beginning to teach them. Thus parents have a unique opportunity to transmit to a future generation of backcountry users, habits that will help preserve the land's wildness. Because children learn by following the example of their parents, when they go with you into the outdoors, they will do what you do. If you show respect for the wildlands, if your activities leave no scars on the environment, your children will accept this approach as the only way.

Many low-impact camping decisions are strictly an adult's responsibility. Still, you can explain to children from the beginning the reasons for what you are doing. For example, one of an adult's responsibilities is to pick the campsite, which should be an already barren spot, a comfortable gravel bar, or a place covered with forest duff rather than with vegetation. You can tell your youngsters that you are not camping in the lovely meadow nearby because your presence would eventually lead to the destruction of all that grows there. As you stand at the edge of the pristine meadow on already impacted land, you can help your children understand that the impacted area also was once covered with alpine plants until people came and camped there.

You decide, too, whether your campsite is appropriate for a small fire at night, and you can share with your youngsters a general philosophy about fire use. You can tell them that fires are fine in some places, such as a driftwood-cluttered beach. However, in the alpine country, where each plant and tree struggles to survive, and in places already stripped clean of usable wood, fires should not be built.

You also choose to carry and cook on a lightweight stove. If you explain to children that the stove is presently the best means of cooking in the wilderness without leaving behind fire rings, they will understand and accept this method of outdoor cooking.

A child's passive involvement and understanding of low-impact camping style is important, but youngsters also can be involved actively in careful wilderness use. Since children often snack to keep from becoming bored or weary, taking proper care of the snack litter is a good place to begin a youngster's education. When you practice low-impact camping, you never leave behind or bury anything; yet the easiest thing for children to do is to drop a scrap of paper or a plastic bag. Putting every wrapper into the litter bag takes thought and practice. If you establish this simple task as family policy from day one in the backcountry, children will learn one important way they can contribute to preserving the wildlands.

Any parent knows that when you take children somewhere, anywhere, they immediately have to go to the bathroom. In the backcountry, teaching youngsters the cat's method of burying feces is another small, yet vital, step in wilderness preservation. Walking that 200 feet away from the campsite and water sources represents an effort. It is not easy, but it is necessary.

When hiking with children, you can stress the importance of staying on the trail and not cutting corners or taking shortcuts. When children brush their teeth or wash in camp, you can teach them to do this away from all water sources. You can be sure that youngsters know not to dump wastewater into lakes and streams.

All of these practices can be easily understood by children. Later you can introduce more complex low-impact principles. If you want these ideas to stick with your children, you must expect to repeat yourself many, many times. Do not be surprised if what your youngster knew at the end of one camping season is forgotten when the next spring or summer rolls around. If you persist in teaching good habits, your children eventually will learn. If you continue to explore better ways of low-impact camping and set an example for your children to follow, you will plant the seeds for their becoming responsible wilderness travelers in the future.

Backcountry trips with children should be fun. A steady stream of "Don't do this" and "Don't do that" is bound to ruin the experience for youngsters and parents alike. Before you start out on a trip, establish the ground rules. At the trailhead, or before you climb into the canoe, or before setting up camp, spell out your expectations. Better yet, talk about careful wilderness use when you are at home choosing gear, trying out equipment in the backyard, or testing yourselves on near-to-home excursions.

Children like consistency. It is easier for them to learn what is expected if you set basic low-impact standards for your family regardless of the place you are visiting. If you are in a multiple-use area where grazing is permitted, entire meadows may have been devoured by sheep. You can still establish that your family does not pick, pull up, or trample the vegetation.

With young children you can make low-impact concepts into a game: you are spies, and if you leave traces behind, enemy agents will discover your location and capture you. You can offer a reward to the best cleaner-upper when you break camp or, at an often-used site, give a treat to each child who finds a certain number of pieces of other people's litter. Any of these inventive approaches helps stress the importance of taking special care of the environment.

Teaching children careful habits is difficult when they see careless wildland use around them. You may have explained the need for staying on trails and for not breaking down trail edges, and then you may discover that a pack of horses has preceded you and ground the earth into a confusion of hoof holes; or, while you are roasting marshmallows over your camp stove, you see that people nearby are building a blazing fire even though the wood supply is scarce. In these cases, simply explain to your children that your family tries to leave the wilderness as you found it. You will be surprised at how quickly youngsters catch on.

If you come across a campsite that has been left messy by another party, you can use this negative situation to underline the importance of careful use. We once backpacked in a multiple-use area where horses were allowed, but where no facility was made available for them at the campsites. A family of two adults and two children had brought two horses to their site, and our youngsters watched both horses and people gradually destroy the usability of an area large enough to accommodate two or three other parties. The ropes tying the horses to the trees rubbed off the bark. The animals defecated throughout the campsite and left manure at the water's edge when they went to drink; they also nibbled and broke off vegetation. Later, after the family left, we wandered through the empty site. The people had strewn watermelon rinds and orange peels on the ground and had scattered about their ripped plastic tarps. They had fished and left the guts along the water's edge where our children had intended to swim. There was no need to explain anything. The destructive actions of the family spelled out the why's of low-impact camping more graphically than hundreds of explanations. The scene taught our youngsters that careful camping means leaving behind a place that others will find pleasant. This site had totally lost its appeal.

Children's noise is something that only parents can love, and even they do not always find it tolerable. Other people do not go into the out-of-doors to encounter noisy youngsters, so use your judgment in determining how much noise is too much. We discovered a mountain-top echo once, and our children were totally captivated by the phenomenon. We had a five-minute conversation with our echo. Each child had a turn, and then we told our youngsters that that was enough because there were other people who had come to the area for peaceful quiet. The outdoors is not a tiptoe-and-whisper kind of place, but children do need to learn to control their noise level as a basic consideration for others.

One way to minimize your children's impact on other people is to choose an off-to-yourself campsite. With a stove and water containers, you need not cluster near water sources. You will be more comfortable in an out-of-the-way perch, and the chances of your family disturbing others, even with pleasant sounds, will automatically decrease. In real wilderness, where no one else is around, children's noise will be less of a problem. Often, though, areas that are easy enough for youngsters to reach are accessible to others too. When you have neighboring campers, your youngsters need to respect their privacy. In nonsolitary places you can aim to create the illusion of isolation for others and for yourselves.

You and your youngsters must become skilled practitioners of the walk-softly philosophy of wilderness use. When children are young and their minds are open to suggestion, parents have a unique opportunity to introduce them to backcountry experiences that will bring no harm to the wildlands.

2

Getting Ready

BEFORE YOU SHARE wildland excursions with your youngsters, you need to acquire a reasonable level of outdoor expertise. To remain patient with your children on trips, you should also maintain good physical condition. If you start small with easy trips close to home, your entire family will learn to enjoy the outdoors and will want to expand into longer, more complex experiences.

Start with Yourself

Taking children on wilderness trips when you, as a parent, have no out-of-doors experience is sheer foolishness. You are asking for trouble. You can get the experience you need by taking backcountry trips yourself. By going without your children, you can test your real interest in the wilderness experience. Only when you discover that you thoroughly enjoy sojourns into the backcountry is it time to think about taking the youngsters along.

It is not the purpose of this book to offer general wilderness travel hints; the following, though, are some suggestions on how to prepare yourself for travel into the wild places.

CLUBS AND ORGANIZATIONS

One of the best ways to acquire sound outdoor skills is to join an outdoors-oriented group. There are many organizations, such as the Sierra Club, with general outdoor interests. Other groups are centered around specific outdoor activities; these include cross-country skiing clubs, hiking clubs, bicycling clubs, and canoeing and kayaking clubs.

Check into what is available in your community. If you have a choice of several groups, you can pick the one that specializes in the activity you think you would most enjoy. Organizations usually can provide you with new-member pamphlets and information. Some clubs schedule new-member sessions or invite prospective members to sit in on regular meetings.

To find out the objectives of a particular club, talk with club officers and members; they will be glad to explain the group's interests and approaches. If you want unpressured recreational fun, for example, a group dedicated to competitive outdoor activities may not be for you.

The advantages of an active outdoor organization are many. First of all, it is inexpensive; no one is trying to make a profit. You pay dues yearly, and club activities are then offered free or at minimal cost. In addition, you become part of a group of kindred spirits. The people you meet through the organization will have outdoor interests similar to your own. For beginners, organizations often sponsor outdoor skills classes. Hiking clubs offer survival training and first-aid instruction while canoeing groups teach boating techniques and water rescue. Fees may be charged just to cover class costs. Regular club meetings provide an informal setting for learning more about the outdoors.

Clubs also keep you advised on the latest developments in wilderness conservation. If you are going to enjoy the outdoors, you must have wilderness to visit. Outdoor organizations help keep you informed about the political struggle for wildlands. Establishing wilderness areas and keeping them intact takes work; it requires regular letter writing to land agencies, policymakers, and governmental representatives. The club may have a conservation committee, or you may learn what is happening through the group newsletter or grapevine.

Once you have found a club that seems right for you, then what do you do? For the beginner, the best first step is to take the basic courses offered. The most useful instruction includes field experiences. In such courses, you do more than talk about an activity; you take easy beginning trips and learn your skills under the guidance of experienced enthusiasts. The best club programs also offer a series of beginner trips. These excursions gradually become more difficult so that by the end of the series you have had a good taste of what is involved in the particular activity. For example, a large, active hiking club may sponsor excursions on a variety of difficulty levels, from easy walks to moderate hikes to scrambling over trailless terrain. There may be day, weekend, and week-long trips. As a beginner, you can start slowly and build up to longer, more difficult hikes.

Later, when you are no longer a beginner, a club continues to be useful. Teaching always sharpens skills, so perhaps you can share what you have learned with the next group of novices. Through a club you also can stay abreast of the latest conservation news. If the group outing approach does not appeal to you, you do not have to travel with the club but can still keep in touch with like-minded people and gather information on places to go.

Outdoor groups exist in the most unlikely places. Some thrive far away from any real wilderness. If, however, you live where no local clubs exist, you can fill that void by joining the nearest chapter of a large national organization. The group's newsletter will keep you informed about trips and conservation issues. Summer excursions with groups like the Sierra Club provide wild country experiences, many of which are designed for people with minimal outdoor skills. You sign on for a trip at your level of experience—beginning, intermediate, or advanced. Then your week or more of total immersion in the outdoors provides a crash course in wilderness skills.

CLASSES

Another way to acquire outdoor skills is to take classes sponsored by junior colleges or adult continuing education programs. These classes may cost more than similar classes offered by outdoor clubs. Be sure that any such courses incorporate the opportunity for field experiences. Without trips to try out the principles and techniques discussed in class, the knowledge gained will be of little use in a real wilderness situation. A one- or two-session course can only whet your interest. The ins and outs of outdoor activity are complex; so to be worthwhile, a course must offer extensive classes and field trips.

OUTDOOR STORES

Outdoor stores sometimes offer activity or equipment clinics. These sessions are part of a store's advertising efforts, but if you keep this fact in mind, you can obtain a free introduction to gear, skills, trips, and activities. Again, if the presentation consists of discussions only, you will acquire theoretical knowledge but not usable skills. Some stores also underwrite courses; you may have to pay for these. The value of a course depends on the amount of practical outdoor activity included.

GUIDES

There are people who make a living by taking parties into the country's wilderness areas. Some of these guides provide everything for you: equipment, food, and expertise. To go with them you need to know nothing. Many guides take such good care of you that you can return still knowing nothing about the outdoors. Guided trips are costly, but if you have the money to spend, you can, on even a very passively oriented trip, get a taste of the outdoor experience.

Guided excursions that aim to teach about the outdoors are becoming more common. On these outings you work and learn. Although the trips are still expensive, you have the opportunity to acquire skills that will provide a basis for more independent outdoor experiences.

Guides know the area in which they work. If your outdoor skills are minimal and you are in an unfamiliar region, the guide's knowledge may be worth the financial investment.

PARK TOURS

In many parks, the land management personnel offer guided trips. Often these are tourist-level outings; rarely are outdoor skills taught. You may, however, gain valuable information about the natural setting from park guides and rangers. Sometimes concessionaires offer more intensive guided trips within parks. You can find out about these longer excursions by communicating directly with management personnel at the wilderness area you wish to visit. A concessionaire's services cost about the same as those of any commercial guide.

FRIENDS AND ACQUAINTANCES

People who love the outdoors often are willing to share their knowledge with others. You may find a person at work or in your neighborhood, a friend or merely an acquaintance, who will accompany you on a trip and provide you with valuable information.

BOOKS

"How-to" books on the outdoors can provide fine preparation for backcountry travel (see the Appendix). They present a variety of viewpoints, and if you find similar ideas expressed by a number of authors, you can be fairly sure that you are learning about accepted practices and

opinions. Reading, however, is not doing. After moving vi-
cariously through an author's adventures and reading his
or her advice, get involved in the outdoor activities
themselves.

MAGAZINES

Many outdoor magazines offer practical, up-to-date advice and information on backcountry travel (see the Appendix). *Backpacker Magazine, Canoe,* and *Cross Country Skier,* which are all commercial magazines, provide
valuable information on equipment and places to go, as
well as greater contact with other wilderness users. By
joining such environmental and conservation organizations as the Audubon Society, Natural Resources Defense
Council, The Nature Conservancy, Sierra Club, and many
other local groups, members receive periodicals with articles of interest to the outdoor traveler. Since magazine
budgets depend on fees from their advertisers, remember
that the advertisements in any of these magazines are not
endorsements; before you buy, check carefully into the features of any products.

FAMILY EXPERIENCES AS YOU LEARN

While learning, you need not exclude your children totally.
Some outdoor groups run year-round or seasonal activities
geared especially to families, and others accept families on
easier trips. If the group you join offers no family activities,
you still are likely to meet members interested in trips for
children. Then you can informally schedule some beginning family excursions. On trips with other adults you can
pinpoint locations for later family outings; for example,
the first mile and a half of a 5-mile day trip you take may
be just right for an outing with children later. Some commercial guides offer family trips; these excursions tend to
be quite expensive but can work well for people who have
more money than time.

KEEPING IN SHAPE

Parental patience is an important ingredient for ensuring successful family experiences outdoors. To keep a positive mental attitude on trips with children, you need to be in good physical condition. If walking 2 miles at a slow pace leaves you panting, you will be too tired to put up with your youngsters and to help them enjoy being outdoors. With children along, a parent is a guide, teacher, storyteller, song leader, and nature expert and must carry the bulk of the load. He or she must plan, navigate, and calculate. The best way to keep energetic enough to cope with these tasks is to plan a regular regimen of physical activity in between family outings.

General Conditioning

Exercising occasionally only leaves you stiff and sore; it does not keep you in good general physical shape. To prepare for the wilderness experience, you must engage in physical activities that help build your body's endurance. With these, you essentially reduce the work your heart must do, and you make your cardiovascular system function more efficiently. Muscles that have been conditioned can more easily extract oxygen from the blood as it circulates throughout the body. One hour of vigorous activity involving use of the leg muscles three times a week is the minimum exercise necessary to improve your body's general physical condition.

For building cardiorespiratory endurance, muscular endurance, and muscular strength, running ranks high as efficient conditioning. Bicycling, swimming, aerobics, power walking, handball, and squash are almost as beneficial. Step machines, stationary bicycles, rowing machines, and cross-country ski machines are only some of the exercise equipment now available for conditioning at home.

What you do for exercise will vary according to your interests. In many communities racquetball, squash, hand-

ball, swimming, and soccer are available for adults. Playing games on a regular basis can make conditioning fun.
If games and group exercise are not for you or if you cannot arrange your time to fit into a schedule of organized
sports, there are plenty of options for do-it-yourself, do-it-
alone exercise.

Conditioning for Specific Activities
Keeping generally fit helps, but it is not the complete answer to physically easy outdoor trips. Once you begin exercising regularly, your leg muscles may be in great shape,
but can you tote a 30-pound pack? If you are going canoeing, your legs may be strong, but are your arms ready
for long hours of paddling? Just as you schedule time before a trip to pack gear and shop for provisions, allocate
time for stepped-up physical preparation for the particular
activities planned.

Finding the Time
Keeping in shape may sound easy. However, it is often difficult for parents with small children to find the time for
exercise.

To give each other the time needed, parents can trade
off staying with the children. If your schedule is tight, early
morning exercise before children are awake and before the
workday starts is a good alternative. For the late riser, it
may work best to exercise in the evenings, after children
have settled down for the night. Whatever you do, make a
firm commitment to yourself to exercise regularly and a
firm agreement with your spouse or an exercise partner to
share baby-sitting chores.

If time trading in the family is impossible, arrange for
baby-sitting with a neighbor or friend who has children. If
you find another parent who desperately wants to get back
into shape, you can exercise while that parent takes care
of the children and then reverse the arrangement. Taking
on a conditioning project with a like-minded friend also

provides excellent motivation, for then the two people involved can help keep each other going. For families in which both parents work full time, regularly scheduled exercise over the lunch hour sometimes provides the most convenient way to stay in shape.

Some parents prefer to take a child along in an all-terrain stroller for outdoor exercise such as jogging or power walking. Two children fit into some models. One version can be converted into a bicycle trailer so that a parent can choose to exercise by jogging or by bicycling. By jogging with the child in a stroller, parents gain flexibility and independence, because they do not need to make special baby-sitting arrangements. Children merely go along at a time that is convenient to the parents' schedule.

If you choose a vigorous-enough activity, your exercise period can consume little more than a half hour to an hour a day. Even the busiest of adults can manage to scrape together that amount of time. Whatever you do—neighborhood cross-country skiing in the winter, bicycling indoors on a stationary bike, running up and down the stairs, or jumping rope—will help make you physically and mentally prepared to take your children into the out-of-doors.

Preparing for Trips with Children

You have done your homework. You have prepared yourself in one way or another to go safely and knowledgeably into the out-of-doors. You are ready to take your children into the backcountry. Your next step is to decide the best ways to provide enjoyable kinds of outdoor experiences for your family.

WHEN TO GO

Children who grow up in or near cities rarely experience the total quiet automatically encountered in deserted backcountry. The increasing popularity of wilderness travel makes finding isolation for your family more of a challenge, especially since youngsters can walk, cycle, or ski only so far. When you travel 5 miles into the back-country, you meet more people than the wilderness should have to bear. Therefore, if you want your children to ex-perience true isolation in the outdoors, you must plan to go when the crowds have left or diminished. Traveling dur-ing low-use periods also helps to spread out the impact people have on the environment.

Weekdays and off seasons are good times to seek a more isolated wilderness experience. Anytime you can arrange weekday trips rather than weekend outings you will en-counter fewer people, even in the summer. During the off seasons, popular places often are empty, and spring or fall can be beautiful times for excursions. Although outdoor travel with young children is taxing, you can make the most of off-season travel while your children are pre-schoolers. Once youngsters start grade school, your fam-ily's freedom to come and go at odd times is more limited. In most communities, school-age children have a spring vacation, which is ideal for some types of backcountry travel. Springtime cross-country skiing, with its milder weather, is perfect for youngsters. You can try snow camp-ing with fewer risks in the spring also. Early or late in the season, hiking and backpacking demand extra preparation and warmer clothes, but these efforts will be rewarded when you have a small piece of the wilderness all to yourselves.

HOW TO GO
Going with Organized Groups
Some outdoor organizations—usually the large, multiple-interest groups—schedule family outings. Trips planned for families include a variety of excursions into backcoun-try areas close to home. Other outdoor clubs welcome families on easier trips. When you are relatively inexperi-enced, you gain the support and know-how of the group

and the trip leader. The families you meet through an out-door organization may make ideal traveling companions later when you begin to take trips independently of the group.

Going with Other Families

Going on outdoor trips with other families usually pro-vides fine motivation for youngsters. The children may be from very different age groups and still have a strong pos-itive impact on one another. A 5-year-old will look up to a 9-year-old from another family; the desire to be like the older child may make the 5-year-old move his legs more steadily than ever before. Older children who feel admired may outdo themselves too; they may show patience and helpfulness they would rarely show to their own siblings.

Having other families around also may make your youngsters forget that some of what they are doing in-volves work. When children have peers to talk with as they go along, walking or canoeing becomes more fun, and the boredom of putting one foot in front of the other or of sit-ting quietly in the canoe all day disappears. Rest stops are more enjoyable, too, and looking forward to playing with other youngsters in camp lends added excitement to the outing.

The adults in another family also can have a positive influence on your children. In every family, children play irritating games to test the limits of their parents' patience. Complaining to a parent is easy, while the slight distance and lack of familiarity between your child and another adult can work wonders in motivating youngsters toward bigger and better accomplishments. Some trading of chil-dren on hiking, skiing, or bicycling trips can provide an extra boost for your child. No youngster wants to say no to someone else's parent, and children like to impress adults who do not belong to them.

On club trips you go with whoever happens to sign up,

while on private outings you choose your companions. For successful experiences, families that travel outdoors together must be highly compatible. If family philosophies toward care of the outdoors or child discipline differ too greatly, your trips may result in trouble rather than fun. To get to know another family's style and attitudes, try out a short day trip. If the day works well, fine; if not, you have lost little. Once you find compatible families, you and your youngsters can enjoy many hours of group fun in the out-of-doors.

Going as a Single Family

When you take outdoor trips as a single family, you do not have to work around the needs, expectations, and free time of friends or acquaintances. You pick a convenient time and a suitable destination, pack, and then experience your outing at a pace appropriate for your family.

Going as a single family also offers precious times of family togetherness. Daily life is full of distractions that keep children and parents from being together, talking together, and enjoying one another. As children grow older, they develop interests that pull them away from their family. You can take advantage of family outings to leave distractions behind and spend long hours as a close-knit unit. These are meaningful times for games, stories, work, and fun as everyone participates in activities together.

The main disadvantage of the single-family outing is that children rarely hesitate to complain to their own parents. If you have youngsters who tend to complain or who are hard to get going, motivation can be more difficult.

Another disadvantage centers on safety. For boating trips or for long stays in totally isolated wilderness, a one-family excursion is not as safe as a group outing since you essentially have no other adult support in case of an emergency. Furthermore, if you are new to backcountry travel and feel insecure, your children will sense this immediately, even if they are very young. In this case, it is wise to travel with others for a while, especially with people willing to share their skills with you.

Even if you prefer to travel with groups or other families for morale or safety reasons, some single-family outings should be planned. These trips are ideal times to get to know your children without the kind of distractions that crop up at home.

The Single Parent

Nothing prevents the single parent from exploring the outdoors with children. However, do not go on a wilderness trip as the only adult. For most adults, traveling alone in the backcountry is questionable procedure. If you are alone with children, the practice is even more inappropriate since you then have no other adult support in the event of an emergency. In most outdoor locations, the work and supervision of young children requires two sets of adult hands and two adult heads.

There are many ways to secure additional adult assistance. A teenager who is highly experienced, strong, and levelheaded can be hired to accompany you on outdoor trips. If you team up with another one-parent family, you can manage safe outings as long as the total number of children is reasonable. Two single parents with one child each will work; if each parent has three or four young children, reconsider. You also could go with organized groups, or you could join a two-parent family. Watch your numbers, though. For children under 7, it's best to maintain a one-to-one or one-to-two adult–child ratio for safety and sanity.

You also might ask a friend to go with you. Be sure, though, that the person has a reasonable degree of backcountry experience. You want help, not hindrance. When judging the suitability of a companion, ask yourself if this person could go for help in an emergency. If you proceed sensibly into the backcountry, the chances of disaster are slim, but you need to be prepared nonetheless.

Group Impact on the Wilderness

When two families with children join together for an outdoor trip, they automatically become a fairly large group. The larger the group, the greater your impact on the backcountry itself and on other people you meet. In delicate areas, some management agencies recommend a maximum group size of six. If your group is larger, you must take special steps to minimize the effects of your presence. First, choose as your destination areas that can more easily absorb people. Fragile alpine country with few campsites should be avoided. You should be particularly insistent that noise in the party be kept low; in camp, close supervision of your youngsters' activities is necessary. If you cannot find adequate space for all your tents without spreading into vegetation, you can establish separate camps for each family.

On trips sponsored by organizations, the group's size must be given special consideration too. To help moderate the people impact, participants can separate into smaller groups, which can then head for slightly different destinations.

EXPERIENCED PARENTS

The inexperienced parent's first job is to learn about the outdoors and to gain expertise before taking children on excursions. The experienced parent's major task is to gear down outings to a level children can enjoy. A skilled outdoor traveler may be accustomed to trips that increasingly test and challenge his or her abilities. When taking youngsters along, the experienced parent must backtrack to beginning-level outings. Wilderness travel that pushes young children too hard will only make them dislike the outdoors. To share your enthusiasm for the backcountry, start small and then gradually work up to bigger excursions when youngsters are older and more experienced. If the thought of curtailing your own grunt-and-push style of hiking or boating is odious, perhaps taking your children along is not for you. You also could try alternating family trips with harder, adults-only excursions to enjoy the best of both types of experiences.

PRE-TRIP SCOUTING

One of the best ways to ensure a successful trip with children is for adults to check out a particular area first. Parents with young children frequently have difficulty finding baby-sitters and the time to scout locations. However, these problems are minor when compared with those that can develop if you take youngsters into an unsuitable area.

On an adults-only backcountry trip, think about covering the same territory in a slightly different way with your children. On a week's backpacking trip of 20 or 30 miles, you may discover that the first 4 miles lead to an off-trail lake. On a day's bike trip of 40 miles, you may find that the middle 10 miles are flat and safe and include a lovely park. In canoeing a chain of lakes with hard portages, you may notice that few people use the main portion of the first lake. Any one of these discoveries can help you to create a suitable outing for your youngsters.

Keep a diary of your trips. Details recorded about a particular area visited will prove valuable years later when you decide your children are ready to share the spot. At home you can establish a trip notebook or card catalogue. Make note of the age at which your children will be ready for a particular location. Jot down any ideas you have about making the trip better for youngsters.

GUIDEBOOKS

With the rising interest in outdoor activity, there has been a proliferation of guidebooks. These usually describe the general atmosphere of a place and give exact details concerning elevation gain, trip difficulties, degree of use, and mileage. Although you can always find this information on topographical maps, the guidebook approach is a fast, easy way to sort through trip possibilities. Short of going there yourself, reading detailed information about a particular hike or canoeing lake or backcountry bicycling route is the best way to ensure picking out an excursion that is appropriate for children. In many parts of the country, guidebooks have been published listing trips appropriate for families with children. If you are going into an unfamiliar area, you can write to the local land managers and inquire about the availability of guidebooks for the region. In your own area, you can find such books in outdoor stores or general bookstores. Most stores will order books they do not have in stock. Some bookstores and publishers specializing in outdoor books have catalogues so that desired materials can be ordered and mailed to you directly. You may discover that some of the guidebooks are published by a local outdoor group, and thus you share in that organization's many years of varied experience. The drawback to the guidebook approach is that too many people have the same easy access to information that you have. You may find more company on these guidebook-described trips than you could possibly want. Local land managers can tell you if the trip you have in mind covers land that is overused or generally overcrowded.

OUTDOOR NEWS SHEETS

In some places outdoor news sheets exist to provide subscribers with up-to-date backcountry information. These serve as an additional source of information for trip planning and generally cost very little.

MAPS

Maps are fascinating once you understand how to read them. A good outdoor skills class teaches both map and compass reading. When you have mastered map-reading skills, you can purchase topographical maps published by the U.S. Geological Survey; Canadian maps can be obtained through that country's Department of Energy, Mines, and Resources (for addresses, see the Appendix).

These maps describe exact details of terrain. You can tell how steep a climb is involved, where lakes and streams are located, and whether a dangerous dropoff lurks around a bend. If you are interested in a specific region, you can order a group of maps and then figure out suitable family trips as your off-season recreation. You should always carry these maps with you on your trips, but their primary value is for studying the terrain before you go on a trip.

CHECKING WITH PARK AGENCIES

Land management professionals can provide you with up-to-date materials on the region they control. Unfortunately, some people do not bother to explore the resources of the parks they want to visit. Instead, they read about an area, talk to a friend, and decide the trip sounds fine. This approach eliminates the possibility of finding out more current information and of hearing about policy changes that affect how you, the visitor, are to use an area.

There are state parks, national parks, national forests, national wildlife refuges, and Bureau of Land Management areas to choose from. Even if you haven't pinpointed a destination beyond being interested in a particular state, you can write to agencies and ask for lists of all the recreational areas they oversee. In return, you may receive a tiny blurb on various areas in a region, or you may get very detailed information.

Once you have chosen an interesting place, write to that park itself. Park personnel usually supply you with maps that outline trails and give an overview of the lands within park boundaries. These are not topo maps, but they do supply general information. They are updated yearly, or new information is included with the maps. When planning a family trip, inquire in your letter about the feasibility of taking a particular trip with youngsters and ask for suggestions. Many times park personnel will have taken such trips with their own families and know the kind of experiences that will suit children.

Park managers will be only too happy to direct you to a less popular area if you have chosen a trip they know to be overused. Take their advice. A trip into a region thick with people is hardly a wilderness experience. Such a place quickly becomes impacted, and you are doing the land a favor by not going there.

PERMITS

When you write for information, find out if the park you want to visit has a permit system. Permit policies differ from one area to another. Some permits are merely for head-counting purposes. The land managers want to know how many people come, where and when they go, and what they do. Other permits are meant to restrict land use and the impact of people. If campsites are overused, the managers may decide on a maximum number of people who can be there at one time. When planning a trip to a park with such restrictions, be sure you understand how the system works and what alternatives suitable to your family exist. In some areas you may merely have to wait to be a first party out the next day. Make certain you have leeway in your schedule for this extra time. Otherwise park personnel may be able to direct you to a less used, available spot.

In other parks there are actual reservation systems. You must sign up ahead of time to go into a region. When making initial inquiries, be sure that space is available at the time you plan to go. Find out the earliest time reservations can be made and plan your trip far enough in advance to get your first choice.

Although ranger stations and park headquarters are not fully staffed off season, they are open to reply to information requests and to give you all the general materials you need. When the season opens, specific details concerning trail maintenance and conditions can be obtained. If you call right before your trip, you can receive up-to-date information gathered firsthand by backcountry rangers.

Trips Close to Home

Once you have assembled a list of potential trips with the help of group contacts, guidebooks, maps, and park agencies, you are ready to try out some of the possibilities.

If you have never checked into potential outdoor experiences close to home, you may be surprised at the number of options you have. If you do your research well, you may discover some ideal spots for family trips that do not require traveling halfway across the country. Trips do not have to be grandiose to please children. A mile-long walk to a small, little-used lake for the day may be just right, while a longer trip through rugged terrain may be too much for them.

Since short trips take almost as much packing and planning as longer excursions, a two-day outing may seem like too much trouble. Sometimes, however, two days are perfect, especially for the very young. Despite a trip's good fun, young children can quickly miss what is familiar at home—the dog, gerbil, room, or friends. Short trips near to home can be used to work out problems and are good preparation for longer vacations.

Backcountry Trips Away from Home

Taking backcountry trips in areas away from home offers the opportunity to broaden your outdoor experiences. Be sure your children are ready to spend a large block of time in the wilderness. When you tack car, plane, or train travel onto a backcountry vacation, the whole family must be ready for this too. Many people find that spending long hours in the car with children is the most difficult part of a backcountry vacation.

Obtaining information and checking its accuracy is more complex when the wilderness is some distance away. If you belong to a local outdoor club, members whose own trips have ranged far from home may be the best initial sources. When you belong to a nationwide club, local chapters in the areas you wish to visit often can provide information. You may even be able to join a club trip to the destination that interests you.

Write to the land agency in charge of the area you want to visit and describe what you have in mind—a number of short day hikes, a week of canoeing, day bicycling trips, or a week of backpacking. Indicate the degree of difficulty you want to take on—whether you want beginning or intermediate trips. You can ask for a number of specific possibilities. If the response you receive is too vague, follow up with a phone call. Talking to backcountry rangers rather than office personnel frequently proves more helpful. By planning ahead during the off season, you have a better chance to catch these knowledgeable people near the phone.

Also ask the agency for a list of guidebooks and background books on the area. If these are not sold in your community, find out how you can order them by mail. If you feel you cannot go into a strange and distant area alone and you belong to no outdoor clubs, inquire about guided trips. Most guides avoid taking young, inexperienced children. There are more possibilities for older youngsters. In some areas, however, you can find guided trips organized expressly for families.

Once you decide on a specific trip, you plan and organize equipment, clothing, and food in much the same way as you would for a local excursion. Buying provisions and packing at home guarantee that you have what you need and that you do not waste time at your destination. However, if you live where very little outdoor gear is available and are going to a gear-selling mecca, you may want to allow for some shopping time. If there are perishables you want to buy at your destination, find out the location of a store from land agency personnel ahead of time. Change your menus if procuring these groceries is too complicated.

Plan well for travel time. If you are car camping on the

way, a separate set of gear helps you avoid unpacking and
dirtying backcountry equipment. At your destination be
sure to make a last-minute check of your equipment. In the
confusion of extended travel, items can be easily misplaced
or moved out of sight.

PRE-BACKCOUNTRY CAR TRAVEL

Car travel before and after backcountry trips can develop
into the worst part of family outdoor expeditions.
Whether you ride for days or merely a few hours, make
careful plans for car activities to keep young minds and
small hands busy. You can organize a car play packet for
each youngster. A tote bag or daypack not in use for the
trip itself can keep play items from being lost or scattered.
A clipboard can hold paper, a workbook, or coloring
book. You can bring crayons, pens, and pencils plus
games, puzzles, and books. Some craft activities, such as
needlework or cardboard loom weaving, also are practical
in the car. On a long trip, introducing something new each
day helps relieve the monotony; even on short trips, taking
along a number of car activities helps to keep your children
happy.

Snacking and group car games help pass the time too.
Some children love such games as counting all trucks of a
certain kind, looking for words on signs that begin with
each letter of the alphabet, and competing to count the
most horses or barns or alfalfa fields along the road. You
can also purchase car lotto games that ask children to find
certain items that can be seen from the car.

Remember, nothing works forever. Change the activities often, preferably before restlessness or squabbling begins. Plan frequent rest stops too.

For day trips, keep travel time to a minimum. An hour's
drive at the beginning and end of each day may be tolerable. A total of four hours in the car may be too much.
Some people find they can carry half-awake children into

the car early and then let them sleep through much of the driving time. Coordinating naps with the drive home also can create a peaceful ending to a day's trip.

During car travel, young children need a safe place to nap or rest or play. Car seats are available to fit infants through grade-school-age children, and special features such as head rests and car seat travel pillows can facilitate more comfortable car napping. Booster seats and safety restraints are designed for the older child. A travel tray that attaches to the back of the front seat and extends over the child's lap allows for games and hand work such as coloring, drawing, molding clay or play dough, and building with interlocking blocks; children can also manage snacks and meals more conveniently. Since many states require safety belts, and young children must be in car seats that meet specific safety standards during travel, youngsters will need regularly scheduled rest stops to break the monotony of sitting.

PRE-BACKCOUNTRY COMMERCIAL TRAVEL

Often families have limited vacation time and appealing outdoor destinations are far away from home. Although traveling with children by plane is expensive, the long hours of driving that are so tiresome for youngsters are eliminated and your choice of interesting wilderness locations to visit increases dramatically.

In many ways, carrying outdoor gear on the plane is no more complex than taking regular luggage. You have to make preliminary inquiries, however, if you want to transport something unusual. Unless a kayak or a canoe can be taken apart and shipped in pieces, you cannot put a canoe or kayak onto the plane as regular baggage. Bicycles have to be taken apart and boxed. You may have to obtain your own boxes through bicycle stores if airlines do not provide containers. Cross-country skis, even when made of fiberglass, need special protection, such as a lightweight wooden box or a heavily padded ski carrier. To be certain that nothing falls out of fully loaded packs and to prevent straps from catching in baggage conveyers, enclose them in heavy-duty plastic. Since fuel for stoves cannot be carried onto airplanes, make arrangements at your destination for obtaining fuel for your trip. Security personnel may consider even your stove suspect; therefore, make whatever advance arrangements are necessary for taking your stove without its fuel. At times when security is tight, even a pocket knife may have to be specially handled. Check with your airlines first before each trip, since each carrier has special procedures and policies change.

Trains, ferries, water taxis, and buses often have routes that go into or near wilderness areas. The novelty of a different mode of travel is appealing to children and may help while away the travel hours pleasantly. Find out in advance from carriers if you can take the backcountry gear you need. Ferries usually have room for canoes, kayaks, and bicycles. A set of wheels can be attached to kayaks and canoes so that boats can be pulled more easily when you move on and off public transportation.

RESTING AFTER TRAVEL

After prolonged car, train, ferry, or air travel, it may be necessary to devote a day to eliminating travel weariness. You cannot expect children to be fresh and anxious to start a strenuous trip when you arrive at the trailhead in the late afternoon after one or more days of travel. In this case, before starting your backcountry excursion, spend some extra time at a nearby car campground. Provide your children with opportunities to run around and stretch their legs, do some tourist-type activities, and relax. You may need and enjoy this respite just as much as your children do.

RANGER STATIONS

Children like to meet park rangers. Often, in the rush of planning and getting to a destination, the extra half hour necessary for a stop at the local ranger station is left out. This is unfortunate because visiting the station provides a good opportunity for your children to meet the people who take care of the outdoors they use. If you have done your homework ahead of time, which you must, you already know what policies are being enforced in a particular area. Stopping at the ranger station helps reinforce backcountry regulations in children's minds. If you are in a national park and nothing can be removed, the child who is a rock collector should realize this beforehand. He or she can look at the rocks but cannot take them away.

Many ranger stations have interesting exhibits that preview the area's natural attractions. Others have magazines, coloring books, and other materials especially designed for children. If your visit is timed right, you may be able to attend slide shows and lectures. The more children know about a region, the more the entire family is going to enjoy the trip.

3

General Gear

AN IMPORTANT PART of enjoying the outdoors is being properly equipped. The variety of general outdoor gear is nearly overwhelming. When you are in the market for equipment, the best first step is to collect catalogues. Write to gear suppliers for the most recent catalogues available (see the Appendix); the more you receive, the better.

Many companies sell through retail stores and through catalogue departments. By looking into mail-order possibilities, you can expand your choices. If manufacturers sell only through retail stores, they can supply you with a list of the nearest stores that carry their products.

What kind of information is included in a catalogue? First of all, there is the sales spiel. Everyone has the "best" and "most useful" product. Ignore that and get into the specifics. You can find out the dimensions of the item, materials used, sizes available, and special built-in features. You also can ascertain the most current price, a detail difficult to keep tabs on as costs spiral.

Since catalogue buying means that you see only pictures of each item, not the items themselves, use catalogues to surface evaluate and decide which items seem appropriate and should be looked at more closely. What you cannot judge from a catalogue are such considerations as the quality of workmanship and materials. If an outdoor store is accessible, you can check out equipment there. You might even rent gear first to see if it suits you. If you must catalogue-shop, experienced acquaintances and friends often can provide practical information about gear. You may be able to try out a friend's equipment before ordering your own by mail.

Once you find out details concerning gear design from catalogues, you can ask more intelligent questions at local outdoor stores. If the stores near you do not carry an item you want, you may be able to get a buyer to order it for you.

Another source of information concerning outdoor gear is *Backpacker Magazine,* which regularly develops consumer reports; these are based on equipment field tests and provide detailed and objective information. Many other outdoor magazines cover gear, but only rarely do they attempt in-depth evaluations of specific products. Through these magazines you can also obtain free additional information about products from their reader service department. Reading articles and books can help make you a more knowledgeable consumer when you buy any outdoor gear. Although equipment details will change with the constantly changing market, the ideas and principles for intelligent buying can be applied to any purchases.

Shelter

In the outdoors, adults should be able to absorb a certain number of problems—a soaking rain that falls suddenly in the night, droning bugs that settle into a site chosen for its wind protection, a whipping wind that causes temperatures to drop drastically, even snow that falls unexpectedly in July. For children, any of these situations can turn out to be an exciting adventure, something the family handles

well, or a disaster. A good shelter provides the best protection possible in a variety of situations.

The best family shelter in the backcountry is a lightweight tent made from synthetic materials. For parents
with a crawling infant or roaming toddler, a tent can serve
as a needed playpen in camp, especially when parents have
work to do. For naptime (and naps are important on trips)
a tent's closed-in space is like the child's room at home and
may expedite sleeping, while at night the tent walls act as
a barrier to stop the youngster from rolling or crawling
away.

Finding the perfect lightweight family tent is a challenge. On a single-family trip, tent gear is carried by the
two adults only, yet it must be ample enough to serve all
family members. Scrutinize skeptically anything in a tent's
design that increases weight. Also determine what your
shelter must do for you in the places that you visit. In hot,
muggy areas with plenty of small-animal activity at night,
the tent should guard against rodents, bugs, and dew and
provide good ventilation. If you warm-weather camp but
aspire to explore the country's mountainous regions, think
ahead to a more versatile tent that will give wind, rain, and
cold protection.

BREATHABLE TENT WITH
SEPARATE WATERPROOF FLY

During one night the average adult exhales approximately
1 pint of water. Picture a family—two adults and two
medium-sized children—in a single-walled, coated nylon
tent. Because of the coated material, the adults would drop
2 pints of water onto themselves and their gear, and the
children would contribute their share too. The breathable
nylon tent with a separate waterproof fly helps solve this
condensation problem. Water vapor escapes through the
open pores in the inner, uncoated nylon wall, while the
coated fly sheds outside rain and dew. An air space is main-

Figure 2. Breathable tent with separate waterproof fly

tained between the two walls. The inner tent is made with a floor and partial side wall of waterproof nylon. This double-walled concept is the basic design used for most lightweight tents.

With one piece of material constructed of a waterproof, breathable three-layer laminated fabric (see Chapter 4, the "Materials" section), these single-walled tents function much the same as a double-walled tent. Three-layer-laminate tents eliminate the need for an outer fly, but they are more costly than a comparable double-walled tent. In unusually rainy climates, it would be wise to field-test this design in a rented or borrowed tent to determine the effectiveness of the dual breathability and rain-shedding features for your family.

SINGLE-WALLED, COATED NYLON TENTS

The single-walled, coated nylon tent presents more of a condensation problem for families than for a single adult. With children, you are bound to be crowded in the tent and to have more than the usual water vapor problem inside. This type of tent, although appealingly inexpensive, does not provide the dependable shelter you need for children in bad weather.

DETERMINING SPACE NEEDS

Tents are classified as two-person, three-person, or group models. Within these classifications, floor size and shape vary. Deciding how much floor space is enough depends not only on the number in the family but also on the size of each person to be accommodated. What constitutes adequate head room is a matter of personal preference. If you camp where bad weather is likely, it may be worth buying a larger (and this means heavier) tent with extra head room for those wet days of family togetherness.

To determine if a particular tent is right for your family, you can rent that model from an outdoor equipment store. Do not, however, take children into the wilderness with an untried tent. Instead, set it up for a night of backyard camping—and remember, the worse the weather, the better the test. Many of the hard-to-answer questions about your needs can be answered this way, and you also find out if the tent is going to be easy to erect. When a child is cold, wet, hungry, and tired, when shelter is really needed, nothing is more important than being able to set up your tent fast.

If nearby stores do not rent gear, check with other families who camp. Ask about the problems and successes they have had with their tents and find out what features they like. You may even be able to borrow a tent for testing. Be sure, though, that the model you are testing is still available. New designs are constantly flowing into the marketplace while old styles are discarded.

When you are buying by catalogue, the tent dimensions listed may mean little to you as you read them. One way to make the numbers meaningful is to get a marker pen and draw out the actual size and shape of the tent floor on an old sheet. Then spread out your sleeping bags on the sheet, stack up the gear you expect to keep inside, gather together the family, and see how you all fit. You will discover immediately that the situation is cozy—or worse. If unbearable, consider the next size tent available.

Believe it or not, as many as two small children (4 to 5 years old or under) and two under-6-foot adults can fit snugly into a two-person tent, preferably the roomier

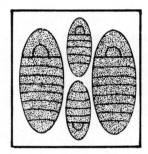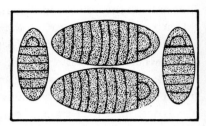

Figure 3. Possible family sleeping arrangements

models. Some of these tents feature special areas for gear that can be converted into sleeping space for children. Alcoves or enclosed vestibules with floors are sometimes just right for accommodating youngsters. When gear space is used for sleeping, a waterproof cover, such as a rain poncho, is needed to protect gear stored outside.

When the family is squeezed together elbow to elbow, you may have to deal with condensation on the waterproof part of the walls. Extending a quarter-inch, closed-cell foam pad up the side walls keeps children's sleeping bags dry if they snuggle against the tent all night (see Chapter 4, the "Pads" section). Past the age of 6 or 7, even one child can begin to cover too much space in the less roomy two-person tents. As children grow, an alternative is to carry two of these smaller tents, or to supplement a main tent with a bivy-sack. However, when you duplicate stakes, poles, and guy lines, you may end up with more weight than you would with one larger tent.

Many types of larger tents are available. A three-person tent can accommodate two adults and one preteenage child comfortably; with some cramping, two older children can fit. Ideally, a family of four, five, or possibly even six should be able to find one tent for all at a weight of between 8 and 10 pounds. Remember that preteenage children rarely share in carrying tent weight. Be especially wary as you look at larger tents to avoid designs meant for high-altitude climbers destined for extraordinarily severe climate. Features added for such conditions usually raise a tent's price and weight with little or no increased benefit in general use.

TENT DESIGN

When choosing a tent design, think about how the variations in space will accommodate your family. Tents come in a variety of floor configurations, wall designs and heights, and pole support systems. The most common models include domes or geodesic domes, hoop-supported styles, freestanding tents, and a few of the once-popular A-frames. Within these designs, support is provided by two-, three-, or four-pole systems. When evaluating support systems, remember that the more poles the greater the weight you will have to carry.

Figure 4. Dome-style tent shown without fly

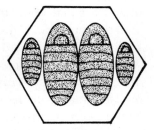

Figure 5. Using gear space in a dome design for sleeping children

Some tent walls are high-ended in the front and low-ended in the back; others, including the dome style, are highest in the middle. In bad weather, the head room of the higher tents makes dressing, eating, and breathing in the tent more bearable. With some designs, the floor space may be wider in the front and narrower in the back while other floors form regularly shaped squares and rectangles, hexagons (six-sided), or octagons (eight-sided). Hoop-supported and dome-style tents are designed to provide the maximum interior space by pulling the walls taut and out away from the tent inhabitants.

Extra spaces meant for gear may create very adequate sleeping room for youngsters. In dome tents, which are supported by curved exterior poles made of fiberglass or anodized aluminum, gear space along the sides may be large enough for children.

Although you will want to match your tent's design to the climate in which you camp, features that encourage good cross ventilation, such as doors with no-see-um net, netted back vents or rear windows, and/or netted tent ceilings, can be valuable additions. The option of zippered storm flaps over these netted openings allows for adjustment to colder weather.

If your tent is to function adequately, the design and cut of the fly are important. A skimpy fly may let in moisture. In rainy weather the drawback to any tent with a tightly fitted fly is that ventilation may be hampered, especially with the entire family inside. Some flies come with a short front extension; a coated storm panel covers the tent door. A longer front extension on the fly can be useful with children. Access is not as easy, which is fine since youngsters need to stop at the tent door to take off muddy boots before entering. Dirty boots can be sheltered under the extension, and the space could be used for emergency cooking in bad weather. Even in a tent with a cookhole and ventilation, however, you are asking for trouble by trying to cook inside with children wiggling around. For any in-tent cooking, only kerosene stoves, which are the safest to operate, should be used. (See the section on "Stoves.") Better yet, leave your youngsters inside the tent where they are warm and dry, and take your stove outside and cook under an extra tarp.

SPECIALTY ITEMS USEFUL TO FAMILIES

Families are always trying to find additional space in the tent. Vestibules, which can be zipped onto the front of a two-person or larger tent, are one way to provide more room; gear or children can fit into this extra space. So that sleeping family members can use all the floor space in the tent, gear lofts or attics, a mesh hammock attached below the tent ceiling, and inside mesh storage pockets along the tent wall can be useful additions. Since wet gear is almost guaranteed with children along, gear lofts can also help with drying out wet clothing or boots. Tents designed for taller people can also provide more floor space and be worth the extra cost and weight.

WORKMANSHIP

The workmanship on a tent is very important to long-term use. When buying a tent from a catalogue, you have no opportunity to inspect such features as the reinforcement at stress points, the kinds of seams used (flat-fell seams are best), and the closeness of the stitching. Some of the higher cost of a better tent is due to the bias cut of the fabric that minimizes general sagging and flapping in the wind. In bad weather, the less sag and flap, the more efficient the protection. To help evaluate such details, you can consult *Backpacker Magazine*'s yearly outdoor gear issue, which provides information based on field tests of new products. You can also rent or borrow tents so that you can examine the quality and thus compare various products and features with your own field tests.

OTHER ALTERNATIVES

If wind protection and warmth are not necessary where you camp, but bugs are a problem, the no-see-um net tent may be worth considering. This design provides a well-ventilated warm-weather tent. Various models feature a coated nylon tub floor and a coated fly that extends low enough to keep out rain if needed. Some netted models provide the option of zipping in a storm flap when a warmer tent is necessary.

Another approach is to carry one tent and use a tarp

(see discussion of tarps, next) for the extra people, probably the adults. Taking a tent fly with poles and stakes is another tarplike alternative. Already partially structured, these set up particularly fast.

Any double-shelter arrangement breaks up the coziness of the family's being together. The bedtime stories children love cannot be shouted out between two structures. Often children—and not only little ones—are reluctant to sleep without an adult, so you must do some careful distributing of the adults in the party.

USING TARPS

A good-quality tent is expensive. If you feel you cannot afford a tent but still want adequate shelter for children, a variety of arrangements can be rigged with a tarp and ground cloth. For a fraction of a tent's cost, coated nylon tarps come with grommets already conveniently spaced; you simply add your own line. Tarps come in various sizes; for a family, 9-by-12-foot and 12-by-12-foot tarps are convenient sizes. A 9-by-12 tarp weighs only about 2 pounds.

Tarps provide moderately effective rain protection. They are less efficient against wind and little help, if any, against bugs and rodents. For bug protection, extra no-see-um netting can be added to the bottom of a tarp either by sewing it on permanently or by using Velcro fasteners to attach the netting when needed.

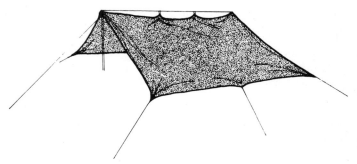

Figure 6. Tarp with guy lines and poles as shelter

If you are new to tarping, practice in the backyard to find out what a tarp will and will not do. Since a tarp sheet is flat, some way is needed to hold up and shape the material. You can use tent poles with a tarp, or you can tie line between two trees (assuming there are two conveniently located trees) as a center support. On canoe and kayak trips, paddles can double as poles unless you plan a base camp and day trips. Stakes or rocks can be attached to guy lines to anchor a tarp. As you try out your tarp, devise a high, breezy setup for clear weather; then decide how you can modify this basic setup so that it can be easily lowered in the rain. Think of a way to keep the wind out, regardless of its direction. (You'll discover that the two-tree method limits versatility when fighting wind and rain.) To use a tarp successfully for your family in bad weather, you need enough practice so that your shelter materializes quickly. Even five minutes is a long time for a child to stand shivering in the rain.

When you carry a small tent into areas noted for rainy weather, take along a light tarp to provide shelter for cooking, eating, and leg stretching. In prolonged rain, children become very restless when confined inside a tent.

SLEEPING ARRANGEMENTS

Creating a sleeping arrangement for a family is an art form in itself. Family politics must be considered. Children may want equal turns to sleep next to Dad. To avoid quarrels and roughhousing, exhausted siblings may need to be separated.

You also want to make the best use of the little space you have. If all heads are one way, shoulders—the widest part of each body—are spread out across one dimension. In a nontapered tent, head-to-foot sleeping makes better use of space, especially with bigger children. You will find, too, that the outer areas where the tent slopes down are more comfortable for children than for adults.

Sleeping with youngsters in close quarters is not guaranteed to be pleasant, especially if your children squirm, roll, toss, creep, and crawl at night. Besides moving, young children can produce an incredible array of sounds. Parents may have to learn to sleep through anything.

YOUNG CHILDREN AND STRANGE PLACES

Some young children are especially wary of a strange setting. Your tent is not home, and if the experience is new you may have a child who won't sleep—or worse. A sobbing child in the out-of-doors is no fun. Ideally, parents will use a tent often enough to create place familiarity for their children. If trips are rare, practice runs in the backyard can be helpful preparation. Some young children will not sleep with parents or siblings in the tent and must be put to bed before everyone else retires. Others will not sleep without parents there, and this means everyone goes to bed together. Backyard outings help you to discover what works best.

It is essential to take familiar bedtime toys on your trips. Whatever your child is accustomed to—a snuggle toy, blanket, pacifier, or bottle of juice—makes the tent seem less strange and more like home.

SLEEPING OUT, THE PURIST APPROACH

The experience of sleeping outside the walls of a tent can be beautiful. Parents who love the out-of-doors sometimes want to share the specialness of night with their children. The quiet is magnificent. The dark, star-speckled sky stretches out endlessly. The moon coats mountains and forests with shimmery light.

Certainly no one in our family will soon forget the tiptoeing visit of deer to the spot where we slept out one night. National park secure, the animals wandered close enough to touch. In a closed tent we would have missed their silent coming and going. Another time we witnessed the midnight play of a family of mountain goats. Seven of them woke us with their cud chewing, and we watched fascinated as they played and butted and grazed.

On any clear night a family can choose to sleep out under the stars. You need a ground cloth and a protective covering over your sleeping bags to keep off the dew. Aluminized plastic emergency blankets, weighing only 2 ounces, work quite well. Especially in the mountains or along the ocean, set up your tent as insurance against a sudden weather change. To function well on outdoor trips, children need uninterrupted sleep. If they awaken in a downpour and have to wait while you rig a shelter in the dark, you may have exhausted, cranky children as well as wet gear. If you are blessed with one of those can't-get-back-to-sleep youngsters who sings and mutters till dawn, he or she can leave the entire family exhausted. When sleeping out, be ready to move children quickly and quietly into the tent.

CAR CAMPING TENTS

If you plan to expose your children to the outdoors gradually by car camping and day hiking, you can use any kind of tent that will fit in the car. However, if you intend to branch out into backpacking eventually, you should definitely be using a lightweight tent. In the comfort of the campground, you can learn how to set up your backcountry tent and how to arrange your family in it, and you can iron out problems before an extended backcountry excursion.

BOAT CAMPING TENTS

People who camp only out of kayaks, canoes, or rafts with their children need not be as concerned about tent weight. Boats can be paddled easily with a heavy load. However, when transporting your entire family on water, space can become an important consideration. The compact, lightweight mountain tent is a space saver. If you are boat camping at low elevations where the weather is mild or warm, a no-see-um net tent may be ideal.

SNOW CAMPING TENTS

Some parents who are experienced snow campers take their children on short, overnight trips in the winter. If you plan to do this, your tent should have useful wintertime features. Tied tunnel entrances are a reasonable addition for winter camping since zippers can freeze in cold weather. A closed vestibule with a cookhole and high chimney vent also are valuable. Many people add a detachable frost liner, an inner wall made of absorbent material, such as cotton; the liner is designed to gather up frost that accumulates during winter nights. Snow stakes, which are extra long (11 or 12 inches), also can be carried, but aren't necessary in the summer.

CARE OF TENTS

To extend the life of coated materials, do not submerge your tent to clean it. (Some tent instructions are ambiguous on this point.) When dry, a tent's slick nylon surface helps grime slip off. If food spills, which is possible if you are forced to eat in a crowded family tent, a gentle wipe-up with a soft sponge and warm water usually is sufficient.

It is better to avoid getting gas or pitch on a tent than to try to clean these substances off later. Therefore, lighting, priming, filling, and storing stoves should be done away from tents.

Taking off boots before entering a tent decreases the accumulation of dirt. Children have to be reminded. If a youngster's clothing is mud and dirt spattered, stripping before entering may mean a few chilly moments, but the rule saves the tent. Carry an extra plastic bag to hold hopelessly soiled clothes; do not let children dump them inside the tent. The waterproofing on a tent is a coating; in time it can wear off. A light (backpack-type) whiskbroom, when gently applied, eliminates dirt and sand that can scratch off the tent's coating.

After you return from a trip, always dry out your tent. Nylon can mildew. A few hours on a sunny day will suffice. If the weather isn't sunny, set up the tent inside and let it air until you are certain no moisture remains. When the tent is thoroughly dry, a gentle brushing and a good shaking will get rid of most dirt.

Nylon is a strong material, but it can be punctured. For mending, carry adhesive-backed cloth tape for coated materials and ripstop repair tape for ripstop nylon.

Zippers are also available for do-it-yourself repair. When you purchase your tent, find out if the company offers repairs, replaceable parts, or any other services to extend the life of your tent.

Applying extra sealer to seams in the coated areas of your tent can help reduce leaks that develop due to aging. Resealing should be done at the beginning of each outdoor season. Improved sprays for recoating tent flies and tub floors can refurbish worn coated materials and increase the effectiveness of your older tent. If your tent fly begins to leak, you can also replace it. Flies can be purchased separately for many tents and are the least expensive part to replace. If you have an old tent, do a complete maintenance check before every new camping season. A night in the yard during a rainstorm or a little garden sprinkler action is a good way to test for leaks.

GUY LINES AND CHILDREN

Even so-called freestanding tents and domes require lines and stakes so that they do not roll away in the wind. Falling over a protruding stake or guy line can be painful. To save children and tents unnecessary trauma, it is wise to make the tent area off limits during playtime. Pounding in stakes so that they are even with the ground also helps avoid accidents.

THE IMPACT OF YOUR SHELTER

Pegs or stakes usually come with a tent and are the part of the tent that penetrates the ground. The more slender the stake, the less damage you do to your campsite. Plastic or wedge-shaped pegs are larger by design, and they cut larger holes. If the stakes that come with your tent chew up a site more than necessary, you can buy slim stakes separately. Long, slender aluminum nails also cause less ground damage.

In theory, the more freestanding your shelter, the less impact on your campsite. Freestanders, however, still must be securely anchored. The greater the number of stakes required, the more your shelter breaks up the earth. To eliminate some staking, rocks can be tied to guy lines, but be sure to move the rocks back to where you found them when you leave. A tent with a coated tub floor can protect occupants as effectively as a drainage moat, so you do not need to dig a ditch around your tent.

If your family uses two small tents or a tent and a tarp, you affect a larger space at your campsite. Be sure the places you visit can absorb more than one shelter. Never spread onto the vegetation beyond your established site.

Choosing an unobtrusive rather than a brightly colored tent lessens the visual impact of your camp. If you are concerned with safety (you want to be found if lost), a bright tent, which could be exposed in an emergency, and a dull-colored fly provide a good combination.

Stoves

ENVIRONMENTAL REASONS FOR STOVE USE

At one time, when the backcountry was little used, whether a party cooked on an open fire seemed relatively immaterial. Today, with the increased popularity of wilderness travel, fires are inappropriate in many places, as you can see by visiting an overused site. You will find that such a campsite and the surrounding woods look stripped; downed wood and the natural debris of winter are gone, having been used for campfires. The place appears unnatural and strange; it no longer looks wild. By using a stove for backcountry cooking, you can more easily leave wilderness areas just as you found them. (See also Chapter 9, the section on "Fires.")

When you take children into the outdoors, you encourage them to enjoy the wilderness as a lifelong recreation. You increase the potential interest in backcountry and help create a new and still larger generation of backcountry users. As a wilderness enthusiast, you have an obligation to teach your children nondestructive habits of outdoor use. By learning to carry and use a stove for cooking, you show youngsters one simple way to come and go without leaving your family's imprint on the out-of-doors.

Backcountry stoves are lightweight, and they are easier to use for meals than a fire. When you cook on a stove, you leave no charred fire ring and no wood-stripped setting behind. You give future visitors more of a chance to experience the natural beauty of the site.

CHILD REASONS FOR STOVE USE

In addition to environmental reasons for carrying and using a stove, the child reasons are so numerous as to make the purchase of a lightweight stove a top priority for any family.

Picture the following scene. You start out on a backpacking trip with your two children. Sunshine filters through the clouds the first half of the day, but by afternoon there is a heavy overcast. The temperature drops and it begins to drizzle. You are prepared, and everyone dons raingear. The hike is steeper than you anticipated. By the time you find a campsite, the rain is pouring down hard, and you have two exhausted young children, who, when they stop walking, start to shiver. As they shake, lower lips tremble and tears well up. If you are really prepared, within five minutes you can have your children inside a tent in dry sleeping bags, and within ten minutes, the time it takes to boil water for soup or hot chocolate, you can hand your children warm drinks to soothe their troubles away.

Imagine the same scene if you arrive at the campsite and have to build a fire. First you discover that wood is scarce. You go a distance and find some that is already wet. You carve off peelings that, even with fire-starter, burn momentarily and then go out. As the youngsters are standing there waiting, they are close to tears. You may be getting miserable yourself from crawling on damp ground to blow on tentative sparks. Your patience level with your children may be hovering around zero.

Even on good days, children who have exerted themselves physically can be fine one minute and exhausted to tears the next. Youngsters who are passengers in a canoe or kayak or raft sit all day in the center of the boat, where water taken in is most likely to drain. A damp child can become chilled suddenly when afternoon coolness sets in. If you are prepared to warm your youngsters fast by cooking something hot on a reliable backcountry stove, you can avoid many unpleasant moments.

Although stoves have their own hazards, the dangers are few. With a fire, which burns first for meals and afterward for sociability, there is always the possibility that a youngster will trip or fall into hot coals. Fire also fascinates children. They like to put wood on a fire and watch it ignite or, worse yet, hold the wood while it burns. If you make the fire circle out of bounds, then some of the reasons for having a fire, such as warmth, work only for adults (see Chapter 9, the section on "Fires").

A stove is used strictly for cooking. Although it has its attractions, such as that friendly hiss of burning fuel, you do not use the stove for warmth or social reasons. You cook a meal and then turn off the stove; it cools in minutes, becoming a harmless piece of metal. The limited time of stove use in itself eliminates much potential danger for children. Since the barely visible flame is not an attraction, you can more easily put the cooking stove out of bounds during use.

Finally, a stove offers another advantage. Stove cooking is clean while a fire leaves pot bottoms sooty. Family camping entails a great deal of work, so that eliminating an extra job, such as soot cleaning, is a blessing.

No one who wants family camping to be pleasant and relaxed should go into the backcountry without an efficient, lightweight stove. By using a stove instead of a fire for cooking, you help leave the environment as you found it and save yourself a lot of worry.

TYPES OF STOVES

Many types of lightweight stoves are available; there are small, white gas–burning models; slightly larger white gas designs with hand-operated fuel pumps; multi-fuel stoves that burn white gas, kerosene, or unleaded auto gas; kerosene stoves; alcohol burning stoves; cartridge stoves that use a butane-propane mixture of fuel; steel cannister stoves that burn propane; lightweight forced-air twig and wood chip burning stoves. When deciding which stove is best, remember that families are essentially groups and that what works well for one person may not be adequate for a group. Also determine the altitude, climate, and seasons when you will use the stove.

You need a reliable stove. You need one that starts consistently in a minimum amount of time. You need a safe stove too. If you plan to camp off season, winter camp, or camp at high altitudes, you need a stove designed to operate in these situations.

For each stove type, there are a variety of models available. No stove is all things to all people; therefore, when you buy one, personal needs and preference will influence your final choice. Whichever model you choose, your decision to use a stove rather than a campfire for cooking helps preserve the wilderness and makes cooking more pleasant on family trips.

White Gas Stoves

These stoves operate on white gas fuel that is sold through sporting goods and hardware stores. White gas stoves can be used year round. The reasonably priced fuel required makes these stoves economical to run and provides excellent heat output, although they rarely simmer effectively.

Almost all models must be primed. To start a white gas stove, heat first must be generated around the tank and vaporizing tube. To do this, you burn a small amount of fuel in the stove's priming cup. When the flame dies down, you open the stove valve and light the escaping gas with a match. Once the stove has been primed and is warm, the vapor pressure inside forces the liquid fuel into the vaporizing tube, where the liquid transforms into a gas. The gas continues moving upward, combines with air at the bottom of the burner head, and burns. Essentially, fuel is kept flowing as a result of the stove's own heat. Once you master priming, operation of a white gas stove is simple.

Although any spilled fuel is highly flammable, it evaporates quickly without leaving greasy stains, and the fuel burns clean. Since fuel can flare up while you are priming, children should be kept away from the stove from the beginning of meal preparation. When you evaluate designs, look for a low-profile style with wide-based support for pots to avoid dangerous spills.

For cold weather, a white gas stove must have a hand-operated fuel pump that provides extra air pressure to force fuel up to the burner. Because white gas has the fastest boiling time even in cold weather, hot food can be prepared and hungry children can be fed quickly—which gives this type of stove a distinct advantage.

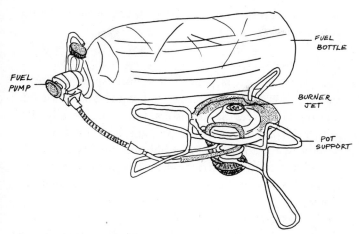

Figure 7. Lightweight backcountry stove with handpump

Multi-fuel Stoves

Many stoves that burn white gas will also burn other fuels, including kerosene, leaded and unleaded auto gas, aviation gas, Stoddard solvent, diesel. Especially if any foreign travel lies in your future, the multi-fuel models represent the most versatile choice. Since you can always use white gas for outdoor activities in the United States, you obtain all the advantages of this fuel plus the versatility of being able to find some other fuel anywhere in the world.

Some multi-fuel and white gas stoves use a fuel storage bottle instead of a built-in fuel tank. Such designs have the advantage of saving some weight and space.

Kerosene Stoves

The safest stoves to use burn kerosene. Since kerosene is difficult to ignite, you have to try hard to create an accident with this fuel; you must also try hard when lighting a kerosene stove. All kerosene stoves are hand pumped and must be primed. Although kerosene burns clean, it definitely stains. Still, if your main concern with children is stove accidents, you should consider the kerosene stove or you could choose to use kerosene in one of the multi-fuel stoves.

Fuel Cannister Stoves

Fuel cannister stoves provide low initial purchase price, simplicity of use, and flame control, which allows for simmering. However, the cannisters, which are usually filled with a mixture of butane and propane, are relatively costly to buy in the long run. In addition, empties cannot be reused and must be carried out; many of these cannisters cannot be recycled. What attracts novices to the fuel cannister design is its simple operation. You attach the stove to the fuel cartridge in one of several ways, depending on the design; then you turn a knob to release the gas; and finally you apply a match to the gas to produce an easy-to-regulate cooking flame. Low-profile styles with wide-based pot support provide the best stability for pots. For a beginning stove user who plans on mild-weather trips, the cartridge stove provides an easy introduction to back-country stove use.

The disadvantage is the longer cooking time required on these stoves. Also although heat from a full cartridge is fairly good, partially used cartridges gradually produce di-

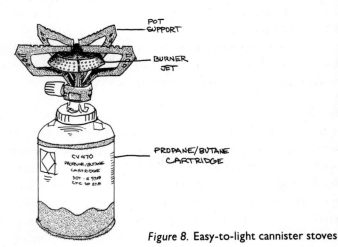

Figure 8. Easy-to-light cannister stoves

minished heating power and, when close to empty, will barely simmer. Even when the heating efficiency has decreased in this way, some of these cartridges cannot be changed until they are completely empty. At low elevations cartridge stoves work well only at temperatures above 32°F; they also will function at elevations above 15,000 feet where the atmospheric pressure is reduced. As a result, they should be considered a warm-weather stove.

Alcohol Stoves

A few stove models use alcohol, which burns the most quietly of all fuels. The low volatility of alcohol makes these stoves very safe, but the fuel is hard to buy and the stoves produce half the heat that an equal weight of other gases would generate.

Propane Stoves

Propane-burning stoves require heavy, thick, steel cannisters and, therefore, are appropriate only for boating, where space and weight are not an issue.

Small Wood Chip Stoves

Lightweight wood-burning stoves with a battery-operated forced-air fan provide a fire without a fire ring. Weighing only 15 ounces, these stoves burn twigs, pine cones, bark, or charcoal and save you the weight of carrying in your fuel. A battery-powered blower creates a miniature bellows effect that produces enough heat to boil a quart of water in four minutes. If you choose this forced-air wood burner, you must be certain that these stoves are allowed where you plan to camp; also remember that these models are appropriate only where fast-growing trees are readily available.

Operation and Maintenance of Separate-Fuel Stoves

Be sure that you become well acquainted with your new stove before your first trip. Practice lighting it outside at home, because a chilly evening on the trail when your children are ready to fall apart is not the time to begin experimenting with a stove's intricacies. Especially if you are just learning to prime a stove, repeated home practice is a necessity.

Once you have learned to operate your stove, you must determine your fuel needs for a particular trip. Most stove manufacturers give approximate burning times for a tankful or cannister of fuel. Check the accuracy of this information as you are learning to operate your stove. Keep a record of water boiling and cooking times to help you calculate your family's fuel needs on trips. When planning, remember that boiling times are longer at higher elevations.

With separate-fuel stoves, you need a good-quality metal container with a spillproof top for carrying your fuel. For these containers you must purchase separate pouring caps. Round, aluminum bottles in various sizes are readily available. Some stove brands require specific fuel containers that attach to the rest of the stove so that no separate pouring is necessary. For extra insurance against spills and fuel drips, enclose the fuel container in a heavyweight plastic bag and seal the top well.

Many separate-fuel stoves are self-cleaning. At the top of the vaporizing tube, a needle is activated to keep the hole open. You clean other models with separate cleaning needles. Before storing a stove with a built-in fuel tank, always empty out any leftover fuel.

Buying the repair kit recommended for your stove is always a good investment. Regular maintenance takes only minutes, while a stove faulty from neglect can cause you hours of frustration on a backcountry trip.

Remember, too, that stoves age. At the beginning of a new camping season, check the condition of your stove. Compare the unit's boiling speed with its boiling speed from the previous season. With some stoves, you can replace worn parts at an outdoor store or through the manufacturer.

Figure 9. Lightweight cooking pots
with lids

Cooking Pots

Sturdy, lightweight, aluminum pots for camping can be purchased in nesting sets or separately. For general camping, nesting pots in various sizes (1-, 2-, and 3-quart) allow for more versatile cooking. For backcountry travel, you can help reduce the overall weight of your gear by taking a minimum number of pots.

FOR BACKPACKING

Cooking simply for the family can save work and time and can cut to a minimum the number of pots needed. With a backcountry stove, only one pot can cook at a time. By finding one basic pot the right size for the meals you plan, you also reduce the weight carried. The pot should have a snug-fitting lid to speed boiling. Usually main dishes take the most water, so check your food packets to determine the maximum amount of water you must boil for a meal. The basic pot can be used for any foods that rehydrate with the addition of boiling water. If dishes must cook in the pot itself, you can serve soup and hot drinks first and then prepare the main course.

Some pots have special features, such as lids that can

double as plates or frying pans. If the sizes suit your needs, this means another weight saving. Some meals, such as eggs, sausage, or fresh fish, require frying. An 8-inch frying pan also can serve as a container for mixing and setting four-person desserts, including cheesecakes, cobblers, compotes, and puddings.

For fish or egg cooking, a nonstick coating on frying pans helps avoid messy cleanup. With nonstick pots and pans, you must use utensils made of materials that will not scratch the surface, and a soft cleaning device. Some of these dish cleaners come with a sponge on one side and an abrasive on the back side so that one pan cleaner allows both hard scrubbing and soft wiping of coated surfaces.

For additional weight economy, you can use your basic pot for dishwashing too. Cooking and cleaning up in this one-step-at-a-time manner works well for children, since without a table they tend to spill if given more than one item at a time. Some people prefer having a second pot for dishwashing; a 2- or 3-quart size that is wide rather than tall usually accommodates camping utensils.

A good metal pot-lifter enables you to pick up a hot pot and pour without burning yourself. Some lifters come with the pots. If purchased separately, a pot-lifter should be sturdy enough to support the weight of your largest pot when it is filled.

For convenience, you can choose a pot large enough to hold your stove. This keeps the "kitchen" in one place and easy to locate in your pack. Careful packing of pots is essential. In a tightly loaded pack, even sturdy pots can bend out of shape. Lids do not fit misshapen pots, and this, in turn, slows down cooking times.

For easy measuring, paint lines on the outside of your pots to indicate cup levels. When traveling with groups, initial your pots, lifter, and other kitchen utensils to avoid mixups with other people's gear.

FOR BOAT TRIPS

On canoe, kayak, and raft trips the weight of your gear becomes less important. Since you have room for canned and some fresh food, choose cooking pots that can accommodate the menus planned. Nesting pots save space and provide a slight size variation. Be sure you have lids for each size pot you carry. Often plates can double as lids, or vice versa.

When you boat travel in groups for safety, you can devise plans for sharing some meals. Many groups assign each family a certain number of meals to prepare for everyone, usually breakfasts and dinners. For this situation, you need pots big enough for large-group cooking.

Plates, Cups, and Eating Utensils

In the backcountry, a child who is handed both a cup and a plate inevitably will spill one or the other. For backpacking, one cup and one spoon per child is practical and saves on weight. A youngster manages better when eating one course at a time. If you serve soup first, you can cook the main dish while the child eats the soup. Warm water set aside at the beginning of a meal can be used to wash out the cup between courses. When the various foods you serve blend nicely into one another, you can dispense with between-course washing.

A child's cup should have a handle that ensures a firm grip and that will not burn a youngster's hand. Stainless-steel Sierra Club cups stay cool around the rim and hold enough food for most children, though they are a bit awkward at first for little hands. Plastic cups are light but can crush and break if not carefully packed. When toting the family's cups together, nesting cups are advantageous.

If weight is not crucial, you may want the luxury of cups and plates for everyone. Camping plates are available in plastic or lightweight metal, and some can double as

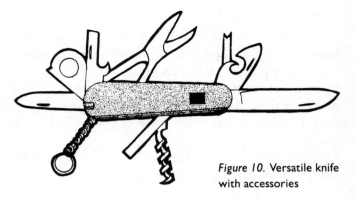

Figure 10. Versatile knife
with accessories

pot lids. Metal plates are heavier; plastic ones are more fragile.

Eating utensils for camping are made of lightweight stainless steel. A spoon, fork, and knife set weighs just 3 ounces. You generally need only a spoon and fork for youngsters. Knives are handy, though, for spreading peanut butter, jelly, and margarine, so take one or two with you.

For cutting, carry a multi-accessoried knife. Tweezer and scissor accessories are indispensable for family trips.

The multi-accessory knife provides a minitoolbox and first-aid implements as well. If you buy a model with a metal ring attached, you can wear it on a string to avoid losing it. Older children enjoy having their own multi-accessory knives, which also should be worn around the neck. Once children own knives, parents need to set unbreakable rules for their proper use.

Food

When planning food for beginning trips and for travel with young children, the best policy is to keep meals simple, quick, and easy to prepare. The time saved can go into enjoying the outdoors with your family.

For backpacking, dried foods form the backbone of meals since they are lighter to carry. In a canoe, kayak, or raft, using some dehydrated food saves space. With a home dryer you can dehydrate your own food, save money in the long run, and provide familiar tastes for youngsters.

HOW MUCH

Planning food quantities for family backpacking trips is especially difficult. Knowing how much a child eats during meals at home helps very little. A child who is hiking every day uses extraordinary amounts of energy. Fresh air also stimulates the appetite of a nonwalker. A parent carrying both gear and a child may experience unprecedented appetite gains. Be prepared for ravenous children by taking maximum amounts of food. Better to have too much, despite the added weight, than have too little, which may deplete your child's energy.

When determining amounts, think about trip activities. A strenuous first day of carrying packs requires more food than later days of pleasure hiking from a base camp. Near the end of a trip, everyone in the family will be in better physical condition and will require less food. At best, food quantity is going to be an educated guess.

YOUR CHILD'S TASTE FOR DEHYDRATED FOODS

Most dehydrated foods do not taste like home-cooked meals. Some children who are usually adequate eaters do not like and will not eat dried foods presented to them as stock, one-pot-meal concoctions. A picky eater almost certainly will bring poor eating habits on trips despite the energy he or she expends. Since many one-pot dried food meals require a starvation-level appetite to be palatable, trying out various combinations at home does not necessarily answer taste problems for adults or children.

Planning separate meals for younger children and picky eaters may be necessary. A child who dislikes mixed foods almost certainly will detest creamy, one-pot trail meals. Dried foods that can be cooked and eaten separately or no-cook dehydrated food may be perfectly acceptable, however. Fruit leathers, dried fruits, jerky, dried peanut butter, noodles, and rice are all home testable. A backcountry trip is no place to try converting the poor eater to better habits. If you cannot establish versatile eating at home, plan to provide separate foods your child will eat.

DINNERS

Food decisions are easy to make for children who will try anything and are not turned off by exotic or previously untried tastes. You can try out one-pot meals on day hikes if your child's eating patterns are unpredictable. A wide selection of prepackaged main courses is available in outdoor stores. You can go exotic and try beef stroganoff, shrimp creole, or turkey tetrazzini, or you can find such traditional favorites as hot dogs and baked beans or chili and hamburger patties. These complete-in-themselves dinners are fairly expensive. The more meat involved, the more expensive the meal.

Prepackaged dried meals are marked as serving two or four people. Since serving sizes vary for different brands, check the weights on labels. If your own appetite is moderate, a two-serving meal may be adequate for two adults plus two light eaters under 6 years of age. As children's appetites grow, two-serving meals become too little for the whole family and four servings may be far too much. If you reseal carefully and use quickly, you can redivide the ingredients of several four-serving meals into the equivalent of meals for three. This quantity feeds two adults plus one or two children between the ages of 6 and 8. By 9, fast-growing children who are good eaters often consume adult-sized portions. Then a family of four needs four-person meals.

When children like certain dishes and have no interest

in variety, you can save by buying in bulk. You can then package each meal to suit your current needs.

Preparing a one-pot meal is easy. Generally, you place the ingredients in boiling water, mix, and then cook. Meats and some other ingredients may require extra re-hydration time. Other one-pot meals are even simpler, because all you do is put a cooking pouch into the boiling water or you put boiling water into the pouch until the meals reheat. For children who want food immediately and often have no patience for waiting once they are hungry, this approach can be ideal. These meals are sinfully easy to prepare, and you have no pots to scrub afterward. If you are looking for shortcuts and time savers, precooked and freeze-dried food may be the best choice for you.

You also can buy dried food ingredients separately and do your own combining. For stew, you can purchase a meat packet and the vegetables you want and add beef bouillon cubes or packaged gravy. For chicken and rice, simply cook instant rice and add freeze-dried chicken and a packaged sauce or gravy. Creating your own dishes often saves you money too. You also can cook ingredients separately for children who want nothing mixed together. You serve youngsters first and then concoct your own one-pot meal. When packaging your own ingredients, include any special cooking directions necessary in each packet. Small plastic bags, carefully sealed with rubber bands or tape, can be used to hold individual ingredients. The entire meal can be packaged in a larger plastic bag and labeled for contents. Plastic sacks stuffed into packs do not have the durability of some of the commercial food packages, however.

When you buy packaged ingredients, always check prices. For future reference, keep a list of one-pot successes and failures and the brands you used. One brand of dinner may not please your family's palate, while the same dish from another manufacturer may be heartily enjoyed. Only trial and error will tell. Older children like to help with meal planning; if you encourage their assistance, you may encounter fewer meal failures. What youngsters choose themselves they often devour with added zest.

BREAKFASTS

Whether your family enjoys sausage and eggs or cereal and toast, you can find camping breakfasts closely akin to whatever you eat at home. The flavors of dried breakfasts are similar to fresh food flavors, so youngsters shouldn't have much difficulty in adapting to the tastes.

If you carry breads, rolls, or muffins, choose kinds that are not flaky or crumbly. The more solid French breads, rolls, and bagels keep their shape and consistency better than average sandwich bread. English muffins hold up well too. If you use cereals, granolas carry better; you can add fruits, nuts, or coconut to make one dish provide a more complete meal.

As you plan menus, think of each day as a whole and work into breakfasts needed nutrients missing in other meals. Eggs or meats at breakfast start the day with protein. Many dried fruits and fruit juices are available, or you can dry favorite fruits at home and carry them with you.

LUNCHES

Lunch can be a no-cook meal. Although hot soups or drinks warm up youngsters on stormy days, planning lunch without cooking gives you leeway to get ready for day hiking away from camp.

Hard, nonfragile breads and rolls pack well for lunches; so do pilot breads and hard crackers.

For short durations in moderate weather, some cheeses and sausages keep well. Jerky, which is dried, will not spoil, and you can dry your own jerky at home. Cheese and meat worked into lunches provide additional protein in the middle of a child's active day, but any nondried foods are going to increase the weight of your gear.

If your children are crazy about peanut butter, even that comes dehydrated. Cheese does too. Fruits come in a variety of dehydrated forms, and many children like granola bars and fruit bars better than candy. Fruit and nut candies also are available and do not melt the way some sweets, such as chocolate, do.

Lunch carries children through the most active part of their day, so don't skimp when packing lunch food. Extras can be used for snacks or worked into other meals.

SOUPS

Soup makes an ideal first course at dinner. In addition to filling out main meals, it can be used as an instant hot food at lunch or an easily prepared food for emergencies. Although individual-serving soups cost more, they provide the family with a greater choice at mealtime and are ready as soon as you add boiling water. Larger soup packages require the addition of three or four cups of water and take some time to cook. Carrying soup for every main meal gives you added flexibility with food quantities. After a vigorous day, serve soup before dinner. For lazy days in camp, wait until the main course is finished and then cook soup only for those who are still hungry. Many soups are salty and help replace the salt lost through sweating.

DESSERTS

Desserts complete a meal and please youngsters. Many dried desserts contain fruits to balance out starchy main meals. Other desserts, such as pudding, add milk to your children's diet. Youngsters often like to be involved in choosing favorite desserts as their part in trip planning.

SNACKS

Snacks are more necessary for children in the outdoors than they are at home. On the trail, snacks are like fuel. They are needed for energy and they are burned up fast. Fats and proteins do not release energy quickly; they are better all-day energy providers. Carbohydrates give fast energy boosts.

If you want a more scientific analysis of the potential energy values of various foods, you can find this information in the U.S. Department of Agriculture handbook, *Composition of Foods,* which contains multiple charts detailing the exact composition of foods. Children, however, like snacks that please their taste buds regardless of the food values. Snacks that work for your youngsters may include sunflower seeds, which are low in carbohydrates, or caramels, which are high.

In the outdoors, foods can provide important motivation for children. For skiing, hiking, and bicycling, snacks can help keep youngsters moving long after they want to stop. They also help pacify a restless child riding in a canoe, kayak, raft, *Fjellpulken,* or child carrier.

You have a tremendous choice in backcountry snacks. If sweets are rarely offered to children at home, candy can have a high motivational value. Caramels, jellybeans, lemon drops, and gumdrops are high in carbohydrates. If chocolate melts, children usually do not care. You can, however, buy what is called "desert chocolate," which remains intact in the heat. To a basic granola you can add child-tempters, such as chocolate-coated nuts and fruit. If you want your children to shun candy, try combining granola with dried raisins, dates, apricots, apples, pears, peaches, or nuts.

Most children like to carry their own individual snack bags for instant nibbling. You may want to ration out particular snack favorites to last through the trip. For any individually wrapped snacks, have a litter bag handy. When you give youngsters their snack bags, provide them with definite instructions on depositing wrappers.

MILK

Some children refuse to drink dried milk. Check your child's reaction to milk in this form before a backcountry trip. You can switch to using dried milk at home if you want the taste to become familiar to family members.

When youngsters dislike the taste of dried milk, you can carry and add chocolate or strawberry mixes or work milk into the camp diet in other ways. Milk poured over morning granola may be perfectly acceptable. Puddings, hot chocolate, hot cereal with milk, or cheese can provide milk in another form if these foods please your children. If a child will drink dried milk cold, but not warm, mixing with icy water or storing the milk in a cold stream can help. Remember, in warm weather milk sours easily once it is mixed. Bottles with milk residue must be thoroughly cleaned.

If your child's milk consumption drops in the backcountry, this dietary imbalance will not hurt on short trips of two or three days. For longer periods of time, ask your physician for advice. To provide the equivalent of milk's calcium you can sometimes use an antacid. Tums chew easily, and other chewable antacids come in fruit flavors.

WATER AND OTHER FLUIDS

Keeping youngsters from becoming dehydrated in hot weather and on physically demanding hikes is very important. Children often ask for water when they do not need it—they walk the first ten steps of a hike and are convinced they are dying of thirst. Later in the day, when they need liquids to compensate for fluid loss due to activity and heat, youngsters forget to drink or drink too infrequently. Therefore, making sure that children drink enough fluids is a parent's responsibility.

Most youngsters like fruit drink mixes, which make up into quart-size quantities. At less cost you can buy larger amounts and then divide as needed. To avoid leaking sugary granules into your gear, carry these larger mixes in screw-top plastic jars or bottles.

With morning and evening meals, many children enjoy

hot chocolate that contains nonfat dried milk. Buying hot-chocolate mix in bulk costs less, but individual serving packets are more convenient.

FINDING CAMP FOOD IN SUPERMARKETS

Supermarkets are a good source of lightweight dried foods. Sometimes, but not always, supermarket prices are appreciably lower than those at specialty stores.

When preparing for the camping season, take time to check out dried food products and prices before you go out and buy them. Take a notebook and research one or more local supermarkets. Wander up and down the aisles and record dried weights and prices of various dishes or ingredients. Check the labels for protein content (meat or protein amounts can account for extreme price variations) and look at the packaging. Some supermarket dried foods come in bulky, difficult-to-pack containers, such as Styrofoam cups. If a meal is appealing but poorly packed, see if you could repackage it for carrying. Besides main meals, soups, noodles, rices, dried fruits, and granolas, supermarkets carry many powdered sauces and gravies.

Keep your lists of what is available and where items can be purchased. They will help you plan trips at home and save shopping time too. Update your lists every year.

NATURAL FOODS

Natural foods stores have proliferated throughout the country. They carry a variety of dried foods processed without preservatives, including vegetarian meals for the out-of-doors. If the same products are available at supermarkets, compare prices.

FOOD FOR BOAT TRIPS

When you pack food for family boating expeditions, weight is not a primary concern, but space conservation is important. Two adults on a boating trip have enough room in a canoe or kayak so that they do not have to take any dried foods. For family trips when storage space is limited, however, you may need to carry some favorite dried foods instead of just canned and fresh foods so that there is more room for children to sit comfortably. On rafting trips, the extra space available often eliminates the need for dried foods altogether.

For main meals, canned meats are a positive, tasty food and are quite palatable to children. Ham, beef, chicken, and tuna come in small cans that occupy little space. Complete-meal canned products, such as spaghetti, ravioli, and chili, are bulky and do not taste much better than dried one-pot meals.

Certain fresh fruits and vegetables carry well on week-long trips. If you take fruit, purchase some of it unripe so that it will be ready to eat late in the trip. Fruits that bruise easily, such as peaches and pears, can be packed in closed, plastic refrigerator crispers. Carrots, celery, zucchini, green peppers, and red cabbage are vegetables that last well.

To save space, take youngsters' favorite fruits and vegetables in dried form and plan main meals that are a balance of canned and dried foods. This is particularly practical if you dry your own food at home (see next section).

For desserts, some home-cooked treats can be carried. Pound cakes, fruit bars, and noncrumbling cookies carry well if packed in plastic containers with lids. Such foods should be kept in your waterproof bags.

When you travel with two children in one canoe, space will be tight. At these times, planning meals as you would for backpacking helps provide additional room.

DRYING YOUR OWN FOODS

With the use of freezers for long-term storage, it is easy to forget that drying is an ancient art for food preservation.

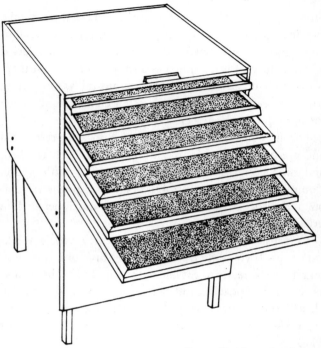

Figure 11. Home food dryer

After the initial investment for a home food dryer, you can provide your family with dried camping foods at a substantial savings. This do-it-yourself approach is particularly helpful if you have children, because you can pick out foods they like and dry them in season. The family can eat some of the dried food at home; this way children can grow accustomed to the tastes, and you avoid introducing strange foods youngsters may be reluctant to try when camping.

By pulverizing fruit you can make fruit rolls or leathers, or you can dry fruit in chunks and slices. Vegetables and meats also dry well. During the year you can plan camp menus and dry the needed ingredients. When preparing for a trip, you simply take the dried foods from storage and assemble the various meals in convenient, labeled packets.

Food drying requires heat that hovers between 95 and 105°F. Temperatures above 110°F will not work. The dryer itself can be built like a small cabinet with removable shelves made of screening materials for ventilation. You can purchase instructions for making dryers, precut dryer kits, or fully assembled dryers from various manufacturers and retailers.

Dried foods store best when carefully sealed away from moisture, air, and light. For long storage, three layers are usually recommended. You can use one layer of brown paper bags and two layers of heavy plastic, or one plastic bag and a glass jar with a lid. Each layer must be carefully sealed. When you pack away newly dried foods destined for camping, arrange them in quantities to feed your family. This way you don't have to repackage them before your trips. Be sure, too, that all foods are labeled.

PACKING FOOD FOR FAMILY TRIPS

Packing meals for family camping trips requires organization. There are many workable approaches. Some parents prefer to use three large plastic sacks marked for breakfast, lunch, and dinner. All the foods for each type of meal are packed together in the same sack. When mealtime arrives, the parent gets out the appropriate sack and chooses the meal from the selections inside.

Another approach, requiring a step up in the amount of at-home organization, is to pack everything for each day's meals in its own separate plastic sack. The sacks are then labeled by day and by meal. A dinner sack would contain the soup, main meal, hot chocolate, juice, and dessert for a particular day. With this approach, food decision making on the trip is minimal. In our family, we pack food in this day-by-day manner to save time during outings and to eliminate confusion and hassles. We avoid debates about which dessert to have, and meals that consist of the least-liked main course and dessert are not put off until last and then complained about.

Whatever system you use, you must pack enough food to take your family through all the days of the trip. You cannot go to the store if children consume more than you allotted. Also bring along meals for at least one extra day to tide you over in an emergency.

PACK OUT PAPER, PLASTIC, AND CANS

When you use dried foods, whether home dried or commercially dried, you will be left with plenty of wrappings after each meal. If fires are allowed where you are camping, you can burn or melt the plastics in a small fire, but remember that this process will produce toxic fumes. These fires are not appropriate for roasting marshmallows. The aluminum layer around freeze-dried foods will refuse to burn completely. Thus disposing of wrappings in camp requires a tedious process of burning and then collecting the sooty residue. Always clean out your fire circle, and carry out these unburnables in your litter sack.

Since dried foods are not messy, some of your plastic sacks are reusable. Especially if you do your own drying, you may find it worthwhile to bring back sacks for the next batch of food to be dried and packed.

Be sure you insist that children get in the habit of using the family litter bag. Show them, by example, how you immediately deposit litter in the sack. If immediate litter disposal is practiced, no stray plastic or paper will be left behind or blown away during an unexpected gust of wind, and children will become as fussy as you are about keeping the campsite clean.

If you are using any cans when boat camping, never bury the empties. Instead, open the cans at both ends, squash them flat, and put the lids inside the flattened cans. Then carry the cans home in your litter bag. In many communities you can deposit cans at a recycling center or in your curbside collection bin.

Incidental Items

TOWELS

You need something in camp for drying. Some people carry a dish towel and use it for everything—for drying pots and utensils, for stuffing in wet boots, and for drying off children after swimming. At the end of the day, the towel is washed along with the dishes and is hung up to dry. If you carry only one towel, you should be sure of having sunny weather. Other backpackers carry a partial roll of paper towels or a half or quarter of a bath towel for drying.

PLASTIC BAGS

Plastic bags in assorted sizes have many uses in camp. The most functional bags are heavier than sandwich bag weight. Freezer bags are adequate for small items. You need larger and sturdier plastic bags for pots and pans with blackened bottoms, children's sopping clothes, dirty sneakers, diapers, litter, leftovers you cannot bury, and toilet paper you will burn later. For repacking food for lunches, especially if you are planning day trips from a base camp, small sandwich bags also are helpful. Garbage bags are roomy but fragile; they do not last.

If you know you will be carrying out an abundance of diapers, plan to buy a strong-grade plastic; double bagging may be necessary to help with smell control. You do not want any leaking from a rip in flimsy plastic.

Litter bags are available in various parks and are strong enough to be useful. Large plastic fish bags work too. If you have youngsters in diapers or if you are in a no-fires area, a large litter bag for each parent distributes the burden better. As you walk along a trail with children, each adult then has a depository on hand for litter. The litter bag is always within reach, and youngsters develop the habit of putting every single snippet of paper into the litter sack of the parent they are with.

TOILET PAPER

For camping, partial rolls of toilet paper are just right to tuck into easy-to-reach places in packs. Each parent should have quick access to a small roll for the I-can't-wait child. Be sure you know exactly where the toilet paper is, and put the roll back in that special place after use. After use, all toilet paper should be encased in plastic bags and carried out or burned later in a small fire.

BRUSHES

Small, purse-sized hairbrushes are good for packing. One brush can be carried for the entire family. A separate set of camping-only toothbrushes is convenient when packing. Taking everyday toothbrushes means waiting till the last minute to stick these in, and the chances of forgetting them are high. The plastic containers toothbrushes come in make good holders on trips. Buy toothpaste in a small tube. To keep these items from getting lost, place them in a small stuffsack or plastic bag. If you expect children to brush their teeth and keep their hair tidy on a trip, you must be able to produce the brushes at the right moment, since youngsters are likely to forget.

SOAP

Unless you are on an extended trip, bathing with soap from top to bottom is probably a luxury your family can forgo. A certain degree of cleanliness keeps sleeping bags and gear cleaner, however. Face and hand washing with small cakes of soap is a good daily ritual for the entire family. Be sure, though, that you take washwater away from any water sources. Heating up a small quantity of water and taking soap, water, towel, and child in the opposite direction from the stream or lake is a good habit to establish in the family. Be sure you explain clearly to children that you do not soap up in the stream because that is your source of drinking water. No child wants to drink soap, so the concept is immediately understood. Dump all washwater away from water sources too. If you are swimming in a lake, you can keep children very clean without using soap. Never take the soap into the lake or rinse off a soapy child in the water.

For dishes, carry biodegradables only, such as the concentrated biodegradable soaps that come in small plastic bottles. These have squirt tops and are available at many outdoor stores.

REPAIR KIT FOR GEAR

Children can pop more buttons, create more three-cornered tears, jam more zippers, split more seams, and thus cause more damage to clothing and gear than adults could ever produce on backcountry trips. You need to be ready to repair when necessary.

For patching and mending emergencies, carry sewing needles. You can stick three or four into a narrow piece of cardboard the length of the needles. (Needles help extract splinters, too.) Wrap cotton-coated polyester thread around the cardboard to eliminate the need for a spool. Adhesive-backed tape repairs most rips in gear or air mattresses. You can purchase ripstop repair tape for mending ripstop nylon in a long roll or in shorter strips, or you can use electrical or adhesive tape for temporary repairs. Since children lose buttons, two or three buttons plus assorted-sized safety pins should be included also. With these items, you can mend clothing, tents, sleeping bags, and packs. Keep all mending items together. A small plastic container, such as a pinbox or 35-mm film can, is about the right size.

The connecting pieces on backpacks sometimes are lost. Check to see if all the packs in the family are held together in the same way. On many packs, frame and bag are connected by a clevis pin and a split ring. Extra pins and rings, and adhesive tape, obtainable in outdoor stores, should be carried in your repair kit.

Lengths of nylon cord (also useful for rigging tarps, stringing up wet clothes, and hanging food away from

bears and varmints) can help with repairs. If the zipper of
a child's frame pack jams, you can tie the pack closed; if a
youngster's favorite hat, which has an indispensable sun-
shield brim, refuses to stay on in the wind, you can add
cord to secure it under the chin; or if a child's boot lace
breaks, you can make a new one from the cord. Strong nylon cord about ⅛ inch in diameter, often called "parachute
cord," is just about right for these uses.

If roomy enough, the first-aid kit is a convenient carrying place for repair essentials. Otherwise you can store
these items in a small stuffsack so that you can locate them
quickly when needed.

Wilderness Essentials

Whenever you move into the backcountry, even for a short
stroll, be prepared to take care of yourself and your children. Most people conscientiously gather together emergency gear for extended trips. But wilderness is wilderness,
and day hikes or short excursions away from a base camp
demand backcountry preparation too. Some of the most
frightening backcountry experiences described to me hap-
pened on short, unplanned jaunts. Do not create bad situations for your family by going anywhere unprepared.

Always carry a pack that contains necessities for emergencies, for weather changes, and for entertaining and motivating children. With youngsters along, a regular-sized
backpack or two daypacks may be needed for adequate
room. For trips from a base camp, children's packs can be
adjusted to fit adults with a small load.

For wilderness travel, you must have the tools for finding your way. A map of the area and a compass are basic.
Enclose the map in plastic to keep it dry. Be certain that
you are able to read the map and use the compass. If you
do not know how, join a class and learn. Older children
enjoy learning compass and map reading; playing compass
games helps teach them and enables you to brush up on

Figure 12. Among the 10 wilderness essentials: flashlight, batteries, compass, map, first-aid kit, waterproof matches

skills too. You might try a compass treasure hunt: after locating a series of marked places with the compass, your youngster finally reaches a treasure or reward.

Two important items to carry are extra clothing for weather changes and extra food for energy. You should be ready for rain or sudden cooling. Taking layers of clothing that can be added or subtracted gradually is the best preparation. Extra wool socks and undersocks for youngsters often are the most needed items.

Some families carry the equivalent of an extra meal on a day trip as well as an overabundance of snacks. Usually children do well for most of the day, but they may suddenly tire in the late afternoon. On overnight trips, you can stop and establish camp even if you have not reached the place you intended to reach. On day trips, however, you have no choice but to force-march yourselves all the way back to camp or the car. In this case, you need ample food to keep up the family's energy.

For family day trips, adults can take along their heavy jackets, which can function as sleeping bags for children in a real emergency. Or you can stuff a child's sleeping bag into the bottom of a pack—it adds only a little weight.

Your first-aid kit should be with you at all times (see "First-Aid Kit" section). Keep a checklist of what belongs in the kit; you can tape the list to the inside of the box lid. Be sure you include special items necessary on family trips, such as children's aspirin or nose drops. Take a few minutes before any outing to doublecheck your supplies. Band-Aids, moleskin, and other commonly used items must be frequently replenished. Remember that children can get sick fast; they can be well in the morning but spike a sudden fever by noon. You need to be just as well prepared to take care of a child's health on day trips as on overnight excursions.

Always carry sunglasses, hats, and sunscreen for children. These are especially important on the water, in high, open country, and on snow. Even just an hour's play on a snow patch exposes children to sufficient reflected sunlight to burn delicate skin.

No one plans to be out after dark, but you will be in trouble if you do not plan for this circumstance. You should always carry a flashlight with extra batteries and a spare bulb (be sure both fit your particular flashlight). You can buy compact flashlights that weigh only 3 ounces and take AA batteries. In the pack and in storage, batteries should be reversed in your flashlight to prevent them from being unintentionally switched on. Lightweight headlamps, which leave hands free for working in camp and for helping children, provide an excellent alternative to hand-carried flashlights.

Figure 13. Head lamp frees hands for work in camp

A versatile knife with varied accessories is indispensable. In addition to standard knife blades and a can opener, its scissors, tweezers, and screwdrivers, including the Phillips variety, can come in handy on any family trip.

Being able to start an emergency fire for warmth, light, and psychological comfort can be vital if you are forced into an unexpected overnight stay. Keep your matches dry in a waterproof container and always carry a reliable fire-starter that you have tried out at home. The heat advantages of a fire, however, are sometimes overrated. To provide allover warmth with a fire, you almost need a rotisserie for body turning. A child who is sick, hurt, or scared will benefit more from other heat sources, such as warm clothes, an adult's jacket, or a sleeping bag. To corral body heat, you can use emergency heat-retaining blankets made of light metallic material, which fold up to the size of a fist, or you can make do by using large plastic garbage bags.

A cache of food that can be heated is another helpful day hiking item to prepare you for sudden cold or for an unexpected night out of camp. Soup cubes, tea bags, sugar cubes, and individually packaged hot chocolate or soup add very little weight. You can keep them in daypacks year-round. Although most people assume they would light a fire in an emergency, your stove is more efficient for cooking and, again, the weight is minimal. You can fill the stove tank and make do with that much fuel or also carry a small fuel container (half-pint sizes are available).

Establishing the habit of taking wilderness essentials on day trips from home is easy. You can keep a day hiking, day boating, or cross-country-skiing checklist to help you remember. When day hiking from a backcountry base camp, however, being prepared takes a little more thought and some gear sorting. You can keep wilderness essentials in a separate stuffsack in a backpack, or you can make preparations easier by keeping a day hike reminder list with your map. Whenever you divide the family group into two for separate outings—one parent with younger children and the other with older ones, for example—you need to be sure that both groups are still fully prepared with emergency essentials for the day's activities.

The Whistle Debate

Some parents provide each child with a whistle to be worn on a string around his or her neck. The whistle is meant to be used to attract attention if a child somehow becomes separated from the rest of the family. The value of this arrangement is debatable. In any case, the cardinal rule in any family should be that children stay in clear view of the adults. When several children are involved, responsibilities for each child should be clearly assigned. One parent, for example, might take the slow-moving preschooler while the other parent goes ahead with the two older children. The group would be slightly separated, but children would never be without adult supervision. This is also a good policy with older children who are about to enter their teens. At this age a child may become overconfident, which can be a more dangerous situation than having to cope with a younger child who is aware that he or she knows very little.

If you feel more secure when your children have whistles, include them as part of your basic safety gear. When you first buy whistles, take your children into the backyard and let them blow their whistles until the novelty wears off. Then establish an absolute, iron-clad rule that no one blows a whistle unless lost or separated from the group. There can be no exceptions, or the whistles will create a great disturbance for you and for other people enjoying the out-of-doors. Even when youngsters are bewhistled, you should still be firm about the stay-in-sight-of-an-adult rule.

To prepare for the unlikely disaster of a lost child, you can teach youngsters to stay put and signal their whereabouts, using either a whistle or a predetermined calling signal. For young children capable of wandering off but incapable of understanding signaling techniques, using a leash is better than losing the child. Close, constant adult supervision of children is the best way to prevent a child's getting lost. No opportunity should be allowed to arise for youngsters to separate themselves from the adult responsible for them.

First-Aid Kit

Never go anywhere in the backcountry without a first-aid kit containing emergency health necessities. This is important for adults-only trips; it is doubly important when youngsters are along. A child can be perfectly well one minute and become extremely ill the next. Often the physical illness itself does not come on that fast; active young children simply fail to notice early symptoms of trouble.

To be prepared for first-aid treatment, you need a box in which to store supplies: 6- by 4- by 2- or 8- by 5- by 2-inch standard sizes are readily available. Aluminum is preferable to plastic, which can be cracked by the weight of other gear. The top should seal tightly so that supplies do not fall out; a short strap with a buckle can keep the lid in place.

You can purchase a prepackaged first-aid kit. If you do not know much about first aid or the type of emergencies you might encounter, you can take the packager's word that the items in such a kit are what you will require. There is a problem with this approach, however. If you are not well prepared to handle emergencies, you should not be taking your children into the backcountry in the first place. Being prepared means specific training. Throughout the country the Red Cross offers low-cost first-aid courses. Some outdoor organizations include first-aid instruction especially geared to backcountry situations in their beginners' courses. In many areas, fire or police departments or the Red Cross offer free CPR (cardiopulmonary resuscitation) classes. This kind of instruction is as important as any other wilderness preparation.

First-aid training will provide you with enough information to organize your own selection of first-aid supplies. You should be ready to cope adequately with a wide variety of emergency situations. A good next step is to talk with your family doctor or pediatrician to find out which standard medications you need to carry. To be fully prepared, you are going to need some prescription medicines. A doctor familiar with your family usually will be willing to cooperate in providing these prescriptions. You can buy small plastic vials with tight, push-in lids for carrying tablets or pills. If your first-aid box has the space, medicines purchased in small quantities especially for wilderness use can be kept in their original containers. Be sure that each medication is labeled and jot down instructions on when and how to use each medication in a notebook small enough to fit in your kit.

If your young children cannot swallow pills, stocking the first-aid kit becomes more difficult. Liquid medicines are almost impossible to carry; some require refrigeration. An alternative is to make arrangements to procure pediatric powdered forms that are mixed with water at the time of use. You also can be prepared to pulverize medicine and combine it with something sweet (sugar or applesauce will do) to make it palatable for youngsters. Other medications come as suppositories to be administered rectally.

SUPPLIES NEEDED

Besides being prepared to deal with sickness, you should be equipped to cope with wounds, large and small; sprains, twists, and breaks; burns; and special problems related to the out-of-doors, such as heat and sun, cold, and bugs. In snake country you should know how to avoid bites and, if bitten, what to do.

Your kit should contain a variety of materials to treat wounds and cuts. With children along, double the number of Band-Aids taken. For some reason youngsters find immense comfort when a Band-Aid is applied to a troubled spot, bump, bruise, or infinitesimally small prick. Even

FIRST-AID KIT CHECKLIST

For wounds and cuts:
_____ Band-Aids
_____ Butterfly bandages or Steri-Strips
_____ 4″ × 4″ gauze pads
_____ Adhesive tape
_____ Kling gauze
_____ Telfa pads
_____ Soap
_____ Neosporin

For blisters:
_____ Moleskin or adhesive tape
_____ Telfa pads (small)

For breaks, sprains, and strains:
_____ 2 elastic bandages
_____ Triangle bandage
_____ Children's chewable aspirin or Tylenol
_____ Pain medication (prescription)

For burns:
_____ Soap
_____ Telfa pads (large)
_____ Gauze
_____ Pain medication (prescription)

For sun:
_____ Sunscreen

For water:
_____ Purifier or water filter

For colds:
_____ Antihistamine
_____ Nose drops

For infection:
_____ Antibiotic (prescription)

For allergy and bug bites:
_____ Antihistamine

For vomiting and diarrhea:
_____ Suppositories (prescription)

For poison ivy, oak, and sumac:
_____ Soap
_____ Lotion for itching

For poisoning:
_____ Ipecac

Incidentals:
_____ Safety pins
_____ Needles
_____ Knife with scissors and tweezers

tiny Band-Aids, which do little to protect, are soothing to the very young.

Any kind of cut should be cleaned before it is covered. Soap, whatever you carry for general cleanliness, is as good as anything for this purpose. As extra insurance, you can boil the water. A topical antibiotic, such as Neosporin, can be applied but is not as vital as the initial cleansing. Soap and water cleaning twice a day helps prevent infection.

It is important to cover cuts and wounds to keep out dirt. For larger wounds, 4- by 4-inch gauze pads and adhesive tape can replace Band-Aids. Kling gauze, which sticks to itself, produces a tidy wrapping. Telfa pads cover a wound, cut, or blister without sticking. Even if you have all these items, a clean, ripped-up undershirt may be the best alternative for a large injured area. To hold together a cut that might otherwise require stitches, butterfly bandages or Steri-Strips are essential.

For either sunburns or fire burns, the best first step is immersion of the burned area in cold water. With a first-degree burn, which shows up as redness with no breaks or blistering, some kind of ointment or sun cream can help reduce the discomfort. Covering these less serious burns is not necessary. With a more severe burn where the skin is broken or blistered, cleaning and protecting the burn area are essential. Soap and boiled water can be used to clean the site. Large Telfa pads, which will not stick to the burn, make a good first layer, and gauze can be used as an outer wrapping. For extensive burns, you should get your child out of the backcountry as fast as possible.

Moleskin is effective in preventing blisters, although adhesive tape can be used too. Any redness on a child's foot should be immediately covered with moleskin. You will have to check your youngsters' feet, however, since they will not notice redness until a blister has formed and prevention is thus too late. Protect and soothe broken blisters with small Telfa pads covered with moleskin, or a preparation that provides an artificial "outer skin."

For sprains, bone breaks, and strains, elastic bandages should be carried—at least two per family. This type of bandage also can be used to keep a dressing in place on a gauze-covered wound. A triangle bandage can be used as an arm sling, but any long-sleeved shirt will convert to this purpose if you tie the sleeves around the neck and do some safety-pinning.

With any injury, know what to use for pain control. For children, chewable aspirin or children's Tylenol, both of which are nonprescription, can be surprisingly effective. Anything stronger than aspirin requires a prescription and careful instruction as to use. You probably will have to replenish your supplies yearly. When you participate in outdoor activities with youngsters, doublecheck that you have put the chewable forms of medication back in your kit.

Many medications that can be carried routinely to cope with illnesses can be obtained only by prescription. For fevers, aspirin and Tylenol will suffice. Check into having rectal aspirin along for situations in which a youngster is feverish and vomiting. Suppositories to check nausea and vomiting also can be helpful. For infections, either from disease or a wound, you should carry an antibiotic; see if you can obtain a pediatric powdered form.

Mosquito bites that would merely itch on an adult can produce excessive swelling on a child. For allergic reactions and bites you need an antihistamine, many of which are over-the-counter drugs and also can be used for colds. A stronger antihistamine will require a prescription.

If your youngster has an allergic reaction to bee stings, consult your physician. You may need to learn how to give Adrenalin with a syringe. The drug comes in compact emergency kits convenient for carrying.

Show children poison oak, poison ivy, and poison sumac if these plants grow where you travel, and warn youngsters to stay away from them. If a child does get into some, wash the exposed areas immediately with soap and water. In an area you know to be infested, carry lotion for itch relief in a plastic bottle with a secure screw-on top.

Most families have ipecac on the shelf at home to induce vomiting if a child swallows something poisonous. Although ipecac comes in a glass container, the bottle is small enough to pack in a kit.

Every child has his or her own peculiar health problems. Discuss with your physician exactly what you should carry to be able to cope adequately with these potential problems. A youngster with general allergies may need a supply of nose drops, antihistamine, and antibiotics, enough for each day out. Your doctor may suggest preventive measures that may require additional medicines. For the constipation-prone child, a diet of prunes, raisins, or apricots in the morning may be an adequate preventive step, or your doctor can recommend stronger measures.

When you buy your medications, be sure to ask how long you can keep each one before it loses its effectiveness. Write this information on your list of instructions so that you can replenish medicines when they are no longer useful.

SNAKES

In snake country people often carry a snake bite kit, but recent studies show that improper use can lead to infections, which are sometimes more dangerous than the bite itself. If you frequently take your family into areas where poisonous snakes abound, check with a physician who is knowledgeable about the latest and most effective immediate treatment for snake bites. Follow this physician's advice about what to carry for treatment and how to treat a victim.

Avoiding snakes by being cautious is a much better tactic than having to treat a bite. A few simple steps can help you protect your children. Never let youngsters take the lead when you are moving through countryside that is likely to harbor snakes. As an adult, you are more alert and can discern warning signs, movements, a disguised form among the rocks, or a rattle that a child might ignore. You know to avoid putting your hands and feet into places you cannot see. When traveling with youngsters in snake country, it is necessary to establish boundaries that are stricter than usual. Toileting is the most common situation in which youngsters might move unknowingly into potential haunts of snakes; you must always go with children and take the lead.

TICKS

Whenever you walk through grass or brush, there is the possibility of ticks climbing aboard, wandering around, and eventually attaching themselves to you. An adult probably will notice a strange lump on his or her scalp; a child almost certainly will not notice. Tick hunts should be conducted at the end of any day during which you have been in and around brushy areas. Check children's clothing; then gently run your fingers through youngsters' hair, feeling for the rounded tick body. Finally, check limbs and bodies. Do not forget yourself. Since you have given your youngsters a tick check, they may enjoy doing the same for you.

If you find an already attached tick, it is important to get out the embedded head and mouth. Theoretically, if you drop insect repellent, white gas, or oil on the tick, it will back out since you have cut off its air supply. This does not always happen. The glowing-match method recommended for tick removal is definitely dangerous with wiggling children. Even the calmest child will feel threatened when approached with a glowing match head or a heated needle.

When a tick does not back out, use tweezers (a versatile

knife should include this accessory). Grab as close to the tick's head as possible and pull very gently so that you do not crush it. When the tick is out, wash the site of the puncture with soap and water.

PURIFYING WATER

Some water that looks clean is not drinkable without treatment. This concept is difficult for children to grasp. If you have any doubts about the water supply, be sure you purify or filter water before using. Areas with large wild animal herds or grazing domestic animals and places where streams flow from civilization are automatically suspect. On a wilderness trip a child only has to be struck once with diarrhea and vomiting to illustrate why you should take no chances.

Depending on the stove you use, a quart of water takes from 3 minutes to about 10 minutes to reach the boiling point at sea level. It takes longer to come to a boil at higher elevations. Then to purify the water you must continue to boil it for as long as 20 minutes if you are at a high altitude. You use fuel and time, and as you wait for the water to cool, you are faced with a thirsty child who really wants a cold drink.

For drinking water especially, a good system for dependable water purification is the use of a weak iodine–water solution obtained from iodine crystals. The procedure is simple. You get a 1-ounce, clear glass bottle with a leakproof, hard plastic, screw-on top. Into this bottle you put 4 to 8 grams of USP-grade resublimed iodine, which can be procured with a doctor's prescription. Fill the 1-ounce bottle with water and shake well for 30 to 60 seconds to dissolve some of the iodine crystals in the water. After the remaining crystals settle to the bottom of the bottle, the resulting solution can be used for purifying your drinking water. You measure and then pour specific amounts of this solution into specific quantities of water and let the treated water stand for a certain amount of time (see chart). For example, treated water must sit for 15 minutes or less at 77°F and for 20 to 30 minutes when the temperature is around freezing. If the water is permitted to stand overnight, the taste is almost the same as untreated water. Iodine crystals do not lose their effectiveness with time.

Iodine Purification of Drinking Water

The concentration of the iodine solution used for purification is determined by the water temperature. The lower the temperature, the lower the concentration, and the more solution that must be added by the capful (assuming a capful of a standard 1-ounce glass bottle is 2½ cc) to 1 liter of drinking water.

Temperature	Volume of Solution	Concentration	Capfuls
3°C (37°F)	20.0 cc	200 ppm	8
20°C (68°F)	13.0 cc	300 ppm	5 +
25°C (77°F)	12.5 cc	320 ppm	5
40°C (104°F)	10.0 cc	400 ppm	4

Other convenient and effective iodine treatment comes in tablet or liquid form. The main objection to iodine purification is the lingering taste of the iodine and the possible still-murky appearance of the water even after treatment. Water purifiers such as Halazone tablets provide chlorination treatment, which cannot be depended on to destroy many of the microbes found in the backcountry water supply.

Water Filters

A variety of effective lightweight water filters are available. Filters strain out large solid impurities so that water takes on a clear appearance. A maximum 4.0-micron-pore filter is required to remove giardia, the most common of the water-borne microbes found in North America, while a filter pore as small as 0.2 micron may be needed to strain out

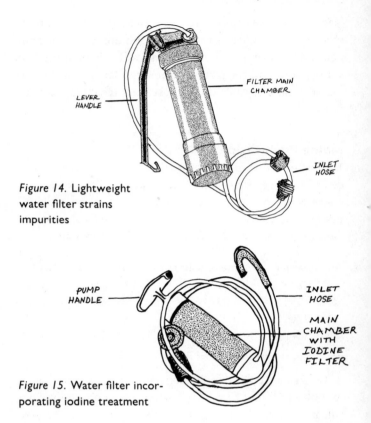

Figure 14. Lightweight water filter strains impurities

Figure 15. Water filter incorporating iodine treatment

bacteria such as salmonella, *E. coli,* staphylococcus, or streptococcus. Some filters also incorporate iodine treatment for smaller bacteria and viruses.

Although pump filters work faster than gravity-feed models, they also have more moving parts that could break or malfunction. Many families filter water in camp while meals are being prepared and thus avoid the frustration of the gravity feed filter's slow-motion approach. The straw filter will not remove many dangerous impurities without additional chemical treatment and thus should be avoided.

When choosing a water filter, determine how much ongoing maintenance will be required; in addition, find out the estimated life of the filter and replacement costs. Ceramic filters have a fairly long life and are easily cleaned by scrubbing and backwashing the surface. Depth filters with carbon strain microbes and absorb chemicals and must be replaced regularly. Regular depth filters must eventually be replaced too, even though you can clean the surface with a brush and backwashing. Some depth filters come with an iodine treatment feature that destroys bacteria and viruses in addition to straining larger giardia cysts. The advantage over other iodine treatment is that very little of the iodine stays in the water after filtering. Membrane filters with microscopic holes are simple to operate and clean; they provide effective filtering and a relatively long life.

No backcountry water supply is guaranteed to contain pure water. Water can be contaminated by wild animals, domestic animals, backcountry travelers, and commercial operators of logging, mining, or agricultural activities. Therefore, you should always take along one of the light, easy-to-carry iodine treatment alternatives as a backup purifier in case a mechanical water filter breaks down.

SERIOUS INJURY OR ILLNESS

In the event of a serious injury or illness, do not hesitate. Get your child out of the backcountry and to the nearest doctor or hospital as fast as possible. If a youngster cannot walk and cannot be carried, the stronger of the two adults should take a cache of emergency essentials and go for help while the other adult ministers to the child.

PREVENTION

The best first-aid "treatment" is to prevent problems as much as possible. Careful supervision of children helps. You can never prevent all accidents, but you can cut down on unnecessary difficulties. Establishing camp boundaries, holding the hand of a child on hard terrain, purifying water, and applying sunscreen and insect repellent before a problem arises help to eliminate many potential problems for children in the outdoors.

4

Children's Gear

THE GOOD CLOTHING and equipment that an adult buys can be used for years, but children constantly change size, a fact that immensely complicates buying gear for them. Such items as children's boots and frame packs are expensive, yet can be outgrown in a single year. A child's growth also affects some of the equipment used by the whole family. A two-person tent adequate one season may become impossibly cramped the next year.

Another problem unique to buying children's outdoor gear is the limited number of choices available. You know just what your child should have, but no one manufactures this item in your youngster's size. The gear that is available may not be at all what you think will work with your child. Often a good piece of children's equipment disappears from the marketplace because the manufacturer sold too few and made too small a profit. Or the outdoor stores near you may not carry children's gear. If this is the case, ask a buyer about the possibility of ordering what you want. Many store buyers are willing to provide this service.

Catalogue shopping is another solution to the problem of how to obtain children's gear. Browsing through the catalogues of major suppliers also will enable you to compare the features of various kinds of equipment and to practice comparative shopping. If you are looking at children's backpacks, for example, you will find that prices may vary by ten dollars. By comparison shopping in catalogues of major suppliers (see the Appendix), you can find out exactly what accounts for the higher price. A heavier pack cloth, sturdier frame, extra pockets, or padded hip belt may be well worth the extra cost. Adjustable features also may increase an item's value. You may find, particularly with clothing, that you are paying for elaborate design features when a simplified version would be adequate for a growing child. Or you may be paying for stylish details that are fashionable on the downhill ski slopes but matter not at all in the backcountry.

It may be difficult to find evaluations of the children's gear you are considering purchasing, since most product testing is concerned with adults' gear. The principles used to evaluate general equipment, however, also can be applied to children's gear.

Instead of becoming frustrated and dismayed by what might seem to be stumbling blocks to finding good equipment for your children, you can derive great satisfaction from being innovative and clever in obtaining gear. You can get together with other families for gear trading and cooperative sales. With only moderate skills, you can sew for your youngsters. You can make do with used clothing or get inexpensive wool from thrift shop hand-me-downs. You can even add on to some items so that they grow with your child, and you can make little changes on the equipment you purchase to adjust it to the size and body type of your youngster.

Clothing

BUYING FOR GROWTH

As noted, a child's rapid growth can be both expensive and a source of frustration to parents who are buying outdoor gear. Costly items—such as heavy jackets, raingear, sleeping bags, and boots—bought to fit perfectly can become too small in just one season. There are ways, however, for parents to stretch out the life of their youngsters' outdoor clothing and gear.

When you purchase ready-made clothes, look for features that allow for growth, such as a full cut rather than a trim cut or pants with an elasticized waistband. When buying clothes slightly larger to permit longer use, suspenders or adjustable buckles on strips can take up extra length in trousers, while elastic or snaps on sleeves keep extra fullness above a child's wrists.

In children's clothing sizes, the width changes more gradually than the length. You can buy clothes long and turn up a hem, which can be let down later when needed. In the summer and for vigorous activities, roomy clothes are more comfortable anyway and do not hinder a child's movements. When you make an expensive purchase, forget appearances. Buy very large for the first year and hope for a perfect fit the second year. When purchased big, heavy jackets and raingear fit better over other clothing layers.

HOW MUCH

For camping in the backcountry, you generally will find that the older the child, the fewer full clothes changes necessary. Even if a baby spends a good part of the day on a parent's back, in camp he or she will be crawling around in the dirt. In camp and along the trail, toddlers manage to soil clothing at a prodigious rate. For any child still in diapers, leaks onto outer clothing are always possible. In a rainy climate or near water, a youngster's clothing needs increase. On a boat trip, though, if a child spends all day in a bathing suit, fewer sets of clothing are required. Consider the place you are going and the age of your children when deciding how many sets of clothing you need to carry.

Young children may require a complete set of clothes for each day out. As youngsters grow older, pants and socks may have to be changed daily, but tops will stay clean enough. For preteens, clean socks each day may still be essential, but young people this age are less likely to totally soil entire sets of clothing.

When camping, standards for what constitutes "clean" are different from what they are at home. You have to decide just how clean your family has to stay for everyone's personal happiness.

For a four-day backpacking trip, the general clothing requirements of a preschooler might include four pairs of long pants, four shirts, four pairs of underpants, plus short pants that can double as a swimsuit. For a preteen, the list might shrink to one extra pair of long pants, four pairs of underpants, one extra shirt, and one pair of short pants for swimming.

Some people take few clothes and plan to wash during the trip. This technique works only in a climate where sun and warmth are guaranteed. Be sure that you wash your laundry with biodegradable soap, away from water sources. Soapy water should be dumped far from any lakes or streams.

Certain clothing works well in all seasons. Cotton or a blend that is primarily cotton with some synthetic is the most comfortable material next to the skin. In the heat, cottons breathe, absorb perspiration, and have no sticky feeling. In the cold, cotton feels good next to the skin as a first layer under warmer clothing. Nylons, on the other hand, create a cold, clammy sensation that gets worse as you sweat from the heat.

Clothes that dry fast are the most useful for children. Real denim jeans, which are popular and easy to buy, are sturdy and fine when dry. However, wet jeans are cold, and they dry very slowly. Jeans, therefore, are a poor choice for trips.

Dark-colored clothes show less dirt. If you carry minimal clothing for your children, you may feel better if the dirt is less obvious.

PANTS

Whether you take long pants or short pants depends on the climate and the expected conditions. Long pants offer many advantages. They protect against bugs, prickly plants, abrasions, and sun. Even in hot weather, long pants that are lightweight and roomy permit the air to circulate for coolness. Some pants pockets are handy for snacks and other odds and ends. A plain style, however, cuts down on weight (pants with four decorative patch pockets are a bad choice) and eliminates extra material that must dry if the pants become wet.

SHIRTS

Many children's shirts and undershirts are made primarily or totally of cotton and work well as next-to-the-skin clothing. The less fussy and decorative the style, the better. Sleeve length depends on the weather. Even in cooler climates, a short-sleeved shirt can be used for daytime and then covered by long-sleeved layers as temperatures drop. Off season, when cold weather is a certainty, long sleeves are necessary.

NIGHT CLOTHES

At night, many outdoor people peel down to underwear or nothing and crawl into a warm sleeping bag. Children can do the same. But if a child's sleeping bag is not warm enough for the weather, wearing warm layers of clothing may be necessary. Changing to the next day's clean clothes helps keep the dirt of the day out of the child's sleeping bag. For people who feel they absolutely must have different night clothing, a child's zip-up sleeper (which also provides added warmth in a bag) or a full sweatsuit can be used for sleeping. Pajamas, however, are just one more thing to carry.

SOCKS

On outdoor trips children never seem to have enough warm socks. You can expect a change of socks a day, but in the rain or on wet, muddy terrain, you may need even more.

If your child wears heavy boots, sweat can soak socks, and this is the first step toward sore feet. To avoid blisters from hiking boots, your child needs two pairs of socks, usually one thin pair and one heavy wool pair. For the inner pair, thin liner socks are available in children's sizes; heavier children's boot socks use wool and/or cotton with nylon reinforcement for longer wear. Some boot socks made for youngsters combine a terry-loop inner layer with a wool outer layer. For a growing child, stretch socks last over a number of years. Heelless or tube socks wear longer too. If you knit, making children's heelless wool socks is a fairly simple project.

BATHING SUITS

Shorts or underwear can double as a swimsuit. Very lightweight nylon suits that dry in minutes are worth having to avoid carting around wet clothing.

DRESSING FOR COLD WEATHER

Warm clothes can be just as essential in midsummer as they are for cold climates and winter. In the mountains and along coastal areas, warm days are followed by cold nights. During the evening, temperatures can drop drastically and stay low through early morning. In warmer climates, storms can cause balmy days to become uncomfortably chilly. Children need protection from the cold; they often require more warmth from clothing than adults do.

Find out the usual weather patterns for the place you are going. This information will help you decide how much warm clothing the family needs. Some youngsters are particularly susceptible to cold and therefore require extra consideration.

Generally, layering for warmth is more practical and adaptable than carrying a single heavy outer garment.

Keeping Clothing Dry in Packs

A brand-new pack made of good-quality coated nylon resists water penetration fairly well. Dampness can, however, seep in through seams, and with a well-used pack the coating on the cloth eventually will begin to wear off. In order to keep your children's warm clothing and extra clothes dry, place them in durable plastic sacks large enough to accommodate the clothing's bulk before you put them in the pack. You can also use lightweight coated stuffsacks in appropriate sizes, and you can make your own stuffsacks at some cost savings.

Layering

The most effective way to deal with the cold is to dress in layers. If you carry only a heavy jacket for a child and the weather is cool, but not cold, you have no way to adjust to the situation. If, however, you carry several thinner layers of warm clothing, you can add or subtract to achieve the exact warmth needed.

Layering works because air is trapped and kept warm between each piece of clothing. Therefore two thin sweaters can create more heat than one heavier sweater. Adding a wind or rain jacket as an outer layer keeps the heat inside even more effectively.

Anticipating the Cold

Movement and work, such as carrying a pack, generate heat. Sitting around can very quickly bring on a chill, especially in children and particularly as sweat cools. Youngsters often do not realize they are too cold until they are already shivering. When the temperature is dropping or when a high activity level has ended, adults must antici- pate a child's potential chill and insist on warm clothes. Mornings and evenings, cloudy days, or mealtime inactiv- ity can produce sudden coldness. To dress a child for warmth at these times and then take off layers later, if ap- propriate, is much easier than coping with an already cold, crying child. If children have become very chilled, put them into the tent and tuck them into sleeping bags. With ex- treme cold, take them into your own bag with you. Do not risk the dangers of hypothermia, which occurs when a person loses more heat than he or she produces and the temperature of the central core of the body drops. This dangerous situation can result in death, and quick mea- sures to warm the chilled person must be taken immedi- ately. Winter cold can chill someone who is not well enough insulated with warm clothing. Hypothermia also can occur in summer when the clothes taken are not warm enough for weather that suddenly turns cold or windy or for situations when a person gets wet and chilled.

For children, who lose body heat more rapidly than adults, it is essential to prevent such chilling by insulating them more than adequately against the cold during all sea- sons. Your child's warm extra clothes, a well-insulated sleeping bag that is kept absolutely dry, and the family tent are the necessities you take into the backcountry to avoid exposing your family to the risks of hypothermia.

Warmth for the Nonwalker

A youngster being carried on your back generates no ac- tivity heat. You may be sweating profusely while your child may be freezing. For nonwalkers, you should carry abun- dant layers of warm clothing. If you do not use them, that's okay; but if you need them, you will have them. Since the carried child's movements are limited anyway, padding the child in many layers does not hinder him or her the way it would an active youngster. Always prepare for the maximum cold that could be encountered.

To start the day, see what you yourself require when standing around, then add more warmth for your child. The inner layer should be regular clothing. Infants and even toddlers do well in one-piecers with crotch snaps for diaper changing. For outer layers, separate tops and pants allow for more temperature adjustments. Woolens, acrylics, or fleece sweaters, pants, and jackets are the warmest fabrics. Synthetics wash and dry out easily and do not have the itchiness of wool that often annoys children to distraction. For colder weather, try a one-piece snowsuit-like arrangement over other layers. If the wind is blowing, a hooded raincoat can provide wind protection.

With small children, hats and mittens must be attached; you do not want these essentials to be lost along the way. Mittens on strings can be threaded through jacket sleeves, or you can safety-pin mittens to cuffs. A tie-on hat should be pinned securely to the back of the jacket collar. A hood cannot be lost unless you misplace the whole jacket.

WOOLENS

Wool retains its warmth when wet. This characteristic makes it an effective clothing material for the unpredictability of backcountry climate. Woolens must be hand-washed with a cold-water soap or dry-cleaned.

Wool sweaters for children are easy to locate. Although expensive when new, they often can be found at secondhand stores for a reasonable price. The sweater style chosen can help with the layering process: a pullover must be removed for a person to cool off, while merely unbuttoning a cardigan is enough to cool someone a bit.

Although you can purchase wool shirts for grade-school-age children, the price is high, especially when you consider that youngsters will be outgrowing them. To procure inexpensive material for homemade shirts, check out thrift shops. You can buy and then take apart adult-sized woolen clothing, using the resulting material to make children's shirts or pants at minimal cost.

Wool pants are especially valuable for fall and spring and for outdoor winter activity, but are difficult to find except as high-priced dress clothes. If you want them, you will have to make them. To simplify, sew pants without a fly and put elastic through the waistband. Cut them roomy and leave a wide bottom hem that can be let down later. For children with sensitive skin, wool pants should be worn over regular trousers rather than next to the skin.

The itch of wool can torture some children, who are not necessarily allergic to the material. One of our youngsters persisted in chanting "itch, itch" any time we put her into our painstakingly collected woolens. We learned to keep the wool far away from her skin everywhere—on her feet and at her neck, wrists, and ankles—and we gave up on wool for her hats, despite its superior qualities.

You can gain the benefits of wool for children and prevent the itchies by using regular clothing as a soft, next-to-the-skin layer. A cotton collar turned over the top of a wool sweater will keep it away from the neck. If necessary, you can even safety-pin a child's cotton shirt sleeve over a woolen cuff.

Some children are allergic to wool and break into an awful rash on contact with it. Fiberfills or fleeces will be necessary for such youngsters, even though layering is then more difficult. You can also buy acrylic clothing, although it is somewhat less warm.

FLEECES

Among warm fabrics, one of the most popular is the synthetic fleece. Pants, jackets, and "sweaters" made of this fabric are available in a variety of colors and weights. Although ready-made fleece clothing is expensive, the fabric can be purchased by the yard and sewing simple designs is easy. Fleeces feel soft, stay warm when damp or wet, are lightweight to wear and to carry, and dry quickly. The cardigan designs that open all the way down the front provide the most flexibility for a variety of warmth needs. Like all polyesters and nylons, fleeces will melt or burn if exposed to fire. Clothing made from fleece should not double as sleepwear.

SWEATSHIRTS

Sweatshirts can be purchased in almost any children's department at a reasonable price. Although the material is warm when dry, it acts as a sponge when wet and is very difficult to dry. For dependable warmth, sweatshirts and pants are inappropriate for children in the outdoors. Some families find sweatsuits good for sleeping; they can be kept dry in packs all day and be taken out only at bedtime.

JACKETS

For the child who is nearly always cold and who shivers in a light breeze on a hot day, lugging a heavy jacket as well as other lighter warm clothing layers may be essential. A down jacket radiates a cozy heat, but when wet it loses its warmth. The various synthetic fiberfills are almost as warm as down for their weight and provide fine, dependable insulation for youngsters. Some thin synthetic insulators combine high heat value with light weight and very little bulkiness. Although this lighter, thinner synthetic is usually found only in expensive ready-made ski wear, the material can be purchased by the yard and used in making a child's warm jacket, at a much lower cost. Many simple patterns for jackets or for pants are available where outdoor or general fabrics are sold.

Outdoor stores sell a variety of outer garments for youngsters, and winter jackets can be purchased in any children's clothing department. Price differences do not always indicate warmth value. Popular design features or fancy sewing details can increase cost. For the out-of-doors, choose a simple design made with fiberfills (see the section "Insulation Materials"). Jackets should have an insulated hood attached.

Buy a jacket larger than necessary to increase the life of the garment. A jacket that comes to the knees of a toddler will be hip length in a short time. Sleeves with tight cuffs stay anchored at the wrist and allow any extra sleeve length to blouse up until the child's arms grow.

HATS

Many people swear by the old adage, "If your feet are cold, put on your hat." These people go nowhere in the backcountry without a wool hat, and their children follow suit. When you dress a child in layers but carry no hooded jacket, a wool hat comes in handy. It reduces heat loss by keeping in warmth that would otherwise escape.

MITTENS

For unseasonably cold weather or for nippy mornings and evenings, extra wool socks can double as mittens for youngsters. Children often are up and about early while the air is still cold. A morning ritual of covering hands with socks can avoid unpleasant chilling.

If you are off-season camping or visiting windy, rainy, or just plain cold areas, wool or fiberfill-insulated mittens may be essential. Because of the separated fingers, gloves generally are not as warm as mittens, and young children often cannot get them on right.

For maximum warmth, use the layering approach—an inner mitten of wool and an outer mitten of nylon (some are coated to shed water)—rather than one heavier mitten. You can adjust to temperature changes by removing or adding the outer mitten. Small adult-sized outer mitts can be purchased for older children. For preschoolers, making mittens of coated nylon may be necessary. You can omit the thumbs in the design and thread the wrists with narrow elastic for general camping. Thumbless outer mitts will

not do, however, for such activities as skiing or bicycling
or for active older children.

By the time children reach school age, a variety of warm
mittens for active use are available ready-made. A mitten
with fiberfill insulation, rather than a glove, will be best for
cold-weather outdoor activities.

VESTS

Children's vests are available in outdoor stores and in children's clothing departments. Making a vest is an easy first
sewing project. For real cold, a vest cannot replace a jacket
since heat loss is substantial when a child's arms are exposed. Vests do provide an extra layer around the chest,
and in any cold weather they increase the effectiveness of
other inner or outer layers.

RAINGEAR

Choosing raingear for children is far less complex than
finding functional rainwear for adults. Children do not
sweat as much as adults, and thus the condensation that
forms on the inside of coated materials is less of a problem.
You can concentrate primarily on finding a material and
design that will effectively keep out the rain.

Slickers for very small children are available in most
children's clothing departments. They extend to the knees,
are usually vinyl coated with a cotton backing, and come
with a hood or southwester that ties under the chin. (Avoid
the old-fashioned helmet hat, a style that prevents youngsters from easily turning their heads.) Slicker material is
heavy, but the total weight of a coat for a small child still
amounts to very little, even for backpacking. Slickers are
effective for shedding rain and they provide extra warmth.
Since they are made for general wear, the price is
reasonable.

In rain and the resulting mud, a coat is not enough.
Rain pants are necessary for children too (see the section

"Making a Child's Rain Pants"). You need to camp with your toddler only once in the rain to understand why covering a child from head to toe is essential. Water draws children; every mud hole and puddle invites investigation, which leads to splashing. The glee of a child in a puddle is a wonder to behold. A total rain suit prepares for such moments.

The smaller the child, the more useful rain pants are. If you are camping with a crawling youngster, you may want to use rain pants, even on a sunny day, as an anti-dirt maneuver. Coated nylon can be hand-washed and air-dried quickly. Vinyl- and rubber-coated materials need only to be sponged on the outside. Because of their slick surfaces, dry dirt particles slide off easily with a good shaking.

With some imported raingear, both jackets and pants can be bought in preschool sizes. Since these outfits are similar to adult gear used for sailing, you can find them in boating stores as often as general outdoor stores. For ruggedness, this gear is the ultimate. Seams are welded closed, not sewn. Such features as rubber under the feet and around ankles and a cozy drawstring hood keep the material from shifting on a child's body. The cold-resistant outer coating does not crack with age, and although the outfits are expensive, they will last through a long succession of children. Our 12-year-old imported rain pants, still in perfect condition, were recently passed on to their tenth owner. A small-sized suit rolls into a compact bundle, and its weight is little more than that of a coated-nylon suit in a larger size. For canoeing and kayaking, a completely suited child can sit in a puddle all day and not get inner clothing wet. Old suits are as good as new. Keeping an eye out for these outfits in thrift stores or among friends is definitely worthwhile.

For children aged 6 through 12, the choice of raingear increases. Ponchos for older youngsters can be purchased. Usually the sizes available have Cub Scout ages in mind; a

Figure 16. Raingear (left, rain jacket worn with rain pants; right, over-the-pack poncho with pants)

6-year-old would disappear from sight under the billowing tentlike shape. By making your child's poncho, you can adjust the size.

Adults who wear ponchos are aiming for ventilation to dry inner condensation. Air sails underneath to dry sweat, but little if any windbreak is provided. For a warm climate, this feature is ideal for adults and children alike.

Before buying a poncho, decide how much warmth your youngster needs from raingear. If the rain comes as a mild shower, a poncho will do its job. When the weather promises to be rainy, cold, and windy, a poncho may let in too much air. A waist belt helps close out the wind, and you can add waist-to-elbow sleeves for warmth.

If a child is helping paddle in the bow of a canoe or doing chores in camp, a poncho's flappiness can be a hindrance. When walking, you can cover the pack as well as the body if the back panel is slightly longer than the front. Ponchos also can be used as ground cloths and to cover gear left out at night. Do not expect one used for multiple purposes to last long; the coating will eventually wear off and its waterproofing value will be lost.

When warmth is needed, rain suits are good windbreakers. They cover children yet allow freedom of movement. Suits should be large so that air can circulate. If inner condensation becomes noticeable, putting a cotton shirt on the outside of a child's regular clothing helps absorb the wetness. Rain jackets are hip length. A jacket with an attached hood prevents loss. Some pants are fitted at the waist with threaded elastic; others come with a bib and straps that adjust. Leg bottoms must be wide enough to allow booted feet to pass through comfortably, so check this feature before you buy.

Some outdoor stores carry lightweight, coated nylon waterproof rain suits. Prices vary, and often the top-of-the-line suit in similar coated nylon materials does not provide increased rain-shedding protection.

Combination polyester and cotton jackets are made for children. They shed snow and light rain, but in a downpour they eventually soak through and take a long time to dry. A cotton and polyester jacket is more expensive (about four times the price of a rubberized rain suit) and bulkier to carry, but it is good for crisp, dry snow and for use as a warm windbreaker.

SUN PROTECTION
Sunglasses

In the filtered light of deep forests, sunglasses are unnecessary for children. The higher the elevation and the greater the glare from water, sun, or snow, the more essential eye protection becomes.

Sunglasses are difficult to keep on youngsters of any age. Therefore, losing them several times during any trip is almost a given. Although sunglasses are made to fit even infants, any child unaccustomed to glasses may find them irritating and take them off.

Effective sunglasses keep out harmful ultraviolet rays. Polarized glass does this. Glasses for youngsters should have impact-resistant lenses, which does not mean, however, that they are totally unbreakable or shatterproof. A few small-sized sunglasses are available at outdoor stores, ski shops, and other stores where adult glasses are sold. To keep good glasses from being scratched, insert them into a hard plastic case before putting them with gear.

To avoid losing children's glasses, use them only when needed. While walking in the forest, keep them tucked away. Once you break into open sunlight, or when you cross snow, or at high elevations, take the glasses out for your youngsters to wear. Parents will have to assume responsibility for collecting sunglasses after use and at the end of the day. For limited use, a better-quality glass in a frame that is slightly too big can be kept on with an adjustable elastic band. Small, round goggles with a stretchable band fit some children's head sizes. They may annoy youngsters for long use but work adequately if worn only when needed.

Hats

Children love hats—cowboy hats, farmer hats, baseball caps, floppy-brimmed hats, hobo hats—any hat that captures their imagination. A hat can double as fine sun protection for a child's eyes and face. A youngster who's an avid Dodger fan naturally wants to wear an "L.A." cap all the time; some youngsters even want to sleep in their hats.

A wide-brimmed hat can be almost as dependable as sunglasses, unless there is surface glare, and the risk of loss is less. Some children's hats come with a string that pulls tight under the chin, an essential feature in a breeze. Floppy felt hats sold in outdoor stores work well for grade-schoolers. You can add a cord to the hat to keep it in place in all types of weather.

Sunscreens

A youngster can develop a high fever from sunburn. You should prevent sunburn instead of having to treat it. Before you start out on a sunny or even overcast day, cover your child's exposed skin with a sunscreen to avoid burns and exposure to ultraviolet rays. If your child is sensitive to PABA, the active ingredient in many sunscreens, choose one of the other sunscreen formulas. During the day, reapply the screen especially after swimming or sweating. Lunch or snack breaks provide a good opportunity to do this.

When picking a sunscreen, first ask your child's physician for recommendations. Then experiment to be certain that no adverse skin reactions occur. To make sure that the sunscreen does not run into your child's eyes, try a preparation made for strenuous sports.

Infants and the Sun

Sunglasses are available even in infant sizes, and with time babies can become accustomed to wearing sunglasses. An adjustable band of elastic or cloth can hold the glasses in place over the child's eyes. Hats with wide brims can be used to provide shade from the sun. Other preventive measures help too. You can choose places to go where the chances of burned eyes or skin are slim or nonexistent. To reduce glare, some parents wear dark-colored clothes when a child is in a carrier on their backs, and they cover the metal on the carrier with dark tape. A large, black umbrella employed as a sun shade is effective also, except in

Figure 17. Brimmed hats and sunglasses to protect infants from sun

the wind. You may feel strange in the backcountry on a sunny day with your umbrella up, but never mind. An umbrella often works better for a baby than any other alternative, and it comes in handy if it should rain. A collapsible umbrella, though smaller, also can be used and fits into a pack when not needed.

When you apply sunscreen on infants who suck on their hands, you must avoid putting it on the areas the babies suck.

BOOTS

For youngsters, there are a minimal number of choices available in real hiking boots. However, most real boots made for adults with small feet would fit older grade-schoolers. These sturdy boots are expensive. The cost is especially distressing when you know your child is going to outgrow the boots quickly.

Since children outgrow boots before significant wear occurs, used boots are the best source of sturdy models at reasonable prices. Over the years a variety of real hiking boots have been available even in sizes for early grade-schoolers. If the uppers have outlasted the soles, the soles can be replaced; thus, a refurbished boot can provide an economically priced solution to a youngster's needs for the protection of a real hiking boot.

Before you search for a used boot or invest in a quality hiking boot similar to your own, think about the terrain you expect to cover with your child. Level, non-rocky trails; smooth lake shores; and flat, sandy ocean beaches do not require real hiking boots. For these conditions, the inexpensive day hiker boots, which are readily available, will be sufficient. A typical day hiking boot is made of heavy-duty nylon and split leather, the upper extends over the ankle and is lightly padded, and the rubber sole has a shallow lug pattern that is glued to the boot upper. When you explore rough mountain territory, however, the characteristics of real hiking boots benefit your youngster.

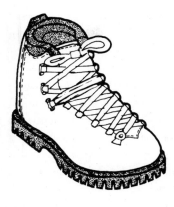

Figure 18. Real hiking boot with lug sole and padded upper

Real Hiking Boots

Good rough-terrain hiking boots should be comfortable and not too heavy on a child's feet. They should guarantee ankle support; give ankle, toe, and arch protection; and provide a nonslip tread. The boots also should keep out water if proper waterproofing has been applied.

If you expect your children to turn into enthusiastic mountain hikers, they need boots that are as dependable as the ones you wear yourself. With dry, well-supported feet and ankles, children will be more sure-footed. Once youngsters carry the weight of a loaded pack, sturdy, good-gripping hiking boots provide general leg, knee, and ankle support. A child in the right kind of hiking boots will become a much better walker. Boots are one piece of equipment well worth the price if you intend to take children into rough, rocky, or steep backcountry.

THE UPPERS. Real hiking boots have extra foot protection, especially in the upper part of the boot. In many designs, inner padding around the ankle and tongue encase the foot. The outer toe and heel are hard; you cannot push down on these with your fingers and feel the foot underneath the way you can on a regular shoe. The advantage of this outer stiffness and inner padding is that rocks, stones, and other hard, sharp objects cannot reach or injure the feet. On rough ground this characteristic is essential. A damaged foot can make a child miserable and put an end to your trip.

SOLES. Hiking boots have heavy soles with a lug pattern for gripping rough or muddy surfaces. For the best wear, the sole and upper part of the boot are stitched together in what is called *welt construction*. Boot tops and soles that are cemented together cost less, but this is generally a less durable construction. The tops of sturdy hiking boots will still be good after the soles have worn out. Resoling children's boots and passing them on to several youngsters in the family is cheaper than buying each child new boots.

BREAKING IN HIKING BOOTS. Although relatively light as hiking boots go, a youngster's hiking boot weighs between 1½ and 2½ pounds. This is more than enough weight for small leg muscles to manage. When your children are using real hiking boots for the first time, it is wise to insist that they walk in them daily for several weeks to break them in and to strengthen leg muscles. Younger children will do this readily, especially if you are encouraging backyard camping play. Start out with a half hour of use and build up to at least an hour or more the last few days before the first trip. (One advantage of used boots is that they are already broken in.) If a child's boots are brand new and an especially stiff design, keep a sharp eye out for blisters; apply moleskin at the first sign of even the slightest pinkness. If an older child feels silly wearing hiking boots at home, make breaking in boots a family project.

FITTING HIKING BOOTS ON CHILDREN. When you buy hiking boots for youngsters, take the socks you intend to use along with you. Outdoor stores often have wool boot socks available, but they are not yours and will alter the fit slightly.

Boots are expensive, and children's feet grow at a prodigious rate. Aim to buy boots as large as possible to stretch out their use for your child. Within reason, you can do this by using layers of socks and by adjusting the thickness of the socks. To avoid blisters, two layers of socks are essential with hiking boots. There are, however, many variations possible with the two layers. For the first year, your child could wear two heavy pairs of wool socks, and these would take up much extra room. You could even try one thin pair and two heavy wool pairs. The second year your child could switch to one light pair and one heavy wool pair. In a cool, dry climate where the warm-while-wet virtues of wool are less vital, you could use two thin pairs. Avoid one pair of socks as an alternative. Heavy cotton sport socks with terry cloth inside are popular with youngsters, but a cotton sock in a boot is more likely to bunch up with hard hiking. These are a poor choice in the rain too (see also "Socks" section).

BUYING HIKING BOOTS. Buy children's hiking boots through a catalogue only if the fit is guaranteed. You must be able to return the boots if the style or size is wrong. When ordering, send along an outline of your child's feet in the sock layers you plan to use for hiking.

In a store, check the fit of boots carefully. With the boots untied, have the child stand on an incline so that his or her toes push down and touch the boot toes. By putting your fingers into the boots behind the heels, you can measure how much room will be left in the toes of the tied boots. The fit should be snug enough to avoid slipping and foot movement that could cause blisters.

Once you tie the boots, have the child walk around, as you would with any shoes. If a youngster has never worn heavy boots, the feeling will be lunky and strange, so do not ask how the boots feel. Ask if the boots slip with walking or if the child feels any rubbing. See if the child can wiggle his or her toes. With the very young, parents have to use their own judgment since the child can supply little useful information.

Once you own children's boots, check the fit before each hike. A growing child's feet can change size appreciably in a month. First put on the sock layers last used; then check the fit on an incline as you did at the store. If the boots feel too snug, change the sock layers and thicknesses until the fit is correct. While you have the boots out, make sure the laces are still strong and are not frayed. Broken laces can be a nuisance on a trip.

For children, owning boots is important. It is part of the thrill of being like Mom and Dad. Capitalize on that excitement and you can add to the happy feeling children derive from going on family trips. One of our girls loved her first hiking boots so much that she wore them with fancy dresses for special occasions. By wearing the boots daily she broke them in nicely and had comfortable feet when we finally went on trips.

USED BOOTS. Since youngsters outgrow boots long before significant wear occurs, looking for used boots is worth the time and effort. Some outdoor stores carry a good selection of used hiking boots for children; you can trade in your youngster's old boots on the price of the next pair. You also can try advertising in your outdoor club's newsletter or asking friends and acquaintances who backpack. If you do not belong to a club, try newspapers that reach other outdoors-oriented people. Community outdoor equipment sales and thrift shops also are sources for used children's boots.

In the past, some of the best children's boots were imported. Since these imported boots have been sold in this country for a long time, many pairs with years of wear left may be lying around gathering cobwebs in people's homes.

Figure 19. Boot with a soft upper

SOFT-TOP HIKING BOOTS. For a dry climate and for moderate terrain that is not rough or rocky, for sandy beaches, and for lake shores, hiking boots with soft leather tops or heavy-duty nylon and split-leather tops are more than adequate. Some of these come with a hard toe and heel; others provide some arch and ankle padding. The advantage of soft-top boots is comfort and availability. You can find them in some department stores and shoe stores and in outdoor stores, where you can try out various sizes on your child. The price usually is slightly less than the price of real hiking boots, but with most models you cannot expect long wear nor can you replace worn-out soles to extend the life of the boot.

CARE OF HIKING BOOTS. Getting leather boots soaking wet is an easy way to destroy them. Since children are capable of sopping their feet in the merest trickle of water, you must take extra care in waterproofing their boots.

When you purchase boots, find out and purchase the appropriate waterproofing to use. Even in a dry climate, occasional rainstorms can occur, and children will find and walk in water anywhere it exists; therefore you need to waterproof a child's boots as adequately as possible.

As soon as you buy new boots, immediately apply the first coat of the appropriate waterproofing. Condition the boots again before the first trip; then establish the habit of cleaning and conditioning boots after each outing. Routine meticulous care helps stretch out the life of youngsters' boots.

Also be sure you dry out boots thoroughly. Warm-weather trips can produce sweat dampness inside. After a rainy trip or an accidental boot dunking, stuff newspapers, old cotton socks, or paper towels into the boots; then dry them at room temperature. Never bake boots near extreme heat. Change the wadding if boots are very wet. Store boots away from damp areas or you may start cultivating some interesting molds on the leather.

On a trip, if your child steps into some water over the boot tops, resist the temptation to fast-dry them over your stove. This can cause permanent damage. On a sunny day, dry the boots stuffed with paper towels or dishtowels (whichever you carry) in filtered sunlight. In bad weather, stuff the boots and keep them in the tent out of the rain. When you have to put your child back into damp boots, use dry socks and watch for redness on the youngster's feet. People sometimes carry boot conditioner with them for in-camp application.

Rubber Boots

When you face mud and water or the regular threat of rain but are not hiking rough terrain, adequate alternatives include children's rubber pull-on boots or leather-top boots with rubber soles, which come in sizes appropriate for larger children. These boots are lightweight and comfortable but give no padded ankle protection. The rubber soles on both pull-on and leather-top styles are patterned to grip. A high-top, pull-on rubber boot can be ideal on kayak and canoe trips.

Play Boots

From time to time, play boots for general wear become popular. Some of them come with lug soles. If you are thinking of these boots for your children, take a long look at the boot tops. A flimsy top will not protect the foot,

Figure 20. Rubber-soled boot with leather top, and full rubber boot

keep out water, or last long. For very small walkers, the patrol-boot style may be the only choice you have in their size. Something is better than nothing, and these boots can be adequate for the amount of walking and the kind of ground covered by a preschooler.

Smooth soles can be slippery. In wet weather, a child wearing play boots with smooth soles may be handicapped, not helped. Sturdy oxfords or saddle shoes, which look as if they would give good support, are often slippery-soled too. If your child wears low shoes, you will have more difficulty keeping his or her feet dry.

If a play boot is fashionable and popular, you may discover that it costs more than a pair of real hiking boots. In this case, you will not save money and will gain little in terms of suitability for rough outdoor use.

SNEAKERS

You may want to allow children to change into lightweight sneakers while they are in camp. A change of footwear rests a tired child's feet. Besides, boots with lugged soles can quickly chew up a campsite; softer soles have less impact on the area. In rugged, rocky terrain, make sure you limit the use of sneakers to the immediate campsite. A child is more liable to injure feet or ankles in these flexible shoes.

Any soft shoes you take should be lightweight. Avoid sneakers or sports shoes with deep cleats; these tend to be heavy and as site-damaging as boots themselves.

Sneakers are not at all appropriate for rough mountain trails. In such soft shoes the chances of a foot injury are high. Sharp objects can penetrate the shoes, a child's feet can get wet and blister, and the feet are not well supported. In cold rain or in wet, marshy areas, sneakers do not keep feet warm or dry. For sandy beaches where clear, warm weather is guaranteed, sneakers are acceptable footwear. In a rainy beach area, however, heavier boots that keep out water still have the advantage.

Sleeping Bags

In the future you may have a wider choice in commercially made children's sleeping bags than you have today. Gear manufacturers are discovering that more and more people with children are going into the backcountry. When a wider selection becomes available, you will want to be more particular about suiting a child's ready-made sleeping bag to your family's camping needs. Now, however, when you cannot always find an appropriate bag for your child, you can make one to suit your needs (see the section entitled "Making a Child's Sleeping Bag").

TYPES OF INSULATION

For the weight, good-quality goose or duck down gives more heat than any other insulator. It compresses into a light, tidy bundle for carrying and has a long life. Down gives off a toasty-by-the-fire kind of heat. There are certain drawbacks, however. The price of down is high and getting higher. When wet, down loses its warmth, so you must go to extra lengths to keep down bags dry (see the section

"Keeping Sleeping Bags Dry"). Even if available at lower cost, down is a questionable choice for diapered children, regular bed wetters, and youngsters with allergies. It is difficult to wash. Improper handling can tear apart the inner structure of baffles, which contain the feathers. In addition, down dries very slowly.

Synthetic fiberfills come close to matching the warmth-for-weight effectiveness of down. These newer insulators are relatively lightweight and reasonably compact especially in children's-size bags.

For children, the new synthetic battings have many advantages. Bags with this type of insulation wash and dry easily. If wet, the insulator retains its warmth; if soaked, excess water can actually be pressed out and the damp bag will still insulate well, a safety feature that is a huge plus. Although adult-sized bags are slightly bulky, a child's synthetic bag compacts down to a reasonable carrying size. It weighs slightly more than a comparably warm down bag.

DETERMINING A SLEEPING BAG'S WARMTH

Despite all the information given by the manufacturer, the exact warmth potential of a particular sleeping bag is difficult to determine. With a child, calculating the youngster's heat needs and the warmth value of the bag are doubly hard.

Infants and small children have more skin surface area in proportion to their body size and weight than adults have. As a result, they lose body heat faster than an adult and require more insulation. Unfortunately, most sleeping bags designed for children have less insulation and less warmth than those made for grownups since the heavy, better-quality bags are costly and manufacturers do not believe that parents will invest a lot of money in a sleeping bag that will soon be outgrown. Manufacturers' doubts about assured profits on youngsters' bags also contribute to the scarcity of choices.

With most brands, sleeping bags are divided into three

122   *The Sierra Club Family Outdoors Guide*
warmth classifications: summer, three seasons, and winter. Within these general categories wide variation exists. By knowing the temperature range of the places you intend to visit, you can at least look at the right group of bags (assuming there is a group of children's bags to choose from). For mountains, where nights are cool or cold even in mild weather, you can forget summer weight. Many temptingly inexpensive children's bags are in this category. Most backcountry weather requires at least three-seasons' warmth.
Gear catalogues list many characteristics of sleeping bags. One means of determining warmth is to look carefully at the "loft" figures. Air that is trapped in a material holds the warmth generated by your body, so an effective insulator has good air-trapping capacity. Loft is the thickness of an insulation material after it has been gently shaken and fluffed to let in the air. The larger the loft number indicated for a bag, the greater the approximate warmth potential. As a rough indication of warmth, you can figure that about 4 inches of loft keeps you warm down to 40°F, 6 inches to 20°F, and 8 inches to 0°F.

Bag design also is important. The tighter the fit of the bag around the body, the less the heat loss and the greater the warmth potential. Mummy-style bags are efficient warmers; open-topped rectangular bags are inefficient. Sewn-through seams let out heat; seams covered with insulation keep heat in. In the fiberfills, overlapping the quilt stitching with a second layer of insulation (sometimes called "double offset quilted construction") provides greater warmth.

If you are not certain about where you are going to camp, buy a sleeping bag that offers flexibility. A drawstring hood can open flat or be pulled tightly closed. A full-length zipper that goes down one side and across the bag bottom allows you to open the bag flat and use it as a covering regardless of its shape. (Be sure a full insulated flap covers the air space at the zipper.) If you elect to add a section to the bag to accommodate your child's growth, the zipper can be detached from the bottom of the bag and then inserted down the side seam of the new section. A two-way zipper that opens both top and bottom can be used for subtle heat adjustments.

In theory, these are some of the considerations to keep in mind when choosing a child's sleeping bag. In reality, so few children's bags are manufactured that you may have to buy whatever you can find regardless of the bag's characteristics.

BAGS FOR THE VERY YOUNG

You will have difficulty finding a sleeping bag small enough to fit infants through preschoolers. Many parents slip a tiny youngster into their own bags. Adults' bags that zip together create extra room, and the space, in theory, seems perfect for a baby or toddler. With this method, however, certain problems exist. Young children often move, moan, creep, and crawl in their sleep. Your child may slumber well, but you may not sleep at all. Children unaccustomed to sleeping with anyone around may entertain themselves cooing, singing, talking, and, when exhaustion hits, crying. The difficulty can be compounded by the touching-close proximity of parents. Another problem is leaking diapers. Not even a thorough airing can totally erase the lingering scent of urine. You could, though, place a rubber-coated pad under a child who is sleeping with you. Finally, there is always the chance that one of the parents will unintentionally roll onto the child sleeping between them, waking or possibly even hurting the child. For the youngster who can sleep anywhere and anytime with no problems or complaints, sleeping with parents may work well. In most families, however, much better solutions need to be found, both for convenience and warmth.

In our family, we solved the infant-through-preschooler sleeping bag dilemma by heading for the sewing machine. With the synthetic materials presently available (see "Materials" section), a good-quality child's sleeping bag can be home-produced at minimum cost and with minimum difficulty (see "Making a Child's Sleeping Bag" section). You can make your small bag to fit and then add on sections at the bottom as your youngster grows (see "Add-On Sections for Sleeping Bags" section). When you make the original bag, sew the bottom seam with thread that contrasts with the color of the lining, shell, and insulation. Taking apart the bottom of the bag will be simpler if you can see the seam threads for cutting. Knowing that you will eventually open the bottom seam, finish off only the side seams on the bag by machine-stitching back and forth three or four times at the end of these seams to prevent opening. Then start a new seam at the bottom with the contrasting thread. You will undo only this bottom seam when you add to the bag later.

It is difficult to keep some young children in standard-style sleeping bags. They will not tolerate the closed-in feeling of a hood tied snugly around the head and under the chin. When bags are loosened or rectangular, the youngsters squirm until, by morning, they are lying outside totally uncovered. One solution we found was to dress our children in warm jackets and place them in small, homemade, waist-high sleeping sacks. The sack, which can taper to meet desired warmth needs, tightens at the top with a drawstring. To keep it in place, you attach large snaps to the jacket at the waist or higher and to the top band of the sack. Suspenders or straps with adjustable buckles also work well. The sack simply goes on and stays on like overalls.

As a first sewing project, a homemade sack of this sort bypasses the need to install a zipper, the single most difficult step in home sleeping bag construction. Such a design also accommodates thumb-sucking, a diversion some babies refuse to do without. You can use a child's regular, winter-weight hooded jacket, or you can sew your own, as we did. Jackets with hoods are not the easiest sewing proj-

Figure 21. Homemade sleeping sack and jacket for the very young child, infants through 4-year-olds

ect. Also, any jacket to be worn for sleeping must be kept dry during the day in the same way you protect a sleeping bag.

A child's comforter made of a fiberfill can also be adapted for outdoor use. Measure the comforter, and then divide it into three equal sections. Mark the divisions (you are not going to cut them) with pins or chalk. The middle section forms the back side of the bag; the two side sections are folded over one another to make a double-weight covering on the front. Fold one side section over the middle section and top-stitch a side and a bottom seam. Fold and top-stitch the other side section at the side and bottom. If you add a casing at the top, you can insert a drawstring. A sweatshirt worn underneath this comforter sack can provide a hood, or the sack can be worn to the waist with a hooded jacket.

A wool blanket can be sewn in the same manner as a comforter. With wool, use a sheet for lining to prevent itching. Anything makeshift must be sewn securely or children rolling in their sleep can undo the sack. Be very sure that young children cannot tangle themselves in any drawstrings used.

You can make do by dressing infants and toddlers in winter snowsuits for sleeping. Some have hoods and insulated feet and mittens. Snowsuits can be purchased in various weights and as one-piece or two-piece sets.

Judging the warmth provided by any of these combinations is tricky. Your infant cannot tell you if he or she is too cold or too hot. Crying could mean anything. Starting with your own warmth needs in a sleeping bag, you should then provide even more warmth for your child to make up for the youngster's greater loss of body heat. To compensate for a bag that is not warm enough, layer for sleeping as you would for daytime warmth. A child in a too-cool bag also could be placed inside a parent's bag and not be excessively warm. For adequate warmth, your child also needs a pad under the sleeping bag (see "Pads" section). Your tent helps to increase the warmth of your child, as does the close proximity of other tent occupants.

In commercial sleeping bags for very young children, your choices are few. The readily available novelty "sleeping bags" are appropriate only for inside or summer overnights at home and should not be considered a real outdoor sleeping alternative.

To obtain adequate warmth, parents must often resort to buying an oversized sleeping bag into which a young child will eventually grow. When a sleeping bag is too long for the size of your child, the extra bottom inches can be tied off to eliminate the heat loss caused by unused space. Although a drawstring around the top of a rectangular bag can help prevent some loss of warmth, these bags are basically for moderate- to warm-weather conditions. A bag must have a tapered or mummy shape with adequate insulation and an attached hood with a drawstring in order to function in cool and cold conditions.

BAGS FOR OLDER CHILDREN

A bivouac sack or a junior sleeping bag will accommodate an average-sized child in the early grade-school years. Some bags are also tailored to fit small adults and run in length from about 72 to 74 inches; the narrower girth of this design cuts down on weight and heat loss. A large child and a small adult are fairly comparable in size. When your youngster grows big enough for you to consider this size, your choice in sleeping bags increases to some of the best lines available. Since a quality bag has a long life, this size could take your child into adolescence and even adulthood. If you must go to regular adult-sized bags, which can be as long as 84 inches, even a child of 10 or 12 carries the weight of a large, unused foot section.

USED SLEEPING BAGS

Both down and synthetic sleeping bags can be obtained secondhand at considerable savings. The estimated life of a down sleeping bag is 10 to 12 years. A down bag which has been carefully used, properly stored out of its stuffsack, and infrequently washed can still be effectively warm when secondhand.

Over the years many child-sized bags or climbers' bivouac sacks have been available through retailers and sew-it-yourself kit companies. You may locate a quality, little-used item at low cost from friends or acquaintances who have sleeping bags sitting outgrown and unused in storage.

STUFFSACKS

Stuffsacks come in a variety of sizes. A child's sleeping bag fits into a small stuffsack, but you can keep a sleeping bag and Ensolite pad together in the next larger size. For carrying, your stuffsack should compress as much as possible. Be sure, though, that you store your child's sleeping bag out of the stuffsack; hang it up or stretch it out flat in a dry place.

An adequate stuffsack is made of moderate-weight coated nylon and has a storm flap, an extra piece of material placed under the drawstring opening to help keep out wetness.

KEEPING SLEEPING BAGS DRY

Of all the gear carried, your children's sleeping bags are the most important items to keep absolutely dry. Although stuffsacks are coated, this is not enough in the rain. For real dryness insurance, you need a second waterproof layer. A large, heavyweight, plastic fish bag or a second stuffsack can be used. Be sure that you reverse the openings on the first and second layers.

For canoeing and kayaking, commercially made dry bags come in sizes large enough to accommodate sleeping bags and pads. Still be sure to use an added layer, either your coated stuffsack or a heavy-duty plastic bag, to ensure dryness especially as dry bags age. Your children's sleeping bags should be able to rest in a puddle of water all day and come out totally dry that night.

Pads, Air Mattresses, and Combination Pads

PADS

Pads used under sleeping bags function as much for insulation as they do for comfort. There are two basic types of pad material: closed-cell and open-cell foam. A ³⁄₈-inch closed-cell foam pad provides little cushion and can hardly be called comfortable; yet it does keep out the cold and dampness. For the child who can sleep anywhere, this style pad often works well. Closed-cell foam comes in several thicknesses—usually ¼, ½, and ³⁄₈ inch—and insulates in weather as cold as 10° Fahrenheit. Some brands are flexible and thus can be tucked conveniently into a pack or in with the child's sleeping bag. Other closed-cell pads have a stiff surface and must be rolled and tied for carrying. Since closed-cell foam is compressed to eliminate air spaces, the material prevents ground dampness from seeping into sleeping bags.

Open-cell foam is spongy feeling and spongy acting. This foam is made of urethane, or polyurethane, and has air spaces. Most polyurethane pads are 1½ inches thick. The material is soft and more comfortable than closed-cell foam, but even short pads are very bulky. Since the foam literally acts like a sponge, the material must be covered or rain and ground dampness will be absorbed. The best covers have a breathable top often made of a cotton-polyester blend and a coated nylon bottom for waterproofing.

Although the two types of foam are fairly comparable in weight, a covered open-cell pad can cost twice as much as a similar-sized closed-cell pad. For a slight cost savings, you can cover your own open-cell pad.

AIR MATTRESSES

Air mattresses provide cushion. Most models are constructed of tubing that is inflated to lift the body off the ground. These mattresses do not, however, insulate for warmth; they do the opposite. Through a convection process, the air circulating inside the mattress cools you by moving warmth away from you. In a warm climate you may want this cooling action. In an area that has cool nights or generally cold weather, air mattresses do not provide adequate insulation.

When you plan to camp on rough surfaces, such as gravel bars, and you do not need the extra warmth, air mattresses lift you away from uneven ground. They enable you to camp in places that would be downright painful with a foam pad. Some manufacturers do make lightweight mattresses for backpacking, but generally an air mattress is heavier than a foam pad. To avoid total deflation, many mattresses are designed with separate air tubes, each having its own valve.

AIR MATTRESS—PAD COMBINATION

An air mattress–pad combination provides the benefits of both of these sleeping pad styles. It fills with air and is made of open-cell foam for insulation and comfort. It can self-inflate, or air can be added by blowing into a valve. These combination models come in a variety of lengths. Valves can be easily replaced, and leaks can be patched effectively. Of all the designs, these are the most comfortable to sleep on, which is a concern for light-sleeping and older children. Although these styles are more costly than the other types, a family of three or four can use two long combination pads placed crosswise; in addition, a thin, flexible closed-cell pad can be arranged below these pads to keep sleeping bags dry and to provide foot warmth.

WHAT YOUR CHILDREN NEED

Many young children do not require the cushion under them that adults feel is absolutely necessary for their own comfort. However, all youngsters in the outdoors need insulation for warmth and protection from ground dampness. You will have to judge your own child's special needs. If a light sleeper rests better on a cushiony 2 inches of open-cell foam, that is what you should provide, despite its bulkiness.

Pads and mattresses come in various widths. A wider pad, even for a small child, allows for night movements and gives extra protection from dampness on the inside walls of a tent.

In a small tent, your family can share pads to spread out the comfort; this way you do not have to purchase thick, full-length pads or mattresses for everyone. You simply buy your cushion and insulation to fit the tent floor. One possible sleeping setup might be a full-length closed-cell pad extended across the tent's width where heads rest and a pillow made by putting extra clothes in a sleeping bag stuffsack; below, a combination pad or a covered open-cell pad placed crosswise for softness in the shoulder-to-hip area of the adults; and finally, below this, a second closed-cell pad to keep feet warm and the foot of the sleeping bag dry. Depending on the length of the soft pad, such a setup could accommodate two adults and two small children. You could share air mattresses in a similar way, but the ribby tubing is less comfortable when slept on crosswise.

Making Do

Since children outgrow gear in rapid-fire fashion, it's worthwhile trying to make do for youngsters whenever possible. Making equipment, buying used gear, and finding thrift shop clothing and materials can help reduce the high cost of going into the outdoors with your children.

With more than one child in a family, gear can be handed down through several youngsters. You may feel less reluctant to buy a child expensive boots if you know you can pass them on to younger children. You can also trade children's equipment among friends or acquaintances. An advantage to membership in an outdoor club is the access you have to other people who have the same problem of children outgrowing equipment. Many groups publish newsletters through which you can advertise your gear needs. In a small club, the grapevine is another source of information.

If you do not belong to a club, but have a group of friends interested in the outdoors, ask about gear their children have outgrown. Often usable equipment is gathering cobwebs in someone's attic. You may want to put in your name for that nice pair of cross-country skis or those hardly scuffed hiking boots when a friend's child can no longer wear them.

Many outdoor stores have used equipment sections where secondhand items that generally have a long life, such as boots, can be traded in on the purchase of new gear. If the trade-in price is good, a large part of the cost of the next size you are buying is reduced. Secondhand items constitute good buys, too, and boots in particular have the advantage of already being broken in. At stores where you trade regularly, you might suggest that the management open a used gear department especially for youngsters' equipment.

Some communities in which outdoor activities are popular sponsor used equipment sales. As one of their annual events, clubs can include a buy, sell, or trade sale. If no such opportunities exist where you live, try initiating a gear sale. The benefits of these sales accumulate over the years as you buy, sell, or trade to procure secondhand gear for your children and for yourself.

Thrift stores sometimes carry outdoor gear, especially if local outdoor stores do not handle used equipment. Thrift shops also are an excellent source of used clothing and materials, especially woolens, for making youngsters' clothes.

Children's gear does not have to be brand new to be useful. Secondhand equipment may have years of wear left, and your child can be very properly attired for backcountry travel in good-quality hand-me-downs.

Making Children's Gear

Commercially made children's equipment and clothing are becoming more readily available every year. However, the cost of gear is high, especially when you consider how fast youngsters outgrow much of what you purchase. You may find that the best solution is to buy what is difficult or impossible to make—such as boots, pack frames, and tents—and then head for the sewing machine to make other items. Even when a store price is reasonable, you may not like the design. When you sew for your youngsters, you can create exactly what your children need.

For making outdoor gear, you need moderate sewing skills. If you have never sewed at all, general sewing instruction is a wise first step. Some lessons in making outdoor gear are available through fabric shops and outdoor equipment stores.

In contrast to sewing fashionable clothing, making equipment is relatively easy. A general sewing machine can handle synthetic materials unless you have an unusually lightweight model. Some machine adjustments may be necessary. If you find that the fabric slips, the stitch size fluctuates, or the needle keeps breaking, you may have to change the tension, stitch length, or pressure of the machine's foot. Try out different adjustments on your machine, using scraps of material. Give yourself a chance to practice on fabric samples before you start the actual project.

MATERIALS

A variety of synthetic materials can be purchased by the yard. Outer fabrics, which come coated and uncoated, include ripstop nylon, nylon taffeta, and various waterproof-breathable fabrics; these materials can be used for clothing, tarps, and tents. Oxford and pack cloth of various weights provide durability in making items such as packs and duffles. Insulation, such as fiberfills or compressed synthetics, can also be obtained to use for sleeping bags and warm clothing. In addition, other warm fabrics such as fleeces are available in a variety of weights.

Synthetic fabrics come in various weights. Numbers on the materials indicate the weight per square yard: "1.9 ripstop nylon" means that every square yard weighs 1.9 ounces. The higher the number, the heavier the material.

Uncoated ripstop and uncoated nylon taffeta work well for tents and for the outer shell and lining of clothing and sleeping bags. When coated, either material can be used for tent flies. Coated nylon taffeta is usually chosen for raingear. The heavier, coated pack cloths are made into such items as stuffsacks, packs, gaiters, and duffel bags.

Fabrics that breathe and are waterproof can be purchased by the yard to be used for such outdoor clothing as raingear. These rather expensive materials are constructed with three layers: an outer layer similar to coated nylon, a porous middle film, and an inner lining. In theory, the middle membrane permits body moisture to escape without letting in outside moisture. Since children outgrow clothing quickly and do not perspire as heavily as adults, these fabrics may not provide enough benefits to justify the high cost.

INSULATION MATERIALS

Synthetic insulators are sold under various trade names. Although these insulators look as if they would be like working with cotton candy, they are easy to handle and cut with no disintegration. All these battings come in various weights. The higher the number, the warmer the materials. Other types of insulators are designed to be less bulky and thus work well for making warm clothing.

The advantages of the synthetics are that they retain their warmth when wet. They wash easily and dry fairly fast. Thus, these insulators are ideal for young children still in diapers, and for youngsters who are inordinately attracted to every puddle of water along the trail.

Down still provides the greatest warmth for the least weight and can be compressed for carrying. It can be purchased in bulk for making down-insulated clothing or sleeping bags but is quite costly. There are many drawbacks to using down for children: the feathers are difficult to handle while sewing, down loses its warmth when wet and is hard to wash and dry, and some children have allergies to the down.

HINTS FOR SEWING ON SYNTHETICS

When sewing on synthetic fabrics, be sure your sewing machine needle is very sharp. Change the needle if in doubt. A size 14 needle is just about right unless you are sewing on exceptionally heavy fabric, in which case you should use size 16 or 18. Sew with cotton-covered polyester thread.

To prevent puckering as you sew, hold the fabric taut but let the machine feed the material. About ten stitches to the inch is the correct stitch-length setting. With fiberfills, sewing with the nylon fabric on top is easier, or you can place tissue paper or wax paper over the batting and rip it off later.

Unless you are very careful, uncoated nylon will unravel as you work on it. To prevent raveling you can sear the seams. A candle in a secure holder, a soldering iron, or a wood-burning pencil can be used for seam searing. Practice first on nylon scraps. Your aim is to sear or melt only the outer threads. Hold the fabric tightly and run about an 8-inch section of seam quickly through the flame of the candle. When using the iron or pencil, stretch the fabric over a clean board and run the implement over the material's edge. It is sometimes easier if one person holds the fabric and another operates the soldering iron or wood-burning pencil. With all synthetics, practice before you start sewing on your actual project.

SEWING ACCESSORIES

Accessories for sewing outdoor gear are available in the same places that sell synthetic fabrics. You can purchase zippers in a variety of lengths, Velcro fasteners, knit cuffs, buckles, nylon web belting, grommets, rings, thread, seam sealers, and many other notions necessary for making outdoor equipment and clothing at home.

PATTERNS

Not too long ago people who wanted to sew outdoor gear for themselves or for their children had to devise the pattern, figure out the materials to use, and manage by trial and error to convert fabric into a functional end product. Now, however, with the availability of patterns and fabrics, sewing your own gear can be accomplished with the experts' advice. If unavailable in your area, patterns, fabrics, and special outdoor gear accessories can be obtained through fabric companies that offer catalogue sales. The catch is that for every dozen adult designs available there is only one design for children. If you are thinking about children's designs of your own but have never worked with synthetic materials, a simple pattern, such as a child's vest or winter mitts, will provide a beginning sewing experience. An easy project helps set the stage for moving into more complex gear making. Another possibility is to sew for yourself; then you can use what you have learned to adapt a pattern to a child's size. A pattern can be constructed if you take apart a similar piece of clothing, such as a fleece jacket, and create a model for the necessary pieces in the desired outdoor gear. When youngsters grow into small adult sizes, they can fit into more of the patterns available for outdoor clothing.

MAKING A CHILD'S RAIN PANTS

Making rain pants for a child requires minimal sewing skills. You can make your own pattern merely by opening out an old, worn-out pair of long pants belonging to your youngster. (Or you can purchase a regular children's pants pattern at a fabric store and then make adjustments to this pattern for size, style, and air and growth space.) Using your child's old pants, cut along the crotch seams and

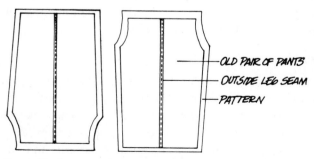

Figure 22. Cut rain pants from a child's old, worn-out pants

along the inner leg seams. Do not open the outer leg seams. To be sure the size is up to date, measure your child from waist to shoe tops. Add 3 inches at the top for encasing elastic, 1 inch at the bottom of each leg for the hem, and several inches on each side so that the pants slide over other clothing and boots easily. The bagginess encourages good air circulation. To avoid putting in a front zipper, make the area from hips to waist wider than regular fitted pants.

Synthetic materials come in widths of about 44 inches. One length of coated nylon taffeta should be adequate, even for a 12-year-old. To conserve space on the material, place one leg pattern with the waist at the top of the material and the other leg pattern with the leg bottoms at the top. To avoid using pins, which leave holes in the waterproofing, draw around the leg patterns with a marker. Draw lines on what will be the inside, or shiny, coated side, of the pants.

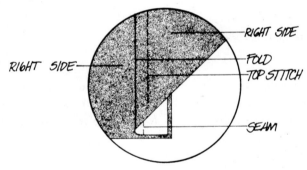

Figure 23. **Top-stitch seam**

To create strong, leak-resistant seams, use what is called a *top-stitch seam* on the crotch and inner leg seams. To top-stitch, place the uncoated (right) sides together and machine-sew the seam ⅝ inch from the raw edges. Then fold both raw edges the same way, and on the right side of the fabric sew an extra line of stitching ⅛ inch from the finished seam.

With right sides together sew the rain pants' front and

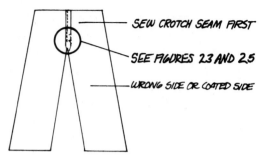

Figure 24. Machine-sew crotch seam front and back with top-stitch seam

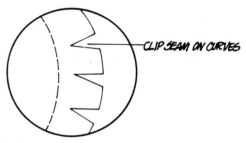

Figure 25. Clip curved crotch seam

back crotch seams first. (The seam will pull on the curve. Clip carefully no more than ⅜ inch into the fabric.) Next, tape the two crotch seams together at the lower edge.

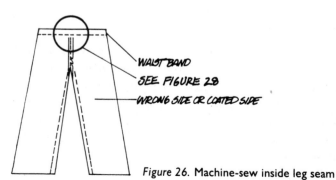

Figure 26. Machine-sew inside leg seam

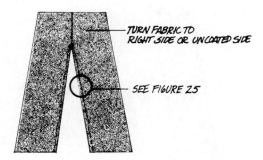

Figure 27. Turn pants to right side and finish top-stitch seams

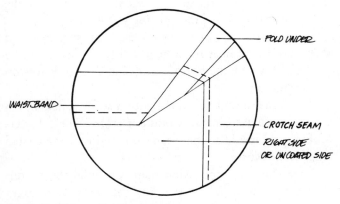

Figure 28. Make waist elastic casing

Then, pin the open leg seams; sew, fold over, and top-stitch.

At the waist, fold ¼ inch, then fold another 1¼ inches of material over to the outside of the pants. Sew this down around the pants top on the uncoated side. At the back crotch seam, leave a 1-inch-wide opening through which you will thread waist elastic.

Use only waistband elastic that is washable; it is sometimes called "swimwear elastic." Measure the elastic around your child's waist. It should be comfortable with a slight stretch. After threading the elastic through the waist casing, overlap the two ends and sew together flat; sew

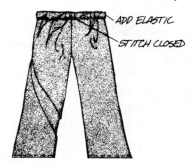

Figure 29. Add waist elastic, close casing, hem pant bottoms

back and forth several times. Tuck the elastic inside the casing, and sew closed the opening you left.

At the lower edge of each pant leg, turn up ¼ inch and then another ¾ inch for a hem and sew. Elastic can be threaded through the bottom hems but this tends to stop air circulation.

All seams should be coated with a seam sealer, which can be purchased in most outdoor stores. For a better-looking end product, coat seams on the inside, or coated side, of the fabric.

Your child's coated nylon pants are infinitely useful: they are indispensable in the rain; they provide an extra windbreak layer against the cold; and, for younger children in particular, they form a barrier between the child's regular clothing and the dirt, mud, and water little ones love to play in.

(*Note:* Some patterns and instructions call for the coated side to be outside. For a child's pants, which receive hard wear, it is better to have the coated side on the inside.)

MAKING A CHILD'S SLEEPING BAG

You do not have to be dismayed that so little choice is available in children's sleeping bags, because you can make a bag yourself. The new synthetics are warmer and more lightweight than the synthetics they replaced (see "Types of Insulation" section); with them you can sew a bag to your own personal specifications. Since practicality, not fashion, is important, even a sewing novice can produce a good-quality, useful bag. A child's bag is easier to make than an adult's bag since its small size eliminates coping with large quantities of material.

Making your own design and pattern is simple. First decide on the shape you want. The less extra space inside, the greater the warmth. The most efficient bag design for trapping body heat is the mummy shape. Essentially this style fits the body; the top of the bag is approximately shoulder width, and the bag gradually tapers to the feet. In making your own design, you can determine how snug a fit you desire.

Growing children need extra length. You can compensate for the subsequent heat loss by creating a tighter fit or by tying off unused foot space.

Some people prefer a rectangular-shaped bag for hot-weather camping. This style allows for more air circulation, and it permits body heat to escape. A rectangular bag is not effective for really cold weather or for nights when temperatures drop appreciably.

To cope with a variety of temperatures and seasons, a tapered bag with a full, two-way zipper that opens from top to bottom provides flexibility. On warm nights you totally unzip the bag; you can even use the opened bag like a quilt on top of your child. In the cold you zip up completely. In moderate weather you open the zipper partially. When making your child's bag, choose a standard-sized, two-way zipper that will extend fully along the desired bag length. Zippers can be purchased at outdoor stores that carry fabric.

A warm bag needs an insulated hood. The hood's drawstring can be fastened tightly to keep in heat or it can be left loose in moderate weather. On warm nights the hood can be left flat. In your own design, a simple half-moon-shaped piece created above the shoulder line on the back side of the bag can become a hood when a drawstring is inserted.

Muslin Pattern

To experiment with both fit and design, you can buy inexpensive unbleached muslin and create a mock-up of your ideas. Measure your child's length and width; add in room for potential growth and an inch all around for seams. With a marker, draw the size and shape you want on the muslin. Cut out a front and back, and sew the two pieces together with a loose gathering stitch. Slip your child into the pattern bag, and see how it fits. Add to or subtract from the pattern until you are satisfied with the size. When you pull out the gathering stitch, you will have two of the three necessary pattern pieces.

To complete your muslin pattern, cut an 8-inch-wide zipper flap. The length should be from zipper top to zipper bottom plus 1 inch at each end for seams and 2 inches for bottom overlap.

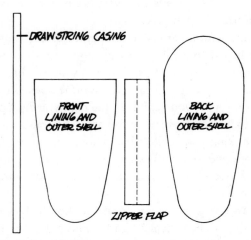

Figure 30. Four-piece pattern for making a synthetic insulated child's sleeping bag

Materials

The lining and outer shell for the bag can be made of un-coated ripstop nylon. For insulation you can choose one of the synthetic fiberfills. Remember, you can vary the bag's warmth by the weight of the insulator you purchase. The higher the weight number, the warmer the material.

Cutting

From the outer shell material, cut one back, one front, and one zipper flap. From the lining material (lining and shell can be the same material and color, or contrasting colors can be used), cut one back and one front. Cut one front and one back from your insulating material; then cut insulation the length, but only half the width, of the zipper flap.

For greater warmth, you can double your insulation or choose to have two top insulating layers and one bottom layer. You are making the bag; therefore you are the designer and can fit the bag to your needs.

STEP 1: ZIPPER FLAP. Make the zipper flap first. Machine-sew the insulator to cover half of the wrong side of the zipper flap. Then fold the flap in half so that right

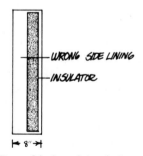

Figure 31. Attach insulation to be encased in zipper flap

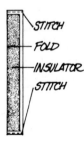

Figure 32. Fold zipper flap right sides together and stitch top and bottom

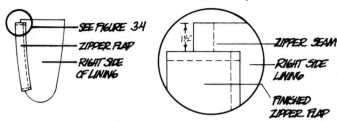

Figure 33. Attach finished zipper flap to right side of front lining with top-stitching

Figure 34. Zipper flap is top-stitched 2 inches in from the lining's raw edge and 1 inch in from the zipper fold line

sides of the material are together. Stitch across top and bottom ends.

Next, turn the flap so that the material is right side out and the raw edges of the top and bottom seam are inside. Fold under ⅝ inch on each side of the long opening that is left and top-stitch so that the insulator is completely encased. (You can trim the insulator for easier sewing.)

Start 1½ inches from the top and top-stitch the flap to the right side of the front lining piece. (The flap will extend over the zipper from the inside of the bag.) Locate top-stitching 1 inch from the fold line for the zipper seam and 2 inches from the raw edge of the lining.

STEP 2: SEAMS. Put together the right sides of the front and back outer shell and sew the bottom seam and the side seam that will be opposite the zipper opening side. Sew the same seams in the lining material. You do not make a regular seam in the insulator; to eliminate some bulkiness, overlap the back and front insulation pieces and machine-sew the bottom and side seams. In all pieces, be sure to leave open the side of the bag where the zipper will go.

(Remember that the raw seam edges of the lining and shell will be inside when the bag is put together. The insulation will be sandwiched between the lining and the shell.)

STEP 3: ATTACHING THE INSULATION. Slip the lining inside the insulation with the lining's raw edges against the insulator. Sew the insulator to the lining 1½ inches from the zipper-side edges and 1 inch down from the bag top. Trim away excess insulation after sewing.

STEP 4: PUTTING LINING AND SHELL TOGETHER. Turn the outer shell so that the raw seam edges are on the inside. Slip the lining with its attached insulator inside the outer shell. Machine-stitch around the top of the bag ½ inch from the raw edges. Leave the zipper seam open.

STEP 5: ZIPPER INSTALLATION. When sewing in the zipper, use a zipper foot. Place the top of the zipper tape 2

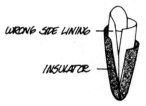

Figure 35. Sew side and bottom seams in lining and insulator; slip lining into the insulator

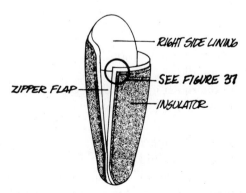

Figure 36. Machine-sew insulator securely to the wrong side of the lining

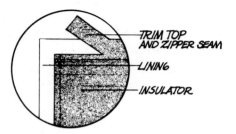

Figure 37. For easier work with casing and zipper, trim excess insulator from still-open edges

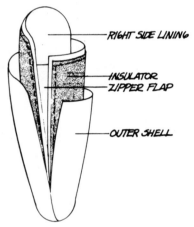

Figure 38. Turn outer shell so that seams are inside; with insulator out and lining in, put lining and outer shell together

inches down from the bag top, and position the seam to go near the middle of the zipper tape.

First put the zipper into the lining only. Fold each of the two raw edges of the lining along the zipper opening toward the wrong side of the lining material. Place the resulting folds on the zipper tape with the zipper pull facing inside the bag (your child can then open the zipper while in the bag). Pin, baste, and machine-sew along both sides of the lining opening. (Once the zipper is securely basted, you can open it for easier machine-sewing.)

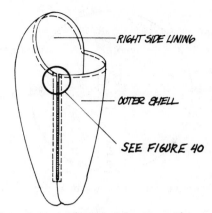

Figure 39. Insert zipper in the remaining open side seam

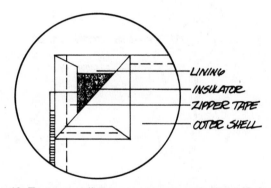

Figure 40. Zipper installation: sew zipper to the lining first, then cover stitches with folded outer shell and sew the outer shell zipper seam

Finally, attach the outer shell to the zipper. Fold under the raw edges of the outer shell and place the resulting fold along the zipper itself. After first pinning and basting, machine-stitch on top of the already finished lining stitches. Take the stitching up to the top of the bag so that the lining and outer shell are sewn together.

STEP 6: DRAWSTRING CASING. For the casing, use a 3-inch-wide strip of the outer-shell material cut long enough

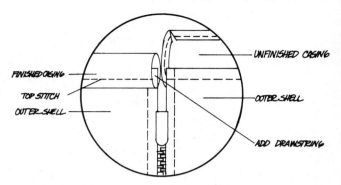

Figure 41. Finish the sleeping bag top by adding a casing

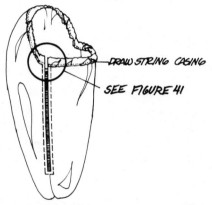

Figure 42. Finished child's sleeping bag with drawstring casing

to go around the bag top, front and back, plus 1 inch at each end for a seam and 2 extra inches for easing the straight material onto the curved hood. (Sear the edges of the casing and the bag top, since the drawstring will be rubbing against these parts of the bag.)

Place the right side of the casing against the right side of the lining. Pin, baste, and then machine-sew. You have to make tiny tucks as you go around the curved edges.

At the two short ends of the casing, fold over the raw edges, wrong sides together, and stitch down near the fold. Trim away all but ½ inch of these casing edges. On the unstitched long edge of the casing, fold over ½ inch of material and sew this down with a long gathering stitch; you can then gather the material slightly on the curve.

Finally, fold the casing over the raw edges at the top of the bag. Put the hemmed fold on top of the stitches you made when you attached the casing onto the right side of the lining. Pin (easing with the gathers on the curve), baste securely, and then machine-sew. Both ends should be left open so that the drawstring can be inserted.

Knot the ends of the drawstring after insertion. Tie a loop of drawstring cord to the zipper pull so that youngsters can zip and unzip more easily.

Add-On Sections for Sleeping Bags

To stretch out the usable life of a child's sleeping bag, you can add on a new section to the foot of an existing bag.

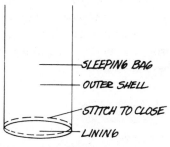

Figure 43. Open the original sleeping bag and then sew the bottom closed to encase the insulation

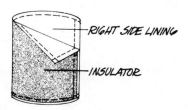

Figure 44. Make the new section to be added; attach insulation to wrong side of the lining piece

For an easier project, use fiberfill insulation even if your child's bag is down filled.

The first step is to open the bottom of the original sleeping bag. With synthetic fills you carefully cut the visible stitches until the bag foot is totally open. To seal off the opening made, fold the raw edges of the lining and shell toward each other so that you encase the insulation. Use a ⅝-inch hem. Pin, baste, and sew ¼ inch from the fold.

Opening up a down bag is a bit trickier. Work in a place where you can save any feathers lost. Snip open the stitching at the foot of the bag just the way you would with a synthetic fill. If the bottom feather baffle is caught in the lining and shell seams, you will have to open that baffle. Try to replace the feathers and baste the baffle closed as you go along. When your bag foot is open, fold under the raw edges and sew to seal it off.

Now measure your child to see how much additional length is needed; allow for growth. The new section will attach 3 inches above the foot opening. Measure the circumference of the original bag at that point and add 1 inch for seams all around. Cut a shell, a lining, and an insulation piece to these measurements.

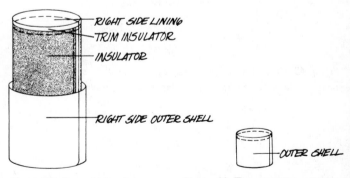

Figure 45. Sew side and bottom seams in outer shell add-on piece; place insulator and lining inside the outer shell

Figure 46. Turn top raw edges inside and top-stitch around the top edge of the new section

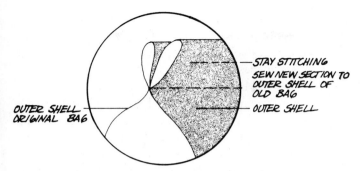

Figure 47. Detail drawing of the seam to attach the old bag and the new section

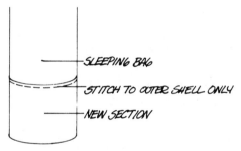

Figure 48. Stitch the new section to only the outer shell of the old sleeping bag 3 inches up from the bottom

Sew the insulation to the lining. Pin and baste first; then machine-sew with the lining facing you. Fold the lining in half with the insulation outside. Sew the side seam and the bottom seam closed. Since you will be sewing right on the insulation this time, place wax paper or tissue paper over the batting.

Next, with right sides together, sew the side and bottom seams of the outer shell. Turn the shell so that the raw edges are inside.

Slip the insulation and lining into the outer shell. The insulation will be sandwiched between the lining and the shell. To avoid bulkiness at the top seam, trim off the top ⅝ inch of insulation. Fold the raw edges at the top of the shell and lining in toward each other. Pin, baste, and then machine-sew together ¼ inch from the fold.

With chalk, mark all the way around the original bag at a point 3 inches above the bottom edge. Along this line fold the original bag under so that the 3 inches are inside. At the 3-inch mark, pull the shell material slightly away from the insulation and lining. Put the top-edge stitching of the new section against this fold you are making in the original bag's outer shell. Pin completely around the bag, being careful not to catch the insulation. Baste and then sew. Stitch ¼ inch from the fold in the original bag shell. Your seam will give the appearance of a small tuck around the bag.

When you finish the seam, push the extra 3 inches of the original bag down so that it extends into the new section on the inside. At the side seams, hand-stitch or tack down securely the 3-inch inside extension from the old bag to the new section you have added. This extension will form a flap under the connecting seam.

Packs

Children's packs come in three styles: small, frameless models that can double as book bags; larger packs attached to an external frame; and internal frame packs also with larger carrying capacity.

FRAMELESS PACKS

A child can use a frameless pack for a variety of day excursions, including cross-country skiing, day hiking, and day bicycling. For backpacking, the child's frameless design holds only token weight. It can accommodate small, light items that a 3- or 4-year-old would carry on early overnight outings.

Frameless packs made especially for children come in many sizes. Most have unpadded straps made of webbed nylon. Many are designed to ride high on the back and have no waist belt. Children are more comfortable, however, if soft packs are belted on. A belt on a frameless design functions as an anchor and makes wearing the pack like wearing clothes; a child can move without the pack shifting or swinging. The easiest way to add a belt is to machine-stitch a ¾-inch nylon web buckled strap (the kind used to cinch a sleeping bag to a frame pack) to the bottom edge of the pack.

Soft-Pack Design

If you buy an exactly toddler-sized soft pack, low cost may be more important than quality features. The shoulder straps should be adjustable and attached close together at the top. Since frameless packs loaded to bulging are uncomfortable, outside pockets provide the best source of additional space. Soft packs close with either a zipper or a storm flap.

For versatility and longer use, the larger the bag cavity the better. When older, a child can carry warm clothes for a day of cross-country skiing or the pack can double as a schoolbook bag.

Making a First Soft Pack

You can make a soft pack for a very young child quite inexpensively. Use coated nylon (you can buy remnants the right size at a reduced price), inch-wide nylon webbing for shoulder straps, and a nylon web buckled strap for a belt. You can design your own pack shape—long or short, tapered from a narrow top, or whatever pleases you and your child.

Fold the material into three sections, like an envelope. Bring the bottom section up and stitch along the sides. Turn this bottom part so that the seams are inside. The top section is the flap; hem its raw edges. Measure the correct shoulder strap length for your child, cut the straps, and at-

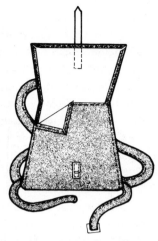

Figure 49. Make your child's first soft pack by folding the appropriate sized rectangular piece of coated material twice like an envelope

Figure 50. Homemade, small soft pack for the small child

tach the tops of the straps close together below the flap fold on the back of the pack. Stitch the strap bottoms to the bottom corners of the pack.

You can add a buckle or sew on large, heavy-duty snaps to close the pack. At the back bottom edge of the pack, stitch on the nylon web buckled strap for a belt. As an extra child-pleasing touch, letter your youngster's name on the pack.

Small Adult's Pack

For the young grade-schooler and the older child, you might consider buying one of the less expensive, small rucksacks made for adults. A 7- or 8-year-old of average build can use a pack like this. Instead of riding high, the pack covers the child's back. To be a workable alternative, the shoulder straps and belt must be adjustable to your youngster's size. These adults' packs basically have more room than soft packs made especially for children, and with adjustable shoulder straps they can be used throughout grade school and beyond for a variety of outdoor purposes.

SLEEPING BAG CARRIERS

Although no longer available new, sleeping bag carriers are another item that can be found used. These carriers can be perfect for the young child with ample stamina for backpacking but the wrong physique to fit into a small frame pack. For some youngsters 4 to 7 years old, especially very slender or short-waisted children, the carrier provides the most reasonable first step in load carrying.

Used commercially made sleeping bag carriers come with adjustable, unpadded shoulder straps. A harness secures the sleeping bag in place below a small zippered pack. This compartment holds the equivalent of a child's rainsuit, warm sweater, and juice bottle. With the sleeping bag attached, the weight is sufficient to make pads on the straps and a waist belt necessary for comfort. Without the sleeping bag, the pack itself has a peculiar fit; it does not double as a usable daypack.

A sleeping bag carrier can be made by using 1- or 1½-inch webbed nylon, which is available by the yard. One set of webbed nylon forms the shoulder straps and attaches to two strips of webbed nylon that extend across the child's back. Adjustable straps with buckles run under these cross straps to encircle the sleeping bag. To anchor the carrier in place, you attach an adjustable strap with buckles to form a belt. For increased comfort on a homemade or commercially made sleeping bag carrier, you can also add to the shoulder straps rectangles of open-cell foam enclosed in coated nylon (see "Making Packs Comfortable" section).

FRAME PACKS

Children's frame packs are essentially smaller versions of adults' frame packs. A child's body is not, however, shaped like an adult's. Youngsters, even husky ones, are built straight up and down. To complicate frame fitting even more, a child's body is constantly changing with growth. No commercially made frame pack is perfect for all children. What you find may be reasonably comfortable—if so, you are lucky. You could discover that your child's body type is close to impossible to fit.

A frame pack consists of three distinct parts: the cloth pack itself, the metal frame to which you attach the pack, and the straps and belt that hold the frame onto the body. When buying a frame pack for a child, you must carefully

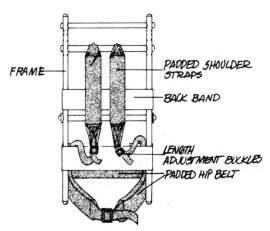

Figure 51. Parts of the frame pack

examine the good and bad points of each of these parts, just as you would when choosing an adult's pack. Then you need to evaluate how well the pack will adjust to the growth of your youngster. Ideally, the same pack that your 6-year-old used to begin backpacking will still fit well four or five years later.

The Frame

The crucial dimension for fitting a child into a pack is the length of the frame between the top shoulder strap attachment and the hip belt. The belt should rest on top of the youngster's hip bone, and the top shoulder strap attachment should be just about level with the top of the child's shoulders. To obtain long-term maximum wear from a pack, you must be able to adjust this important dimension to accommodate your child's growth. The more adjustment potential a pack has, the longer your youngster will be able to use it.

Different packs adjust in different ways. To be sure the adjustment is easy to make, try it in the store before you buy.

Used External Frame Packs

Over the years many adjustable pack frames have been available for children. The best of these were built sturdy enough to last through many generations of use. With these older models, adjustments could be made easily in a variety of ways, by loosening two screws and moving the crossbar up or down, or by moving the crossbar to a number of fixed locations where clevis pins anchored the crossbar in place. Other used frames provided even more size flexibility, because you could purchase a conversion kit that included side members and vertical bars in a larger size to expand the frame size to fit your growing child. These high-quality used frame packs can often be located through advertising in outdoor club newsletters or by contacting outdoor people whose children are grown.

Straps and Belts

Although, in theory, the weight of a pack rests on the hip belt, padded shoulder straps are especially important for children. On a slender youngster in particular, the hip belt will not stay dependably in place; it will move and shift and slide. Even husky children face this problem. Since the pack's weight falls on the child's shoulders more than you would like, the straps must be comfortable. Most children's packs, even the less expensive ones, have built-in shoulder pads. The padding, however, is usually hard. The padded straps do not cut into the shoulders as plain straps would, but for the typical child they still do not provide enough of a soft cushion (see "Making Packs Comfortable" section).

Look for shoulder straps that are easily adjustable. The straps need to be comfortably snug on a youngster. With the hip belt tightened, you should be able to fit your fingers under the straps. Ideally, a child should be able to manipulate strap-adjusting buckles without help.

Not all children's packs come with hip belts. Some have narrow, nylon web belts. A padded hip belt is essential if a child is to carry the pack's weight where it belongs—on the hip bone rather than on the shoulders. Even with padding, a hip belt may still feel uncomfortable to a child when it is cinched tightly enough to be useful. The pads are made of hard foam, and the child has little or no body padding for cushioning. The belt slides; keeping it in the right place is difficult. Most children, especially young beginners, will not tolerate a belt (padded or not) as tight as it needs to be for effectiveness (see "Making Packs Comfortable" section).

Encircling the pack frame are one or two back bands. Some are padded, and some are made of wide, webbed nylon. These bands hold the metal frame parts away from the child's body. Since they do touch the youngster, the padded variety provides slightly more comfort. The padding here, however, is not as important as it is on the shoulders and hips.

The External Frame Pack

When you evaluate a frame pack for your child, do not look at the pack itself first. Examine instead the frame and its adjustability; the straps, their padding, and length adjustment; and the hip belt and its padding. Be sure, too, that you can move the tops of the straps closer together or farther apart. Then go on to consider the pack itself.

Your child may be attracted by a pack's bright color and shiny fabric, but you need to decide how usable the space is. Children's frame packs come in two basic styles. One has a storm flap for closure and the other zippers shut.

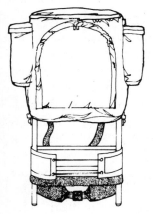

Figure 52. Zipper-closed frame pack

On a zipper-style pack, the zipper curves around the top and sides of the pack. You open a zippered pack completely, the way you would a suitcase. The zipper gives easy access to the entire pack and eliminates rooting down into the bottom for lost items. Even from an early age children can operate a zipper easily. The zipper-enclosed cavity, however, limits your space. You have only so much room,

Figure 53. Storm flap-closed frame pack with sleeping bag attached to frame; packs should fit with the hip belt just above the hip bone and the shoulder strap tops level with the shoulders

which you zipper shut. There is no way within the cavity to expand that space. If you cram a zipper-style pack full to bulging, you run the risk of catching something and breaking the zipper.

With a storm flap, a piece of material falls over the pack opening. You secure the flap by tying down the drawstrings that thread through the sides of the flap. With a small load, you pull the strings tight; with a larger load, you can expand the usable pack space by tying down the flap more loosely.

Most children's frame packs have room under the pack for attaching a sleeping bag. However, a small, light youngster may prefer to carry the sleeping bag weight high. With a storm flap design, you can stuff the sleeping bag into the top of the pack, pull the flap securely over it, and provide the beginner with more comfortable load distribution. None of our children were able to tolerate the sleeping bag low until they were about 9 years old.

When youngsters are older and stronger, the sleeping bag can be attached to the frame below the pack and the extra cavity space can be used to hold other gear.

Outer pockets on a pack provide extra carrying room. A young child may fill only one pocket; an older child, who can carry more weight, may fill all the pockets to capacity. Many packs come with two outer pockets; some have three. The more pockets available the better, for they provide another means of extending the useful life of a pack. Outer pack pockets zipper shut. A child is less likely to jam zippers on outer pockets than he or she is to catch something in a main cavity zipper.

You must also consider the combined weight of the pack and frame. For a child, every ounce counts. If possible, you want the weight to go into gear carried rather than into the pack itself.

If you want your child's pack to last for many years, make sure the pack cloth itself is highly durable. You can compensate for worn waterproofing by using extra plastic sacks to hold clothing. Tears or rips are another matter. Most packs are made of a heavyweight nylon pack cloth. Some inexpensive packs (the type found in variety stores) are made of a very lightweight nylon of questionable strength.

Don't forget that packs, like boots, can be used for more than one child. Sometimes a secondhand pack in a style no longer manufactured can provide an economical alternative for outfitting your youngster. Check with friends and acquaintances who enjoy the outdoors.

Internal Frame Packs

Although children's internal frame packs have not flooded the market, there is a child-size version. The internal frame has the advantage of synchronizing with the body's movements and is thus easier to manage in active outdoor activities such as climbing, cross-country skiing, cross-country hiking, and rock scrambling. The internal frame pack hugs the body and thus provides no ventilation; this feature creates a disadvantage, as does the price, which reflects the costly technology needed to create an effective and comfortable design. Until youngsters are involved in the active outdoor sports for which the internal frame pack was invented, this style offers little advantage and will add to the cost of buying a pack, especially if you purchase a small adult size for an older child. Once youngsters are involved in off-the-trail outdoor sports where the pack movements should synchronize with their actions, they may be more comfortable and safer wearing this type of pack. Then adjustable features, which will allow the pack to grow with the child, are important to assess as you evaluate the internal frame packs available.

Making Packs Comfortable

For most youngsters, even well-fitting packs are uncomfortable in two places: at the shoulders and at the hips. Much of the problem stems from a child's lack of natural padding (a very skinny adult can face the same predicament). To help alleviate the discomfort, you can make nylon-covered pads for your child's pack.

To make your own padding, take 1½- or 2-inch thick open-cell foam padding (the cushiony, spongy kind) and cut it to the size and shape you need. For a hip pad, the piece should cover the place of contact with the hip bone plus several inches on each side. The shoulder strap pads should cover any areas where the straps touch the body. The padding should be somewhere between 6 and 10 inches long and at least 2 inches wide.

Next, make a casing for the pad from coated nylon pack cloth. Cut the cloth twice the size of the padding. Allow for inch-wide seams all around and for the pad's thickness.

To attach the extra padding to the pack straps, use Velcro fasteners. Velcro is a rough-textured material. The fastener comes in two parts; when you put the two pieces

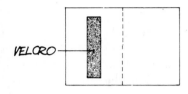

VELCRO

Figure 54. Sew one part of the Velcro strip in the center of one side of the pad casing

Figure 55. Put right sides of casing together and sew the side and bottom seams

1½" FOAM

Figure 56. Turn so that raw edges are inside and insert the soft foam pad

together they interlock. First pull the Velcro strip apart. Sew one side of the Velcro to the underside of the pack straps (either the shoulder or hip straps). You will need to hand-sew if the straps are already padded. Sew the other side to the middle of one half of the nylon pad casing on the uncoated side of the material. Fold the casing cloth in half, with the Velcro on the inside, and sew along the side and bottom seams. Then turn the casing so that the seams are inside and the Velcro is on the outside. Insert the padding through the top, fold over the raw edges, and top-stitch the casing closed.

The extra padding goes against the child's body and is secured to the straps with the Velcro fasteners. With more hip belt cushion, you may even be able to pull your child's belt tight enough to stay in place.

Adjusting a Pack on a Child

A frame pack should fit a child just right. Try as best you can to approach that ideal. Before you load your youngster's pack for a trip, put the empty pack on him or her. Position the hip belt so that it sits on the hip bone, then tighten. Look at the crossbar where the shoulder straps attach; it should be approximately level with the top of the child's shoulders. With an adjustable frame, move the crossbar, if necessary, to achieve this proper placement. (With a nonadjustable frame, you are stuck with whatever frame size you purchased.)

Before you remove the pack for adjustment, see if the straps are attached close enough to each other. A narrow-shouldered youngster requires the closest strap spacing, while a wider-shouldered child may be more comfortable with wider strap spacing. Be sure that the back bands, which can be shifted, are located properly to keep the metal frame away from the child's body.

Take off the pack and make all your adjustments. Tighten the back bands; some buckle on while others are secured with cord. Then try the empty pack on your child again to see how it seems to fit. At this point, your youngster may be totally annoyed by all this fitting. Before you leave on your trip, however, you should load the pack with all you expect the child to carry and look at the fit one more time.

On the hike itself, you should also carefully observe the pack's fit. As your youngster moves, make sure the pack is at its optimum adjustment. Make changes if you see any flaws. Some trial and error will be necessary. The time taken for on-the-trail pack adjustments provides a break from hiking. At that point your child may appreciate the rest.

When to Change to the Frame Pack

In theory, you change to a frame pack when your child's size and body shape fit into available frames. You also must take into account a child's desire to have a frame pack of his or her own. Last summer our 6-year-old, who still has a questionable physique for a frame pack, declared that the sleeping bag carrier she had used for two years was for babies. She demanded a frame pack. Such a moment in a child's life is the right time to provide the frame pack and to begin using it. If you take time to add a great deal of extra padding, you may be able to make even a poor fit work reasonably well for your youngster.

When you are trying to stretch out the life of a child's frame pack, think of the time span involved from the first frame pack at 6 or 7 until a child reaches the teens.

In their teens youngsters usually graduate into adult-sized frame packs, and manufacturers make these in small, medium, and large frame and pack sizes to match a person's body size. Teenagers often are strong enough to handle a large pack (not necessarily a large frame) with its extra weight-carrying capacity. Many backpacking parents dream of the day when their children carry a larger load than they do. The catch is that many teenagers decide at that point not to go hiking with their parents.

Toys and Diversions

A familiar object or favorite toy often bridges the way between a child's world at home and the new world introduced on a camping trip. If a child usually sleeps with a toy, stuffed animal, or blanket, having this item on overnight outings is essential and may even be necessary on day trips for napping. Some children can make do with a strip cut from an old blanket, but a young child may require the exact item from home. Older children in a strange environment sometimes need the familiar more than you might guess, too, especially at bedtime.

Practice moderation when carrying toys along. A heavy, metal toy truck, even though a favorite, is out of the question. A very small doll or 2-inch-long toy car can fit in fine.

When youngsters first start camping with you, set a toy limit of one or two items per child. Children can choose their own toys, but you must have the final say, especially for backpacking. To stress the advantages of lightweight items, some families make it a rule that children carry their own toys. The need for toys in the outdoors is minimal, and after a few trips youngsters realize that it is not necessary to take the kinds of toys they have at home.

Older children who are avid readers enjoy carrying paperback books with them. These are light and provide diversion on rainy days or at bedtime.

Being prepared with rainy day activities is helpful. Many games come in miniature or small sizes. You can find undersized decks of cards, tiny chess and checkers sets, and small versions of Master Mind in novelty stores. If you are confined to your tent during a storm, you can fill the time with these diversions. Small notepads and a pen or pencil slip easily into a pack and enable children to devise their own games in bad weather.

Special Needs for Babies

Parents who bring infants along on outdoor excursions must provide for the baby's special needs. In addition to considering general camping gear, you must determine which diapering, feeding, and child-carrying equipment is most appropriate for your infant.

DIAPERS

Since diapers add extra weight when dry and even more weight when wet, plan to suffer a bit from overloading when children are still in diapers. Most people who camp with diapered babies use disposable diapers. In reality these diapers are not disposable, because you must carry out all the used ones. No matter how far into the wilderness or how isolated your location, never bury these diapers. Some day that wild country may support a steady stream of travelers, and such quantities of paper decompose very slowly. All feces from diapers must be buried in the same careful manner you use to dispose of any human wastes (see Chapter 9, in the section "Toileting Children"). In areas where fires are acceptable (see Chapter 9, in the section "Fires"), you can dry out disposable diapers (it takes a long time) and then burn them (that takes a long time too). The fire you employ will not do for marshmallow roasting or pleasure.

Disposables come in a variety of sizes and weights. Since preventing leaks into other clothing is important, those made with extra-absorbent quilting may be helpful. At night, more diaper layers than usual helps prevent the disaster of a soiled, wet sleeping bag.

If you decide on a new diapering routine for the backcountry, try it out on your baby for at least a week or more before your trip. See how a different style or material works on your particular child. Be sure your selection does not irritate the baby's skin.

If you use cloth diapers, these can be washed and dried in places where clear, warm weather can be expected. For washing, take a non-irritating soap—the one used successfully at home is your best bet—and a wash container of adequate size that will not be used for cooking. When calculating fuel needs, allow for boiling your diaper washwater.

Do your washing away from lakes and streams, and empty the dirty water away from these water sources and away from camp too. This is toileting water, and feces carry bacteria that will contaminate. The 200 feet or more away from the campsite where you go for toileting is the location for diaper washing and water dumping.

Your strong nylon cord can be used as a clothesline. Nonfolded diapers dry fast; prefolded styles take longer. By washing diapers daily, some people manage with only one day's supply of diapers plus a few extras. On a trip, doing the laundry is extra work, but it can reduce the weight you carry.

For carrying out soiled diapers, either cloth or disposables, you need abundant plastic bags. To reduce odor, wrap individual diapers in small, sturdy plastic sacks. Use a large, durable plastic bag similar to your litter bag for the accumulated diapers. Garbage bags, even double, are too flimsy to hold the weight. Keeping the dirty diaper bag outside prevents accidental leaks into your pack.

For covering cloth diapers, you should bring plenty of extra waterproof pants. These wash and dry quickly. Some are designed to provide ventilation into the diaper area. For additional insurance, you can put them over disposables at night.

BOTTOM CLEANING

To prevent uncomfortable rashes during trips, you must keep your baby's diaper area clean. A variety of cleaners are available in plastic containers. At home, try out the brand you plan to take on your trip to be sure that your child's bottom tolerates the product.

If you don't want to use a commercial cleaner, you can wash with warm water and mild soap, using rolled absorbent cotton to clean. Changing diapers regularly also is essential; put on dry diapers at least as often as you do at home.

Make sure you carry along the rash ointment or powder recommended by your physician so you can treat diaper rash if it develops. Some of these medications work for prevention too.

BOTTLES

All babies travel heavy. Bottle babies travel extra heavy. You can cut down but you cannot totally eliminate this extra weight.

When camping, never try anything new for feeding your

child; test it out at home first. For bottle-fed babies, use the same nipples that work at home. Plastic bottles, though, which are lighter and less breakable, can replace glass bottles.

Bottles and nipples must be washed with boiled water and soap and need careful rinsing. Some plastic bottle holders have disposable plastic bags to hold the formula or milk. You dispose of the bags, and only the nipples need washing. If you know you will camp often with your baby, you might choose these as your basic bottle equipment for both home and camp.

Powdered formula or powdered milk can be mixed when needed. Use water purified with a solution derived from iodine crystals (see Chapter 3, the section on "Purifying Water") if you have any doubts about the purity of the water source. Some already diluted formulas come in sealed glass containers; these are heavy, though, and can break.

Feed your baby milk or formula at the approximate temperature he or she accepts at home. If your infant accepts room-temperature milk, you can avoid the fuss of heating. When you must warm ice-cold water, your stove can do the job quickly and efficiently.

BREAST-FEEDING

The breast-fed baby is much easier to take on backcountry trips than the bottle-fed baby. You eliminate bottle carrying, bottle washing, formula mixing, and water purifying for the baby, and for children up to 6 months old you eliminate the need for strained solids. With only a few adjustments, even babies from 6 months to 12 months old can go back to almost total breast-feeding on trips. By that time the child's solids can consist of the softer foods usually carried for adult consumption, such as breads, cheeses, cereals, and fruits.

Nursing mothers find that having their infants with them in a double sleeping bag makes night feedings more convenient. You might think of clothing combinations to facilitate nursing on the trail. A jacket with a two-way zipper or a shirt with buttons will open from the bottom so that you can tuck your child underneath for easier feeding.

Although a nursing baby requires no extra water, the mother has extra fluid needs. A good rule of thumb is to drink every time you nurse or urinate, then drink some more to compensate for sweating. You are carrying your child or more; even in cool weather your activity level will be higher than usual. Activity, heat, and nursing make high fluid consumption particularly important.

BIBS

For feeding, bibs are even more important than they are at home. Carry the large shoulder-to-waist bibs; the plastic types work especially well because they can be wiped off after each use.

SOLID FOODS

Do not experiment with your baby's diet in the backcountry. Any new foods or food combinations that sound workable should be tried at home first. One or two weeks may be necessary to familiarize your baby with the tastes.

Most commercial strained baby foods come in glass jars. For outdoor use these are both heavy and breakable. You must carry in their weight and bulk and then cart out the still weighty, bulky empties. When you use these jars of food, what the baby cannot consume must be thrown out. To avoid waste, you can organize your child's menus so that you use one whole jar for each meal rather than feeding the baby small portions from two or three jars. Anything a baby eats warmed at home should be heated on the trail too. Again, your stove can do the job quickly. To prevent breakage and in-pack spills, carry the jars wrapped in clean diapers.

Some families find that they can save on weight by using

dehydrated food for infants. Home drying works best for accommodating a baby's tastes and needs. A good way to create strained foods is to make leathers. A leather is made from food pureed in a blender or ground in a food mill. For drying, you spread the puree about ¼-inch thick on plastic wrap and place it on the dryer shelves for about two days. These leathers can be rehydrated back into purees. Fruits make excellent leathers, and so do chicken and turkey. *Dry It—You'll Like It,* a book about home drying (see Appendix), contains recipes for many dried food combinations, including leathers, that are suitable for children of all ages.

Before you try any leathers on a trip, however, be sure your baby will accept the tastes. Making dried leathers at home regularly will familiarize your child with these tastes. At-home experimentation also can show you what particular foods do to the baby's stools. New combinations that obviously cause loose stools can then be avoided.

Cereals for babies are easier to pack than other solids. They come in dried form and can be purchased in one-meal, easy-to-carry boxes. Eventually your baby can eat the same morning cereals, breads, and fruits that you eat. You can always squish food a bit before offering it to babies who are new to lumpier consistencies. For solids, do not forget the baby's spoon.

FINGER FOODS

When children nearing a year old are able to eat finger foods, the choice of foods that can be carried for them becomes greater. Hard breads, such as Instant Toast or Zwieback, do not crush in packs. Individually boxed dry cereals are handy to have, and the empty boxes make good camp toys. At this point children can eat home-dried leathers with minimal mess. Since mess is synonymous with the finger foods age, you may find the dried leathers concept particularly helpful in camp. Chunk or sliced dried bananas, apples, apricots, and pears also may be pleasing to a child this age.

Some people carry canned foods for older babies, but the 8½-ounce cans of fruits and vegetables are too much for one child, and the containers are bulky and heavy. With cans, you are always faced with packing out the empties. Open and flatten cans to reduce bulk, but never bury them.

BABY CARRIERS

With a baby carrier, you can transport a very young child in the outdoors until the child's weight becomes more than your back can handle or until you are ready to introduce trail walking. There are two basic carrier designs: the front carrier, for the very young, and the frame carrier, appropriate from the time the baby has developed enough to sit up. Baby carriers are a joy to children. For the infant in the front carrier, the closeness to the parent creates a feeling of secure comfort. Older babies in back carriers have a great vantage point on the trail—they can see everything the adult sees. Regardless of the child's age, the adult's movement soothes and lulls. Most children sleep as well in a carrier as they ever do at home.

When you invest in a child carrier, you can use it everywhere—for shopping, neighborhood walking, gardening, and comforting sick children. In the outdoors you can carry the child on the trail and keep the baby secure on your back as you work in camp. In the process, you develop a strong set of back muscles.

Front Carriers

A front carrier provides head, neck, and back support for an infant. The parent's hands are free to touch and hold the child or to do any work necessary. In one way or another, a front carrier ties the baby onto the parent's chest. You put on the child and carrier the way you would a piece

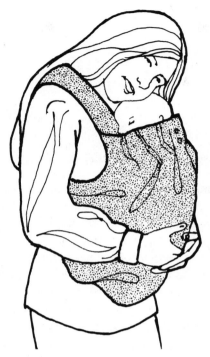

Figure 57. Front infant carrier made of cloth

of clothing. Some front carriers are easier to get into than others. All require practice.

There are a number of front carriers available. The most elaborate, designed to literally snuggle the child to the parent, has features that accommodate the growth of the child. Snaps can be adjusted and tucks or darts can be opened to create the proper fit. Later you can resew the tucks for a second baby in the family. The design allows for easy nursing. As children grow too heavy for front carrying, it can be used as a frameless back carrier. Some people even carry 2- and 3-year-olds this way. The carrier is available in a light seersucker material for warm weather and in a heavy corduroy that functions as an extra warmth layer in cool weather.

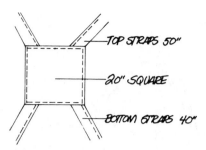

Figure 58. Easy-to-make Chinese baby carrier

Other choices include traditional carriers from various cultures around the world. You can often find these at import stores. Generally, they are simple arrangements of cloth and straps that tie a child onto the parent. The Chinese carrier consists of a square of material with long straps extending from each corner. The bottom straps tie around the parent's waist; the top straps go over the shoulders, cross in the back, and tie in the front. The baby's bottom rests in a pouch created at the waist edge of the square. The top of the square supports the infant's head. This type of carrier can be made inexpensively at home in a material that suits your warmth needs. To a simple, lined, 20-inch square you attach (at a slight angle) two 50-inch-long top straps and two 40-inch bottom straps. Presto—you have an excellent cloth carrier.

The Japanese Komori band is a cloth 10 inches wide and 12½ feet long that wraps around both child and parent. If you buy one, have the sales clerk show you how to tie it on. You will need some practice to master the band's complexities.

The one drawback to the soft-style front carrier is extra unneeded warmth in hot weather. The material encircles the child, and the walking parent also generates heat. If you are making a simple version, such as the Chinese carrier, you might consider meshy materials that ventilate in the summer.

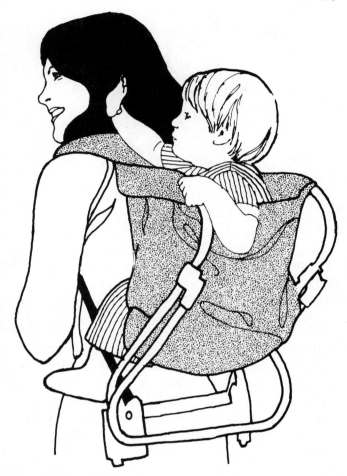

Figure 59. Frame baby carrier

Frame Carriers

A youngster old enough to sit up can be toted in one of several frame carrier designs. Check with your physician about timing the introduction of a non-supporting carrier to the development of your particular child. Since the child ready for the frame carrier will be reasonably heavy, the carrier is designed to be worn on the parent's back.

Figure 60. Frame carrier with a stand that creates an in-camp child seat

Various brands of frame baby carriers are available to transport children on an adult's back. These carriers should feature padded shoulder straps, padded hip belts, and storage for carrying items needed during the day. A carrier must also have a safety belt or harness that buckles around the child. Usually youngsters cannot climb out; if a parent should fall, however, the safety belt keeps the child from being thrown. A stand, which opens out, provides a seat in camp, and although caution must be exercised, this seat is convenient for feeding youngsters. Other conveniences in carrier design include a built-in pad or pillow so that the child can sleep comfortably with ample support for the head and neck. Young children like to explore with their hands, and since a parent's hair and ears are right there to be touched or pulled, some designs have a padded barrier that extends between the child and parent to prevent this sometimes painful happening from occurring. Since the carrier frame pack designs provide varying degrees of comfort for the parent, and deluxe features increase costs dramatically, it is wise to try out brands before investing.

Carrier Safety

With a child on your back, you need to take extra care in many situations. When brush or trees overhang, be sure that twigs and branches do not hit your youngster. In muddy weather take precautions against falling. Carriers can be used with bikes and skis, but be certain that you pick routes that are child safe. It is unwise to try out steep hills on cross-country skis when you have a child on your back, but you could find a level trail that is safe enough to ski.

A belt or harness around your child will keep him or her in the carrier if you should ever fall, so check to see if your carrier has one. In camp, be cautious about using a carrier stand. An active child can tip over a carrier seat. When you use the stand, stay with the child.

WHY BOTHER?

Taking babies and toddlers on backcountry trips is hard work. You may be asking, "Why bother?" Many people go backpacking with their very young children to avoid cutting off their own outdoor experiences. Baby-sitters are not always available, and those who are can be very expensive. In addition, young children need to be with their parents; separation at some ages can be difficult. Parents usually decide that, despite all the extra work and bother, going with very young children is preferable to staying home and missing the backcountry they love.

5

Hiking and Backpacking

Y OU CAN START backpacking with children of almost any age. Many parents are back on the trail as
soon as their infants' night feedings are over, if not sooner.
Some parents wait until children are good walkers without
carrying a pack, while others take their youngsters only
when they can assume the responsibility for their share of
the load. The timing is an individual matter, and readiness
pertains not only to children. Taking youngsters backpacking is hard work for parents, and the adults in the
family have to be absolutely ready to go too.

When your particular family can begin enjoying the
out-of-doors together depends on the number of children,
their ages, and their closeness in age. Toddling 2-year-old
twins are going to be difficult to take. One child at age 2
may be manageable.

You also must consider your youngster's temperament.
An easygoing personality—a child who takes life in stride,
sleeps anywhere, eats anything, and rarely cries—will be
an excellent traveler in the outdoors. The child who is difficult to get to sleep at home will be the same in the backcountry; exhaustion and fresh air may not help to get that
child to sleep any faster. The poor sleeper frequently becomes cranky and tearful. Children who eat poorly at

home may need more food in the outdoors but refuse to take what is available. They, too, can be trying traveling companions. Stand back, look at your children objectively, and be sure they are personality types who can adjust to new situations. Then look at yourself as objectively as you can and decide honestly if you have the temperament to survive the complexities of planning and taking a backpacking excursion with your youngsters.

A child's age greatly affects the ease of your outdoor experience. Infants often are easier than toddlers. An infant spends most of the day on a parent's back. An infant cannot walk off and does not get down in the dirt and eat it. A crawler, who is highly motivated toward movement and does not want to be restrained in a pack or tent, can be an impossible companion. A teething baby who cannot get comfortable regardless of what you do also is a poor risk for backcountry trips.

Some parents find that they manage well with their baby; then the child turns 2, is a walker and stumbler, and becomes too difficult to make camping expeditions worth taking. A child who at 2 had a predilection for tantrums can become, at age 4, a delightful companion on the trail. A 4-year-old who could not walk 6 inches without complaining can, at 6 or 7, develop into a strong hiker. Your child must be an agreeable backcountry traveling mate for you, so wait until an age when you are comfortable taking the youngster with you.

The number of children you have also influences when your family is ready for outdoor trips. One child is relatively easy to take. Two children can compound the work and difficulties beyond endurance. If your two are very young and close in age, you may need to wait longer than a family with only one youngster. When one child is 9 or 10 and the second one is an infant, the older youngster will help. Taking two then can be pleasurable.

I met a woman who, with her husband, regularly took

their six children, ages 2 through 12, on backcountry excursions. They managed beautifully. I would have had a nervous breakdown. What other people do can provide you with guidelines, but only you can decide when your own family is ready to venture into the out-of-doors.

As a parent, you must have a keen desire to travel in the backcountry; then your own enjoyment of the outdoors will compensate for the hard work involved when children are along. Remember, too, that being in the backcountry with your youngsters often is no harder than being at home with them.

Ways to Manage with Young Children

Infants and other non-walkers must be carted on backpacking trips (see Chapter 4, the "Baby Carriers" section). For the bottle-fed baby, the family must manage milk or formula, bottles, any solid foods needed, and the paraphernalia for diapering in addition to the weight of general outdoor gear (see Chapter 4, the "Special Needs for Babies" section). You also must add in the weight of the child to be carried. The mother who is successfully breast-feeding can eliminate bottles, formula, and some solids.

People who take infants devise a carrying system they personally can tolerate. In a family of mountain climbers, the stronger parent stuffs all the gear into an expedition pack, grunts, and heads up the trail lugging the usual 75 pounds, while the other parent takes the child and light odds and ends of gear that fit into the carrier. Most families cannot manage this kind of performance.

The weight carried can be divided in many ways. An infant still light enough to be front-toted can be put into a soft, frameless carrier. One parent then takes the child on front and a regular backpack with the lighter of two loads on back. The other parent takes a heavier pack to accommodate the child's equipment.

An alternative for short hikes is to lug the gear to the campsite in two trips. Two packs are evenly loaded. One parent takes a pack, and the other takes the child in a carrier. Once a good campsite is reached, the most energetic of the two parents goes back to the car, gets the second pack, and walks in again. Coming home requires the same two-step operation. For the vigorous hiker, the two carries equal no more than the number of miles covered on the usual adults-only trip. Be sure, though, that everything you need for the child and for a temporary camp is in the first carry. You can set up the tent and partly organize your camp before going back for the rest of the gear.

TAKING A FRIEND OR FRIENDS

If you have hiking friends who have no children and who enjoy being with your family, you might arrange to share equipment and load carrying with them. You all can use the same stove and set of pots. You might even share one larger tent (although this arrangement could end quickly if your child keeps your helpful friends awake all night). You can divide the total load among all the adults except for the mother, who would carry only the baby. Before you negotiate, be reasonably certain that sharing backcountry tasks will not destroy an otherwise lovely relationship.

TAKING A BABY-SITTER

There are teenage baby-sitters who would enjoy the opportunity to go backpacking. Perhaps their own families have no interest in the outdoors but they always have wanted to try out a backcountry trip. A teenager who does have backpacking experience might find an outdoor trip the ideal way to earn summer spending money.

You will find that someone else's teenager can be a pleasant addition to your family's trips. You have three backs on which to carry the gear and the child, and in camp the baby-sitter can be with the child or help with chores and setting up gear. While the sitter stays with a napping youngster, parents can get in some short wanderings of their own. Be sure, though, that you carry your wilderness essentials for any outings away from base camp (see Chapter 3, the "Wilderness Essentials" section). With a sitter it becomes possible to make excursions with toddlers who have acquired lightning-fast mobility but little or no sense. In the car coming and going, the baby-sitter can help entertain your youngster. If you have more than one child, a sitter can be a sanity saver with chores and when youngsters become difficult. Children also may be more positively motivated around someone who is not a family member. If your sitter has no equipment, you can rent such gear as boots and backpacks.

PACK ANIMALS

Parents who backpack with children feel so much like pack animals themselves that they acquire deep longings for relief, so a mule, pack horse, llama, or donkey may seem ideal. Before you consider a pack animal as an alternative, however, consider the impact these creatures have on trails and on campsites. A pack animal's feet chew up trails, and the hoof holes invite erosion. In camp the animal's movements are equally destructive. Many areas permit animals but provide no separate corralling for them. Your family could come and go in the wilderness for years and years and not damage the environment as much as one pack animal could on a single trip.

Unless you are a long-time horse handler, you'd do better to consider other options. Animals demand knowledgeable handling and care. Instead of reducing the total work, they create additional jobs for you other than the tasks involved in making your children happy and safe in the outdoors.

When you resist the temptation to go into the wilderness with pack animals, you do more than your share to help preserve the backcountry. If you cannot manage the necessary gear with children, try other alternatives or wait a while to begin your trips. As children grow older, their gear needs decrease, and older youngsters can begin to carry some weight of their own.

What to Expect on the Trail at Different Ages

Hiking with infants is a totally different experience from hiking with young walkers or with grade-school-age children. Parents need to adjust their expectations and prepare mentally and physically to cope with the changes that evolve as children grow older.

YOUNG BABIES

A good-natured baby comfortable in a pack is easy to handle on the trail. The parent's movements lull the child. Some babies nap more easily on a parent's back than they do at home in bed. For a small baby, looking around may be entertainment enough. When babies start to reach out and touch, you can attach a few hand toys to the carrier. Babies of all ages like to be talked to, and they may enjoy your singing as you walk. Schedule eating and diaper changes along the trail as frequently as you would at home. If you usually change diapers every two or three hours, keeping your baby in wet pants longer can result in an unpleasant rash, something you want to avoid on outdoor trips.

Be particularly careful about the sun and bugs. A wide-brimmed hat and sunscreen can provide sun protection (see also Chapter 4, under "Sun Protection"). Ask your physician to recommend a sunscreen for your infant. Be sure you apply sunscreen and bug repellent so that babies cannot lick them off; avoid putting these too close to the mouth or on the hands of a child who sucks fingers or

Figure 61. For rain add an extra hood to an adult's poncho for a child in a carrier

thumbs. If an infant tolerates mosquito netting that dangles from a hat brim, you can devise a net arrangement for bug protection. Sew the top of the netting to the hat brim; then hem and thread a drawstring through the bottom to tighten the netting below the carrier rim.

When the rains come, you must be prepared to keep your baby dry. To do this, you could cover your infant with a specially sewn two-hooded poncho. For this you need a poncho with an extra-long back panel; you wear the hood already in the poncho and make a second hood behind you to go on the baby's head (see also Chapter 4, "Raingear" section). When rains cause temperatures to drop, you must be extra sure that your baby is still warm enough (see Chapter 4, "Dressing for Cold Weather" section).

Also available are infant- through toddler-size ponchos meant for use in child carriers or for a small child who is walking.

If you adequately handle sun and bugs, rain and cold, and manage regular feeding and diapering, your baby can make a tranquil trail companion.

OLDER BABIES

When a baby develops the desire to move, keeping the child in a carrier for long stretches of time becomes more complicated. Hands reach out to touch and explore a parent's ears, hair, and hat. The baby's feet and legs push and kick and bounce. This increased activity on your back and the added weight of a baby raise the price paid by the carrying parent.

The slightly older baby may not sleep in the carrier as easily as the smaller infant. The likelihood of tiredness turning into crankiness and tears increases. Finger foods can help keep your child in good spirits as you walk. Be sure you carry plenty of treats and keep them in a place that is easy to reach. Crackers, Instant Toast, granola, raisins, apples, and other foods liked at home help babies pass the time. Children this age like handling their toys, but they also derive great pleasure from studying the laws of gravity. They will drop anything loose and expect you to pick it up as your part in the game. Tied-on toys sometimes work for a while. A sleeping blanket in the carrier can give comfort, and babies usually do not drop these.

You still need to allow time for regular diaper changes and feeding, but stopping is no longer easy. The crawling child demands more attention. Some crawlers put everything in sight into their mouths, including dirt, pebbles, leaves, and grass.

TODDLERS

The toddler years, from 1 to almost 3, can be the most difficult times for families in the backcountry. Youngsters this age must be watched constantly when out of the carrier, even when they're on the trail for just a few minutes. Toddlers may want to walk but be unable to go more than a few yards before losing interest. They may dislike the restrictiveness of the carrier and become bored or restless. Even if a toddler takes regular naps at home, he or she may not sleep at all in the carrier—and a tired child is a crabby child.

Changing activities for your toddler can help. You can organize the child's day so that he or she walks a little (very little) and then rides. You can stop often and play. You can offer food and something to drink every so often. Each activity should be planned to last only a short period of time, ending before the youngster becomes restless.

Expect the walking toddler to explore every grain of sand, every pebble and rock, every blade of grass, and all the dirt in between. After you tell your child what and why about each item, he or she will ask you what and why again. This is how toddlers learn and gradually come to understand the natural world you are introducing to them. Toddlers love talk; they like to sing and to hear songs. The more entertainment you provide as you walk along, the better the day with your toddler will go.

BEGINNING TRAIL WALKERS

Most toddlers are leg stretchers, not trail walkers. Sometime around the age of 2½ or 3 you can begin to expect some hiking from your child. The pace will be excruciatingly slow. The time you spend stopping will be longer than the time you spend walking. Small children quickly become bored with putting one foot in front of the other, and their short legs tire. Remember that for each step you are taking, your child may be taking four.

Rest stops must come often and must provide entertaining play. The more you do to keep your child's mind off the work involved in hiking, the more successful the beginning walker's days will be. Games, songs, stories, treats, rewards, and water play help make the experience fun. While you can plan longer hikes when a child is being carried, trip lengths should be cut down if you expect a youngster to walk all the way. A sturdy 3-year-old accustomed to regular neighborhood walking may manage to cover half the distance you usually plan for family hikes.

At about 4 years old children begin to show signs of developing into strong walkers, and by 5, well-motivated youngsters can be a joy to take on the trail.

From Child Carrier to Hiking

If a child has been carried on trails as a baby, weaning him or her from the child carrier can be more difficult than you might imagine. For the small one just beginning to walk trails, having the carrier along is essential. On day hikes, a child who walks a mile one way cannot always manage the same distance coming home. When backpacking, the first mile may be easy but the second mile impossible. Piggybacking a heavy, wiggling 3-year-old is uncomfortable for parent and child alike. With the carrier along, you can provide a pleasant ride and might even encourage sleep. On a day hike you can use your frame carrier. If you are backpacking, put a cloth carrier in with your gear to prepare for a possible energy crisis; though not a perfect solution, emergency use of the cloth carrier for a child 2 or 3 years old can get the tired child into camp. There is a catch, however. Any smart child knows that being carried is much easier than all that hiking business. Seeing the empty child carrier is a constant reminder of the good days when life was less work.

Very short walks on level ground are useful until youngsters have become strong enough for more ambitious hikes. Any building up of distance or difficulty should be gradual. Many people find that day hikes pave the way for later backpacking trips, and they put aside overnight outings for the heavy-to-carry 2- or 3-year-old.

At some point you will have to make the judgment that your child has outgrown the carrier. Base the decision on your child's capabilities. Also consider your back. If your youngster's bouncing 40 pounds wipes you out, the carrier on your back must go. If you are ready, but your child is not ready to walk, you will have to adjust your trips. A morning-only hike may be all your youngster can handle.

Do not worry; in time, he or she will become stronger and thus more able to handle longer trips.

The age at which the metamorphosis to hiker takes place varies from child to child, even within the same family. Know your particular youngster's capabilities so that you can plan your trips accordingly.

Learning to Walk

To the modern child, walking is not necessarily a natural activity. Hopping in the car and riding the half mile to the grocery store is natural; being driven three blocks to a friend's house is routine. To make hiking trips an extension of daily experience, have your young children begin walking regularly in the neighborhood or in the parks near your home.

You begin slowly and gradually build up the length of your walks. Make the walks fun, not just a chore. Create interesting destinations, such as a friend's house, a park, or a store where your youngster can pick out a treat.

Once you increase the distance covered, carry snacks and juice. Breaks for treats can help a child reach a more distant location and get home too. A youngster who walks regularly builds up the stamina eventually needed for backcountry hiking. These walks also help you ascertain how much walking you can realistically expect from your child.

Starting Pack Carrying Pleasantly

Getting children to enjoy carrying a loaded frame pack requires some parental ingenuity. Toting gear is work. Parents must somehow disguise or soften that fact for youngsters.

A good principle is to begin small, both with pack size and weight, and to start young children with some kind of soft, frameless pack (see Chapter 4, in the "Frameless Packs" section). If youngsters carry something every time the family hikes, they will grow up thinking that pack toting is perfectly natural.

A toddler can start with a small pack of his or her own. You can make an envelope-style pack inexpensively at home (see Chapter 4, "Making a First Soft Pack" section). The weight of such a pack amounts to only a few ounces, and you may find that your little one refuses to take off this new possession that is so much like Mom's and Dad's. One of our youngsters even slept with his first pack, which had been made with his name lettered across the flap.

The first frameless pack for a young child should be something to play with. When your youngster sees you carrying a pack, he or she will want to imitate you. At home, encourage young children to play at hiking. Let them load their soft packs with lunch or snacks and hike around the house and yard. By playing with their packs at home, children can practice opening and closing fasteners, putting the pack on by themselves, and buckling the waist belt. All these tasks are a challenge to little fingers. At first you will have to help, but youngsters feel proud when they learn to handle these jobs by themselves.

Hopefully, all this playing at outdoor experiences will create a pleasant picture of hiking, camping, and toting gear in your child's mind. Creating a positive attitude in a child is an important first step for later backcountry trips.

When you introduce a child under 4 to a real outdoor experience—a day hike or a backpacking trip, for example—a feather-light pack load is essential to success. The pack you choose will depend largely on the size and body shape of your youngster (see Chapter 4, "Packs" section). Only a very large 4-year-old will fit into a frame pack. There are many soft packs to choose from, however.

What a child carries in a small load also is important. Most youngsters love to tote a sack of trail snacks or their own candy. Although the weight is practically nothing and the effort required is close to zero, you have associated pack carrying with something very pleasant for the child. A soft pack should fit like clothing. If you belt a child into the pack and are sure the shoulder straps will not slip and annoy, youngsters often are content to wear the tiny load all day.

Be sure that your beginning pack-toting walks are sufficiently short. Sometimes a light load feels heavy and a comfortable pack irritates only when a child's legs have been strained beyond their capacity. Even when pack carrying is a principle in your family, nothing is wrong with relieving a youngster of the pack every now and then, especially at the weary end of the day. When a child's candy is in your pack, he or she may quickly see the advantages in asking to carry it again. Do not be inflexible, but if you want children to carry a load eventually, do not be conned into letting them give up too soon. Think through the day you have had with your child: perhaps you chose a walk that was too long or too steep; maybe you went late in the day, too close to nap time, or perhaps your child had enough of pack toting for the day. In this situation, instead of forcing a pack on a child who is exhausted and tired of everything, try the pack again on your next outing.

As a child grows older and more accustomed to the pack, gradually add a little more weight. Some children love having their own juice bottle; a pint-sized plastic container is ideal. A child's favorite toy or blanket stuffed into the pack may make carrying more fun. Try to keep the pack comfortable. Any items next to the child's back should be soft. The front pocket of a pack is the best location for a rounded juice bottle or blunt-edged toy. A sweater, extra socks, or anything soft is appropriate next to the child's back. Avoid loading the pack to capacity, even with an older child. A bulging lump against a youngster's body can make the feeling of the pack hateful.

Graduating to a Frame Pack and Bigger Load

Children become ready to use a frame pack at different times. No youngster will carry more than token weight in a soft, frameless daypack. A child's size, body shape, weight, and desire all influence when the frame pack becomes appropriate.

A sleeping bag carrier (see Chapter 4, the section "Sleeping Bag Carriers") is one in-between alternative. It enables a youngster who is old enough, but not big enough, for a frame pack to carry a sleeping bag and some light, non-bulky items if the carrier has a zippered pouch.

Somewhere between 5 and 7 years of age most youngsters can fit into a child-sized frame pack. Do not be influenced by what other people's children can do. Find the right time for your own youngsters.

You should never overload a child who is wearing a frame pack. Somewhere between one-fourth and one-fifth of a youngster's body weight should be the maximum load. Go even lighter with a beginner, any beginner. Before a trip, always weigh your child's pack. (You may feel better if you do not weigh your own, however; parents taking children are doomed to labor under an excessive burden.)

In our family we camped and day hiked with our children when they were preschoolers. When our older two youngsters reached 5, they were tall, broad-shouldered, and strong. At that age they both were ready for a frame pack and could, with minimum complaining, carry their own sleeping bags plus raingear and a few clothes. The load totaled about 7 pounds, which was much less than one-fifth of their body weight.

Even if your youngsters have day hiked regularly carrying soft packs, the distance they are able to walk will be cut approximately in half by the presence of a real load in a frame pack. If children can walk 5 miles with token weight, they may manage only 2 or 3 miles when harnessed into a frame pack.

Practice at home can help. Put less weight in the pack than your child will eventually carry and take the youngster on pack-carrying walks in the neighborhood. These outings condition youngsters and also enable you to discern problems with the frame pack so that you can fix them before a real trip. Gradually increase the weight in the pack until you reach the child's load capacity. If a youngster falters under the intended weight, you know to decrease your expectations on the trip. You can carry your own pack with a load (not necessarily camping gear, just weight) to get yourself in shape too.

The fit of a frame pack on a young child is bound to be imperfect. Sometime around the middle-grade-school years, a youngster's frame pack will begin to mold better to his or her body. If backpacking has been a regular family activity, a youngster will be a strong hiker by this time. As a child's stamina increases, parents must decide how much to increase the weight carried. A 5-year-old wearing a frame pack walks at a painfully slow pace. Each mile consists of strolling a few steps, sitting down, taking off the pack, drinking some juice, and strolling a bit more. With an older, stronger child, the option of moving faster may be more pleasing to you than the advantages of receiving more help in load carrying. Just because a 9-year-old youngster can carry 15 pounds does not mean that you must pile on that much.

For safety, you want all children, regardless of age, with the adults. If a strong child carries too little and you carry too much, keeping the family together can be difficult. Experiment with the weight the older child carries until your youngster moves at the pace you desire.

Try the maximum weight at the beginning of a hike, when your youngster is fresh and full of energy. At the day's end, if your child is exhausted, take something that will lighten the load. Frequent stops are to be expected with any children; if the stopping rate is more than you can bear, take on a little more weight yourself to speed up the family's movement.

For a family beginning to backpack with older children, do not expect too much. Being used to carrying is often more important than being old enough and strong enough to carry. The older child catches on fast that lugging a load

is work. If you want backpacking to become a family recreation, you must make the trips enjoyable. Start relatively
slowly, just as you would with a younger child. When the
activity catches on, you can gradually add greater distances to your hikes and increase the weight load to be
carried.

First Backpacking Trips with Walking Children

The first backpacking trips for a walking child must be
short. Your 4-year-old may walk only 2 or 3 miles the first
time out. Your chances for increasing distances are better
on more level ground. Ocean beaches or flat lake shores
are ideal locations for small beginners. If no climbing is
involved, that same 4-year-old may cover as many as 5
miles. If you force-march a child farther than he or she is
willing to go, you make the youngster hate hiking, and the
purpose of going in the first place is defeated.

When a trail gains in elevation, the distance a child can
hike is cut down considerably. Unless the trail climbs
steeply for only a short time before you reach your destination, it is best to choose a hike on which there is a gradual elevation gain along a gently contoured trail. Occasionally you can find a trail that actually leads downhill to
a choice location. Children delight in the ease of a descent.
Getting them back up the trail again will be harder, but
generally the lure of home provides good motivation.

Your backpacking destination should have child-
pleasing attributes. Although spectacular views may
please you, scenery does not necessarily excite a young
child. For a youngster, water is the most dependable en-
ticement. Thoughts of a lake or an interesting stream at the
end of the trail can make little legs move with amazing
speed. If you hike along a lake, stream, or ocean, a child's
step-by-step interest is bound to be high.

In the mountains, a spot with lingering snow patches
can provide high motivation on the trail and hours of en-

tertainment once you get there. Sliding, fort building, and snowball fights have great child appeal. Places with remnants of old-time mining operations also can stimulate a child's interest. A manned fire tower or backcountry ranger station can be fascinating, especially if the rangers are friendly (they usually are) and willing to explain their jobs and to show youngsters around. You can find out where backcountry rangers are stationed by contacting the park you plan to visit.

When you pick your destination, be sure the terrain is child safe and that no unusual hazards exist. In a mining area with abandoned shafts that drop into nothingness, you will want to pass through quickly, holding your child tightly by the hand. Lakes with sudden dropoffs, steep cliffs that are easily accessible to youngsters, and snowy areas that slant sharply into dangerous territory are inappropriate locations for family trips.

You can check out the feasibility and safety of locations through park rangers, outdoor groups, and guidebooks. The only way to be absolutely certain that an area will suit your own children is for you to go there first and scout it out.

When you are hiking with your children, be flexible. Plan your trip carefully at home, but if youngsters fall apart on the trail, abandon the day's agenda and find a nearby campsite. One key to success in family backpacking is for parents to develop a sixth sense that tells them when a child's day has ended long before the day actually ends.

Gradually Extending Backpacking Trips

On your first trips you may want to start out with just two days and one night on the trail. A short trip automatically reduces the weight carried. You tote your basic gear, but you carry less food and fewer clothes. Unfortunately, the time required to prepare and pack for a short trip is about the same as for a longer stay. When you first try out the backpacking-with-children experience, however, you are better off with a short trip that ends too soon than a lengthy expedition that does not work out. For young children, two days can be a long time.

Once you are certain that backpacking is right for your family, you can extend your trips. Still, do not jump immediately into the two-week-long trek; four days may be more appropriate at this point. You also can add more miles to your trips. Consider the ages of your children and how much weight you are asking them to carry as you determine the number of miles they can walk. An 8-year-old with a 10-pound load may cover no more ground than a 4-year-old in a feather-light soft pack. Children can walk longer distances if coerced, but afterward they may remember nothing of the trip except the misery.

As you extend your hiking trips, the pace should continue to be slow and relaxed. Allow your youngsters time to experience all that surrounds them. When you find a pleasant place appropriate for your family's enjoyment, the number of miles you cover on an excursion becomes immaterial.

Base Camps

To cover more ground, a family can establish a convenient base camp one day's walk into the backcountry and then take day trips in the surrounding area. Although children carry packs coming into and going out of the backcountry, they can walk without a load during the rest of the trip. With the base camp approach, a young grade-schooler can cover as many as 25 miles in five days yet only have to walk 4 miles with a pack. When day hiking, be sure that you are prepared with your wilderness essentials (see Chapter 3, in the "Wilderness Essentials" section).

When you change campsites several times during a trip, allow for rest days. You might spend two days in one camp, then hike farther for the next two days. As you go along, adjust your plans to avoid exhausting youngsters. Tired children can become accident prone. Be sure you allow time for play as well as for work.

Children carrying packs must be strong hikers to change camps each day. Many families save that approach until youngsters are in their teens and thrive on the physical challenge of pushing themselves hard.

Motivating Children Along the Trail

Motivating children to walk a trail demands patience, ingenuity, determination, and a large bag of parental tricks. Watch your 4-year-old playing in the backyard and you will see that youngsters hop, run, jump, and skip and cover miles on a typical active day. Put a child on a trail, however, and that energy mysteriously disappears. Ten steps and the cry begins, "I'm so tired . . . I want to rest. . . . When will we be there?"

As an adult, I love the feeling of walking on and on in a beautifully steady rhythm. But children get bored. Even older children who are strong hikers need diversion in order to reach their destination.

MOTIVATING YOUNG CHILDREN

What you do to lighten the monotony of hiking will depend on the ages and interests of your children. For very young children, 2 and 3 years old, your aim may be to get them off your back and onto their feet for as much of the hike as possible. A child's pride in being big enough and old enough may help this process along. Praise of each small accomplishment should be lavish. Stopping often is important. If you time your rest stops to happen before a toddler demands a rest, you will be way ahead in the game.

Finding something interesting to play with at each stop helps divert a young child's mind from the labor of walking. Little children love little things. An anthill can provide long minutes of fascination. Sand or dirt that runs through the fingers and creates rounded mounds can be equally absorbing. A typical walking program might run something like this: Walk and talk for a hundred steps or so. Children often start out fast, too fast. As the pace slows, suggest a stop. Insist on a real rest; have the child sit down. Explore whatever happens to be there. Get out the juice bottle, offer a drink, and tangibly reward your youngster with a trail snack and with praise. Something to the effect of "Look how far you have walked already; good job, we're proud of you" will surely help to keep the mental attitude positive. After five minutes, start off again. Set a goal that is child-sized small: "See that great big tree up there? Let's go that far and then you can have another snack. Maybe we'll find some pine cones under the tree. Let's go look."

If you hear something interesting along the way—a distant woodpecker's tapping or the whomping noise of a grouse—stop and listen. Encourage your child to keep ears open for woodland sounds.

When observing wildlife, adults often confine their attention to larger creatures, such as a deer, mountain goat, or herd of elk. Youngsters, however, are just as fascinated with a centipede, tadpole, or frog at their feet as they are with a large animal, which because it is wild naturally runs away from approaching people.

As you look at the natural world—the plants, rocks, and animals—underline for your children the need to leave behind all these interesting backcountry lifeforms. Touching must be gentle or not at all.

To take a child's mind away from tired feet and legs, you can use games, stories, and singing. Many children love to sing. Just as a young child can sit for hours and listen to a record over and over again, a hiking child can chug along singing the same favorite song and be completely amused. Do not be surprised if the selection happens to be "Jingle Bells" in the middle of summer. Be thankful for anything that works. Stories fascinate children. Telling a story, either a favorite one you have read with your child or one hatched from your own imagination, can make the minutes fly by. Once you sense that your child is moving well, you may be surprised at how clever your storytelling can get. It is a small price to pay for the pleasure of easy walking.

When motivating children, nothing works forever. Variety and change are the keys to reaching the child's mind and spirit. Do not be dismayed when an activity such as storytelling fails to entertain after 15 minutes; simply change to some other activity. Do not hesitate to break your routine; stop for lunch even if the clock says ten in the morning, not noon.

Some children like being leaders. Even a very young child will stride along with extra vigor after being appointed first in line. Pretending can be a great diversion too. Let your youngster's imagination run wild and your entire family can be transformed into a chugging train, a formation of fast-flying planes, or a caravan of trucks. Although such fantasies are not what most adults want to think about in the outdoors, children enjoy pretending; so if a game gets you where you want to go, use it. If introduced to backcountry experiences early, youngsters will play at hiking and camping some day too.

MOTIVATING OLDER CHILDREN

As children grow older, you must change on-the-trail diversions to suit their interests. You still need regularly scheduled stops and high-energy snacks, and do not forget the praise for accomplishments.

Games are still appropriate, but the types that work are going to be different. A school-age child enjoys keeping a mental list of objects seen in the natural world. Guessing games are fun too. "I see something" requires the child to pick an object and tell the first letter. Then everyone tries to guess what has been seen. A memory game can occupy children for a long period of time. One person starts by saying, "I went to the mountains (or ocean or river) and I saw . . ." Then this person mentions something he or she might have seen or, for fun, something it would be absurd to see, such as a hippopotamus. Each person adds something to the list and must remember and recite each preceding object. Older children can recite a long list. Young children can play an abbreviated version of this game; when someone misses, a new game is started.

Stories can still captivate older children. Some youngsters amuse themselves by telling long, drawn-out tales, or parents can tell stories while everyone walks along and listens. Tales of past adventures, of places Mom and Dad have been, and of places the entire family will go when everyone is old enough are pleasing to older children. A game can be made out of storytelling too. Someone starts a tale, and then each family member adds a small segment to the story.

Older youngsters may just want to talk while hiking. Children who like to read may enjoy summarizing the latest books they have read.

For families with children covering a wide range of ages, splitting up into a younger and an older group, an adult with each, can help set an appropriate pace and help parents adjust activities to different ages and interests. However, if younger children are keenly motivated to keep up with older siblings, staying together can be just as helpful.

Children are happier on the trail when they forget the strain of walking. Whatever you do to amuse and divert your youngsters will take the work out of hiking and make the trip more fun for them and for you.

Day Hiking

You can expose children to the outdoors without taking long, complicated trips if you start by day hiking. For the very young, a one-day venture can be as simple as wandering along in a nearby wooded park. In larger, wild areas, short trail walks in the backcountry periphery can provide a good introduction to the outdoor experience.

On day hikes you can try out new equipment and test theories on taking children into the outdoors. You also can ascertain how old your youngsters must be before you can enjoy longer stays. If one day on the trail with your infant leaves you filled with anxiety, four days will be four times as bad; such a day hike experience tells you that you are not a backpack-with-infants person.

The drawback to the day hike is that you must go out and come back in one day. You cannot cover much ground. Day hiking is tasting the wilderness; you have no chance to devour or savor it. When you day hike, time your return cautiously. You will not want to travel with youngsters in the dark as a result of having left too late.

Always be well prepared. Pre-trip planning is as important for a day as it is for a week. Know where you are going, how long and difficult a walk it is, and what you can expect at your destination. Carry wilderness and child essentials in your pack. On day trips you motivate youngsters to hike just as you would on long backpacking trips. You start slowly and gradually build up to longer endeavors.

On day hikes you can see lakes, streams, waterfalls, ocean beaches, historical spots, backcountry ranger stations, wooded glades, and all the flora and fauna of the wilderness scene. You also may come across innumerable places that would make ideal beginning backpacking destinations. In this way your day hikes double as scouting expeditions.

Car Camping

With a little effort you can make car camping a reasonable facsimile of backpack camping. For the rank beginner, car camping (which is not trailer, camper, or mobile home "camping") is a logical first step. When you car camp as a prelude to backcountry travel, use your lightweight wilderness gear and look for special, hardly touched kinds of places. If you go at off-season times, such as spring and fall, you have to yourselves areas that are people-packed during the summer. Even civilized state parks can exude an aura of isolation during these periods.

For successful quasi-wilderness car camping, pick the least civilized of the established camps. Many parks designate certain sites as primitive. At these sites you use stream water; there are no flush toilets or electricity. If such a place is rarely used, you can have an off-to-yourselves outing. Other parks separate trailer camping from tent camping. In the tent section the atmosphere can be wooded, rough, and only slightly changed by civilization.

Sometimes you can find places that require a bit of walking. We once discovered a camp where wheelbarrows were provided for people to push gear out to sites far from the parking area. Another time we spent several pleasant days at a campsite reached by hand carting equipment a hundred paces from the road. We were camping with a teething 9-month-old and a mischievous 2-year-old, and that was all the distance we felt like carrying anything. But during those four days we hiked 30 miles with both of our youngsters in carriers.

A car-camping spot more crowded than you would like still can make a fine base for day hike activity. Your time in camp can be minimal. You can spend full days on the trail and return only for dinner and sleeping. The next morning you can explore another day hiking location. By rising early you can start out for the day before other campers are out of bed.

6

Backcountry Bicycling

DAYLONG BACKCOUNTRY BIKE TRIPS are relatively easy with young children. The infant can ride in a carrier on your back (see Chapter 4, "Baby Carriers" section). Another option suitable even for a young infant is traveling in a trailer that attaches behind the parent's bicycle. For the child strong enough to sit up, you can attach a bike seat over the rear wheel of your bike. In choosing from the seats and trailers available, both comfort and safety are important. Often young children will nap in a bike seat or trailer, making full-day trips more manageable. With a roomy trailer, experienced parents can carry even an infant plus the baby equipment, such as bottles, diapers, and extra clothes, needed for overnight and extended backcountry tours. The beginning bike rider must learn bicycling skills and gain experience before venturing out on backcountry trips. Once youngsters are competent bicyclists, they can join the family on a variety of short outings geared to the child's skills and endurance, and older children can travel on their own bikes on longer trips and overnights.

Choosing a Bike Seat

Think safety when you choose a bike seat for your child. The seat should have a harness that will secure the child to

Figure 62. Child's bike seat with foot guard

the seat. The fastening device must be child proof so that even dexterous little fingers cannot undo the harness while you are bicycling. The child's feet should be secured with straps in foot wells deep enough to prevent the feet from slipping out into the wheel spokes. A high back to the seat and adequate padding create a comfortable support for the child's head and neck. Some families like seats that adjust to several positions so that a napping child can lean back rather than have to sit in a straight upright position. For convenience, a seat with a quick-release feature allows you to leave behind the fittings on the bike and remove the seat easily and quickly.

Children can be carried in a bike seat until their weight is too much for the rear wheel's rim and tire. For most youngsters this happens around 4 or 5 years of age; an especially skinny child might last until 6. An adult's bike with a slightly heavier wheel holds up better under the weight of a preschooler.

Choosing a Trailer

Often families prefer the many conveniences of pulling young children in a bicycle trailer. Bicycle trailers attach to the back of the parent's bike with a hitch. The child or in some designs two children sit inside the trailer and are pulled along. When evaluating trailers, look for safety, comfort, and flexibility. A safe trailer will have sides high enough to prevent small hands from reaching out and a child seat with a harness that fastens securely and cannot be undone by small fingers. A wide-base design with a low center of gravity creates a solid running vehicle that is fairly easy to pull. For families serious about extensive touring, look for durable construction and high-quality materials that produce as light a trailer as possible. The trailer should also be easy to collapse for transporting. A cover with windows keeps children dry and warm and interested in the passing sights. In addition, a top will provide sun screening and protection from flying objects thrown up from the road. Younger children benefit from seats that adjust for napping. Most trailers will carry up to 100 pounds and thus can accommodate young grade-school children plus gear for longer tours. Another feature that appeals to adults with multiple interests is the ability to convert the trailer into a jogging stroller or a cross-country skiing sled.

The In-Between Years

Bicycle trailers will transport a single child and gear through the early grade-school years. Most children outgrow a bike seat as many as several years before they are strong enough to cycle far on their own bikes. The beginner on a two-wheeler cannot manage backcountry biking with you. Even when biking skills advance, endurance will be minimal. If backcountry bicycling is your primary interest, you will have to be patient and wait before it can become a family activity. Don't forget, though, that other outdoor activities, such as day hiking or backpacking, can be enjoyed with the younger child.

Early Riders

As a prelude to actual touring, help your young child accumulate hours of traffic-free bicycling time. Bike trails separate bikes from cars and are growing more popular throughout the country. Many trails found in cities and suburbs wander through parks; they are pleasant and safe and provide a good starting point. A child can ride a long distance and concentrate only on cycling skills. Some communities establish bicycle days during which streets are closed to car traffic; such occasions also give youngsters the opportunity to safely acquire riding experience and to build endurance.

For children between 5 and 7 years of age, bicycle day trips must be short. You should avoid areas with such hazards as gravel or traffic. Learning cycling skills is enough for a child this age to handle; having to deal with other concerns can be too distracting. Even if biking ability develops quickly, judgment concerning bike safety comes only with age and experience.

Somewhere between 7 and 9 years of age, bicycling children can begin to fit into family backcountry bike touring plans. These early trips should be geared to youngsters. They should be relatively short and include stops along the way that are interesting to children: river banks, parks, lake shores, and historic landmarks. The country you tour can be farmland or wooded terrain. City youngsters enjoy seeing plowed fields and farm animals as well as magnificent forests. Plan enough time for lengthy rest stops. Fourteen miles is a long trip for a 7-year-old, but seven miles of riding followed by a two-hour play stop and then another seven miles can be tolerated.

Choosing a Bike

For beginning trips, a bike without gears is perfectly adequate for a young child. On a first two-wheeler, a youngster learning to ride will not use the gears even if he or
she has them. Some bikes made for children aged 5 to 7
do feature gears; for these you will pay more and gain
little. A small bike usually is outgrown before a youngster becomes confident enough to manipulate the gears
effectively.

Youngsters 9 through 12 years old can benefit from
geared bikes in the same way that you do. An experienced
cyclist this age will be strong, so you can begin to take
challenging trips. You can ride on hilly terrain and increase
the mileage covered. At this point, gears are a good,
though expensive, investment. Watch out, though. With a
quality geared bike, a strong child has a powerful machine
to ride and will be able to cruise along more efficiently than
ever before. Be sure, therefore, that you still enforce the
same safety rules you taught your child at an earlier age
(see "Bicycle Safety" section).

Despite the adjustable features on bicycles, a child can
outgrow three different-sized bikes between the ages of 5
and 12. With the increased popularity of bicycling, there
is a healthy secondhand bike market. Through newspaper
ads, bike shops, or club newsletters, you should be able to
locate good, revitalized, secondhand children's bikes to
save you money.

To determine if a particular frame size is correct, have
your youngster straddle the bicycle bar; in a perfect fit,
both feet should touch the ground. (On a girl's model, you
will have to visualize where the bar would be to see if your
youngster fits the frame.) Other parts of the bike, including
the handlebars and seat height, are adjustable.

Beginners' bikes are more sturdily built and have thicker
tires than adults' bikes. The sturdier the first bike, the better it will absorb the child's inevitable falls. Novelty bikes
are fine unless they cost you more money. Downturned

handlebars are sporty, but they encourage the beginner to look down instead of ahead; even an older child can have trouble remembering to look ahead with this style handlebar. Start out with the simplest bike to ride and keep this model until your child has acquired long hours of cycling experience.

Bicycle Safety

All children—infants being transported in a bicycle trailer, youngsters riding in a bike seat, and young bike riders—must wear a safety-certified helmet. In many states bicycle helmets are mandatory, and a variety of models are available with size-adjustable features that extend the use for the growing child.

While your youngsters are learning to cycle, see if your community offers a bicycle safety course. In these classes police officers or firefighters teach children the rudiments of bike safety. When someone else explains the importance of safety practices you have been trying to teach, youngsters often absorb the information more readily. Even on out-of-the-way back roads, bicycles share the road space with motor vehicles. Children must understand the need for caution.

Once you begin bike trips with youngsters, establish and strictly enforce your safety rules and make sure your entire family can be seen clearly when riding. Choose brightly colored orange or red outer clothing. Inner clothes that may be exposed later as the day warms also should be brightly colored. Use clips on long pants to keep them out of bike chains. Strips of material tied above the ankles often are more comfortable on children and work as well as metal clips. A bike flag on the rear of each bike draws attention to your presence on the road. If you take the flags off when transporting bikes, the devices will last longer.

When touring, line up the family with an adult at the front and the rear. Be sure children stay in line near the edge of the road. On backcountry roads traffic will be minimal, but teach children to ride as if there were cars. As you ride, talk to your youngsters to make them aware of potential hazards. The lead adult should tell of any approaching difficulties; the adult at the rear should keep youngsters aware of anything coming from behind. On a quiet country road cars make a horrendous noise, but a child intent on handling a bike may not even notice. Call out any time a vehicle comes in either direction. Give youngsters ample opportunity to situate themselves safely on the road. For a dump truck or logging truck (sometimes they are the only vehicles you see on back roads), have children stop at the side of the road and wait until the vehicle passes. A small child can be blown over by the wind from a large truck passing even at moderate speed.

Before you go out to ride, remind youngsters about the hazards you could encounter: abrupt road edges or loose gravel that could throw them off their bikes, country dogs determined to protect their territory, side roads or driveways where vehicles can appear unexpectedly. As you go along, alert children to potential problems and give clear instructions on what to do. Since you rarely ride fast with young ones, stopping to walk the bad stretches may be the best alternative. With unfriendly dogs, get off your bike and keep the bike between you and the animal; then situate yourself between the dog and your children. Once you stop, most country dogs will back off; they resented your wheels more than your presence. A watchdog is obedient; in your sternest voice, order him to go home. Some cyclists come prepared for war against canines. If you respond aggressively to a dog, however, you may be asking for trouble. I personally like to stop and talk to dogs, and in long miles of backcountry travel I have yet to be attacked.

Downhill runs are exciting, but insist on moderate speed with brakes applied and bikes under control. When the lead adult sets a cautious downhill pace, children will follow the example.

Children mimic what they see. If you are a careful cyclist, your youngsters will learn good cycling habits, and family backcountry trips will be safe and enjoyable.

Packs for Bicycling

A frameless daypack can be used for bike trips. With a minimal load a soft pack is not uncomfortable as you cycle. However, you can free yourself of a backpack by using bike pannier bags, which hang on either side of the rear wheel; you can buy a good-sized pair in a heavy, coated material. The bags attach to a rack that hitches onto the bike-post clamp or seat stays. If you contemplate overnight cycling, pannier bags can accommodate the necessary gear.

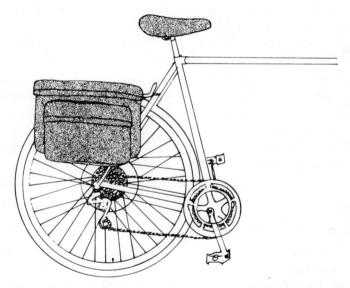

Figure 63. Back wheel pannier bags for gear-carrying on bikes

What to Take in Your Pack

Although backcountry roads are accessible to motor vehicles, a bicycling family is dependent on people power. On the best trips you are in quasi-wilderness, so you must

come equipped to take care of your family's needs. Be sure
that you carry your wilderness and child essentials (see
Chapter 3, "Wilderness Essentials" section).

A bicycle is a machine; therefore you also must pack the
necessary tools for repairs. If you are riding a foreign-
made bike and your youngsters are on U.S.-made models,
be sure that your tools work for both. With adjustable
wrenches you can avoid carrying separate sets. Taking a
spare tire that fits the adults' bikes will not help if your
child's tire gives out. If you check tire wear on each bike in
the family before trips, you usually can avoid replacing
tires on the road. With regular pre-trip bike maintenance,
emergency repairs can be kept to a minimum. For repairs,
make sure that you have your multi-accessoried knife,
spoke wrench, small pliers, tire tools, screwdriver, chain
tool, and tire-patching kit.

You can get tools at bike shops and outdoor stores. Be
sure you know how to use all your repair tools. You should
know how to patch or replace a damaged bike tire. On
geared bikes, which can be slightly temperamental, you
need a basic understanding of how to adjust and fix the
gears for maximum performance. If you are going to undertake extended bicycling trips, you should learn how to
do total repairs on your bike. Some bike shops and general
outdoor stores offer bike maintenance and repair courses.

Where to Go

Recreational bicycle clubs can introduce you to touring
possibilities for the area in which you live. You may be able
to find bike-touring guidebooks for other areas. County
maps indicate back roads that are not included on general
car maps; study these and you can discover miles and miles
of appropriate backcountry bike touring territory. On
adults-only trips, keep your children in mind. Look for
portions of longer tours that are relatively flat, free of traffic, and child pleasing.

Overnight Bike Camping

With one child in a bike seat, parents still can manage overnight touring. The rear space on one bike can hold the youngster. With a bike trailer, extra space is available for both the child, the youngster's extras, and some overnight gear. If you are taking two young children in one trailer, some of your storage space will be limited by the weight-carrying capacity of the trailer. Still, the bike trailer offers the most effective way to transport children on overnight backcountry tours.

To carry camping and child gear, you can try several approaches. Front-wheel pannier bags (you need a special attachment rack), handlebar bags, and midframe bags are available. Moderately loaded soft packs are not as comfortable but can hold what normally would go into the child-carrying adult's rear pannier bag. By going with other adults, you can share some camping equipment and thus reduce your load. You can use dried foods or, if your route passes a store, you can buy provisions late in the day for dinner and breakfast. Lightweight, compact backpacking gear frees space.

If riding a loaded bike is new to you, log many hours of adults-only overnight touring to become accustomed to the feeling of carrying gear before taking your child. For trial runs with a youngster, start out with two-day, overnight trips; then build up to longer endeavors.

You also can tackle overnight bike touring with an older grade-schooler. The youngster must be a strong and experienced cyclist. Before you tour, find safe, traffic-free roads and have your child practice riding with his or her contemplated overnight load. Then try a one-night trip. When your youngster shows confidence and strength on the loaded bike, longer overnight tours are possible. Be sure the pannier bags fit your child's bike properly.

7

Backcountry Water Sports

Y OU CAN TAKE CHILDREN as young as infants on day hikes and backpacking trips. Wilderness travel in a motorless boat is not, however, for younger children. With older youngsters, canoes, rafts, and some double kayaks are dependable transportation on backcountry waterways—that is, if you yourself have had long hours of paddling experience.

Backpacking starts with an already established skill: anyone can walk. For the backpacking trip, you need good judgment, proper equipment, conditioning, and wilderness carrying and camping experience. Water sports require these as prerequisites, but they also demand a wide variety of highly developed water safety and paddling skills.

Some paddle-propelled boats, including many long, flat-water canoes, can accommodate children. Some long, flat-water double kayaks that can be paddled like a single from the stern can hold one child and one adult. In a few decked canoes, a middle storage cockpit can accommodate one child rather than gear.

Inflatable rafts are safe for family backcountry trips only if parents are highly experienced rafters. Double kayaks meant for tandem paddling in unison are not designed for two adults and a child or for stern paddling only.

Preparing Yourself

Water travel has its hazards. On clear, windless days on protected flat water, the experienced canoeist or kayaker faces no great danger. Water weather is changeable, however. Smooth, calm water can become menacingly choppy with the introduction of an afternoon wind. When traveling on water, you must be skilled enough to handle any boating problems. Do not take your children along until you have become a truly skilled paddler.

Clubs, classes, and supervised first experiences are even more important for water sports than for other outdoor recreation. To be valuable, a class must offer extensive boating experience. Short-term instruction is only a beginning. Accidents can happen to anyone, but a majority of boating mishaps occur when inexperienced boaters discover too late the necessity for skills, knowledge, and experience.

Preparing Children

When you have become a competent paddler, you can consider trips with children. Before you take them, however, make sure they are good swimmers. They should be both comfortable and skilled in the water. Children should be able to float, tread water, and generally relax. As a prerequisite for going with you, you can establish a minimum skill level, such as doing ten laps of crawl stroke in a pool.

Swimming lessons for babies are available in many places throughout the country. If you plan to take your preschoolers boating, you can enroll for early instruction. Babies less than a year old have no fear of water and can learn to paddle and go underwater with amazing aplomb. This type of program requires that the parent learn to teach the children. A baby and parent must swim together regularly or the child's confidence and skills are quickly lost.

Most pools start 3- and 4-year-olds with regular swimming lessons. Through relaxed games and play, young children learn skills and confidence in water. The youngster who is as calm as a fish in the deep end of a pool may be ready to join the family for canoeing activities.

On family trips everyone should wear a life preserver at all times. An adult who puts on a preserver before ever touching a paddle sets an important example for children. Grownups believe in a life preserver's ability to support them; a child, however, may not trust the device's flotation potential in the least. Before taking your young swimmer on a boat trip, demonstrate how the life preserver works. Go to a nearby pool and work with your child at the deep end. (You may need the pool manager's permission, and you may have to certify that your life preserver is absolutely sanitary.) Show your child how to relax and let the life preserver do the work. Be certain your youngster can swim in the device. Two or three short sessions in a pool or warm-water lake should increase the child's trust in the preserver.

Before their first trip, introduce children to proper boat deportment. With an aluminum boat you can start practicing in the backyard. For boats made from other materials, you can go to the shallows of a warm lake or see if your boating club can arrange a pool session for practice. Children must learn to enter a boat with their weight down low. For a youngster with short legs and arms, climbing over seats and thwarts while holding on to the gunwales requires practice. In the floating boat, children must learn what their various movements do. No one sits completely still in a boat. With time and experience youngsters come to understand which moves are permissible and which invite tip-overs.

LIFE PRESERVERS

On the water, every child should wear a Coast Guard–approved life preserver that fits his or her body size and weight. The preserver must be properly fastened and worn at all times. To encourage children to use life preservers, always wear your own.

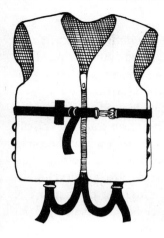

Figure 64. Closed-cell foam life preserver with leg straps

Approved life preservers for children use thick, closed-cell foam for flotation. These devices come in different sizes that correspond to youngsters' body weights. Most close with zippers and also buckle. So that the preserver fits snugly around the child's body dimensions, the cords joining the front and back pieces can be adjusted. When putting on the vest, a child steps into attached, adjustable leg straps designed to keep the preserver from riding up as the child floats in the water.

Always try the life vest on your child in the store. It should fit properly, the way clothes do. Body weights are clearly marked on flotation devices; the labels also should say the preservers are Coast Guard–approved. A child nearing the upper weight limit of a preserver may need the next size.

You should also try out the preserver in a pool or warm-water lake to be sure it supports your youngster correctly. If a child is knocked unconscious in an accident, the device must keep the youngster vertical and tilted slightly backward in the water. To test for effectiveness, have your child hang limp and totally relaxed in the life preserver. Check the life vest's efficiency every year, or more often, depending on your youngster's growth rate.

WATER SAFETY DRILLS

The chances of a tip-over on a family canoe trip are slight—that is, if you have developed sufficient paddling skills and experience, if you have chosen a suitable protected location, and if winds and weather cooperate. Still, you should practice what your family needs to do in a tipover emergency. Boating instruction can teach you rescue maneuvers. What is possible with two adults becomes more complicated, however, when a child is along. Tipover practice does several things: it helps you develop usable skills, it decreases the panic that develops in a real emergency, and it increases your child's confidence and understanding of the boat.

To begin, work on your youngster's self-assurance. Even a good swimmer can be frightened in a canoe or kayak. In warm, shallow water or in a pool, have the child roll over the gunwale feet first into the water. Gradually move the boat to deeper water and, as a second step, have the lifepreservered child swim to shore or to the side of the pool. Then work on getting the child back into the boat from the water. Start in the shallows and again work up to deep water. You will learn how to keep your weight wide-based in the bottom of the boat, and your child will discover how to kick the water for an extra boost and how to roll over the side into the boat without unnecessary rocking.

Only when a youngster is totally relaxed in the water and in the boat are you ready to stage an actual tip-over. You will have to adapt the rescue methods you have learned to a family situation. One adult in the water must assume the role of child comforter as the other adult rights and empties the boat and then retrieves the paddles and secures them inside. For draining water, sand buckets with attached handles work as well as anything (they double for beach play too). With these you bail—a long time if other emptying techniques have failed, or a little while if you are down to 4 or 5 inches of water—the dregs on the bottom. Do not frighten your child with ineptness. Be sure you can climb back into the boat yourself before you include your youngster in practice.

Also try towing your boat to shore after tipping it. You should have ample line attached to both ends of the boat for this purpose. Get together with another boating family and practice two-craft techniques. With two boats, get your child out of the water and into the rescue boat before righting and emptying the overturned craft.

Accident prevention is the key to small-boat safety. You should avoid rivers; cold water; rough water; long, open, windy crossings; and strong wind in general. Look for flat, protected water, and use it on fair, windless days.

Day Trips

A logical first step in preparing youngsters for enjoyable backcountry boat trips is to start with regular day trips in pleasing locations. Avoid driving long distances. A youngster who has sat for hours in the car will be reluctant to sit more hours in a boat. Car campsites on lakes or protected salt water provide good takeoff points. You camp at the established site and then venture off for the day in your boat. Locations near to home also can introduce the family to trips on the water.

Day trips help you determine when youngsters are ready for overnight boat camping excursions. When children can sit long enough and enjoy the boat, the family can graduate into short overnight stays. If these work well, the next step is to consider places suitable for more extended wilderness trips.

CLOTHING AND FOOTWEAR

On any day trip, you must carry clothing that can protect children if the weather changes. Raingear and the layers of warm clothing appropriate for overnight outings should be taken on short trips, too, and always carry your wilderness essentials (see Chapter 3, "Wilderness Essentials" section, and Chapter 4, "Dressing for Cold Weather" and "Raingear" sections).

In warm weather, a bathing suit is appropriate garb for a child in a canoe or kayak—as long as you carry warmer clothes to be used when needed. A cotton shirt over a bathing suit protects a child's tender skin from the sun's rays and reflection off the water. Many children need long, yet cool, pants for an entire day in the boat. Hats, sunglasses, and sunscreen are necessities. After a swim, reapply sunscreen.

On cool days, long pants and a shirt made of an easy-to-dry material are a good first layer. Cover these with a warm wool shirt or sweater. Use additional warm layers if needed. Even if the weather is clear, raingear protects clothing from water on the boat bottom and is a good windbreaker. As temperatures change, add or subtract warm clothing (see Chapter 4, "Layering" section). On day trips, carry an extra change of clothes for each child.

Neoprene wet-suits are also available in children's sizes in either full-length versions with long sleeves and pants or shorty styles with short sleeves and pants extending to above the knee. For the youngster sensitive to the cold or for the extra wet or chilly trip, these options provide protection from both cold water and cold air.

When a youngster sheds clothes as the day warms, put these extra clothes immediately into your waterproof bags; otherwise they may end up soaked in the bottom of the boat.

Choose your child's footwear to suit the climate in which you are boating. In cool waters or during the cooler seasons of spring and fall, leather-top rubber-soled boots or high rubber boots keep feet dry and warm. You can buy these large enough to wear with several pairs of wool socks. Neoprene (wet-suit material) boots come in adults' sizes, but you can buy the material and make them to fit children's feet. With these the feet are wet, but body heat warms the water.

For warm weather, sneakers work well. The soles protect the feet, and any worn-through areas permit water to drain out, but the day must be warm enough for wet feet to feel good. When a child travels wet-footed, extra dry sneakers or rubber boots should be carried for camp use or for cooler weather.

KEEPING GEAR DRY

When you decide to go boating, invest in adequate waterproof containers for your gear. On a day trip one or two such bags are enough to keep clothing, lunch, and wilderness essentials dry and usable. On long trips place anything that water can damage in carefully sealed, watertight containers and dry bags.

Many brands, styles, and sizes of dry bags are available through any water sports supplier. You merely have to match the size of the dry bag with the amount of gear you need to keep dry. In an open canoe, be sure to secure these bags with line.

For portaging—which is not the most desirable maneuver with children along—choose dry bags with straps for easier carrying. Wheels, which can attach to the stern or midsection of your boat, are available so that you can pull rather than carry your canoe or kayak to the next put-in spot. Better yet, find destinations where your family can avoid the complex logistics of the portage at least until your children are strong enough to help in the hauling.

KEEPING CHILDREN OCCUPIED

In many ways boating with children is easier than backpacking or cross-country skiing with them. A young child in a canoe or kayak is a passenger and does not have to work hard as he or she must when hiking or skiing. However, to make sitting in one place for long periods palatable, children need to be kept busy enough to prevent boredom from creeping in and ruining a trip. Many of the games and diversions suitable for car travel also work in a boat (see Chapter 2, "Pre-Backcountry Car Travel" section). Snacks help, and even very young children can amuse themselves by paddling. Half of a two-part kayak paddle is usually the right size for a youngster; small paddles are also made commercially for young grade-schoolers. At first the paddling does little to propel the boat and may last only a few minutes, but children find it fun. Establish from the beginning that the paddle can be used only for forward motion, never as a brake or drag. Other youngsters like to fish. Having a rod in hand occupies such a child for long periods of time, even if he or she catches nothing.

Frequent stops are a necessity; the younger the child, the more on-shore diversions you must provide. With a 5-year-old, a half-hour stop for each hour spent in the boat is not unusual. Stop before children become overly restless.

The shoreline naturally attracts youngsters. On protected salt water, tide pools teem with fascinating sea life. Gravel bars and sandy beaches offer the opportunity for exploration and play. Children like to wade or swim, but be sure the location is safe. Youngsters can swim wearing their life preservers as an extra precaution. Old, beat-up sneakers can protect feet from sharp objects.

If you expect children to enjoy riding in a boat, be sure they are reasonably comfortable. A "life preserver" boat cushion makes a good seat for a child; it is meant to get wet and floats if dropped overboard. About 3 inches thick, the cushion pads a small bottom and insulates against the cold and wet (it should never be used as a flotation device, however). On any trip, the space you leave for your child must be adequate. Most people find that even on a week's trip they can, if they pack a canoe sparingly, fit in two adults, one small child, and all necessary gear. With two young children, you can expect crowding (see later section, "Ways to Gain Space").

CHILDREN AND PADDLING

Even young children can learn to position their hands on a canoe paddle, execute a forward bow stroke, and feather the paddle (turn the blade horizontal to the surface of the water) on the return stroke. The 6-year-old may tire after a dozen strokes but, with a paddle available, may try again later. Older grade-schoolers can learn the basic canoe strokes. A strong 10- or 11-year-old can take on the J stroke, used in the stern. Endurance comes later, but youngsters enjoy learning paddle skills early. On flat water, canoeists change sides to avoid tiring. Encourage your children to develop their strokes for both sides of the canoe.

At 54 inches, the shortest standard canoe paddle is too long for a child 5 or 6 years old. On early trips, half of a two-part wooden kayak paddle is the right size. If you are clever with wood, add a top handle for easier grasping. Most young children paddle so little that a make-do paddle with a slightly uncomfortable top or an excessively long paddle is no problem.

When youngsters are interested and strong enough to learn more, a standard 54-inch paddle should be adequate. The correct length for a paddle is nose high on your child. If you choose lightweight paddles for your youngsters, they will tire less quickly and provide more help on family outings.

Boat Camping Trips

By scouting out boating country before taking your child on a trip, you can avoid unsuitable spots and structure your trip to accommodate youngsters. Portages can be very trying for a family. Loop trips commit you to specific distances that can be too long for children. Plan boating that will be comfortable for the entire family.

Allow for flexibility in your family boating trips. Mileage that takes adults five days in a boat can take ten days with youngsters. Children need shore time; an all-day, 14-mile push with camp arrival at dusk is not for them. They thrive on breaks during the day and early stops to make camp. Youngsters enjoy extra days in one place; they can play instead of sit, and you can add walking and exploring to your trip activities. Always play it safe. Never be forced onto water that has turned rough and menacing; instead, stay ashore and relish that extra day in camp.

WAYS TO GAIN SPACE

For boat camping, parents with one child must do some juggling and squeezing to get everyone and everything in. With two small children some crowding is inevitable in one boat. To conserve space, you can boat backpack style. Use a compact mountain tent, dried foods, and minimal pots and utensils.

An 18-foot open canoe has the best and most accessible room for a family. Traveling with a second boat is another way to provide adequate room. If you have two children, you could travel with a boating couple who do not have children. You could put one of your children in the boat with the other two adults or you could divide up your gear between the two boats to leave space in your boat for your two youngsters.

A strong paddler can put a child in the bow and propel either a specially designed double kayak or a canoe from the stern. Youngsters in the upper grade-school years often are strong enough to paddle the bow (an older child will be bored just sitting anyway). When that happens, you can move into two boats if both parents are confident paddlers. In a one-child family, a single kayak for one of the adults and either a double kayak or a canoe for the other adult and child will work. For two older and larger children, two double kayaks or two canoes are needed. With a weak paddler in the bow of a canoe, a double-bladed kayak paddle compensates for the paddling deficiency. In a canoe, practice the kayak paddle technique before you use it on a trip. With a bow paddler of questionable strength, trips should be modified so that long, tiring days are eliminated and heavy weather is avoided.

RIVERS

A flat-water paddler is not automatically a river paddler. For rivers, you must have special paddling skills and must practice them regularly. You must understand the characteristics of moving water, including gradient, currents, and eddies. To undertake river trips with children, you need to be a highly experienced *river* paddler. Rivers, no matter how benign they look at the put-in, are not for beginners.

SUPPORT ON BACKCOUNTRY WATERS

Never go alone on backcountry boating trips. Other families with children provide fun and companionship for your youngsters. With others along, you also have adequate support in emergencies (see Chapter 2, "Going with Other Families" section).

KEEPING SLEEPING BAGS DRY

Even if sleeping bag containers lie in a puddle of water all day, the bags should be absolutely dry when you pull them out for sleep that night. To keep bags and pads dry, you need a large dry bag designed to hold these items. Be sure to encase the sleeping bag in its coated nylon stuffsack and for extra insurance, especially as dry bags age, you may want to add a third waterproof layer of heavy-duty plastic.

Most people find that fiberfill-insulated sleeping bags are the best choice for youngsters in general and for water trips in particular (see Chapter 4, "Sleeping Bags" section). Fast-drying fiberfills do stay warm when damp. When soaked, water can be pressed out and the bag made usable. Even more comfortable, however, is a cozy, warm sleeping bag that you have kept totally dry.

Selecting a Boat

A good canoe or kayak is expensive. It can, however, last a lifetime. Shop around before buying.

When selecting a boat, spend time in as many models as you can. Through your canoe or kayak club or your boating classes, arrange to borrow boats for testing. You can rent boats at canoe liveries or water sports stores. To get to know a canoe or kayak's capabilities, you need to spend at least a day on the water with it. You also should see how the craft reacts to wind and rough water conditions. Try out a second or third time the one or two boats that most interest you. Then rent the model boat you think you want to buy and use it for a week-long adults' trip.

A boat's design makes it suitable for particular types of use. When shopping, decide if the design characteristics of a craft help or hinder flat-water paddling. Also examine the space. Can the boat hold children, gear, and adults safely and comfortably?

You need a long boat for family trips. Fortunately, given a quality design, a longer boat is more efficient on flat water. Boat-paddling efficiency means that your efforts are rewarded with easy forward motion. In an efficient boat, a hundred well-applied paddle strokes could move you twice as far as the same number of strokes in an inefficient design.

There are a number of different long boats to consider. Each has its own virtues and drawbacks. There are open canoes, decked canoes, and double kayaks to choose from. Various materials are used in fabricating these boats. The materials, too, have both positive and negative qualities.

OPEN CANOES

Open canoes are made in a variety of materials (see "Boat Materials" section) and designs. Some are made for river running, in which case the design emphasis is on maneuverability. For efficient flat-water cruising, the more boat length in the water the better. (A canoe with excess rocker or curve will put less length into the water.) Other design features are important too. A blunt-ended bow must push the water aside; a sharper-ended bow cuts through the water. In boat-building jargon, the sharp-ender is described as having a fine point of entry. A high-ended canoe, the classic shape that people associate with canoes, is a wind catcher. In many modern designs the ends are built straight and relatively low. The style may look odd to you, but it can provide greater flat-water paddling efficiency. A deep canoe with high sides keeps out water, but it also gives you more wind resistance.

The longer open canoes can hold as many as two smallish children and two paddling adults plus their gear. You need a 17-foot or 18-foot craft to accomplish this feat. For cruising, the added length works for you in a well-designed canoe.

DECKED CANOES

In a decked canoe, the top of the craft is covered and the paddlers kneel in bow and stern openings, or cockpits. Gear is stored under the decking, and the canoe is loaded and unloaded through the cockpits and a middle storage opening. Ads often show a child seated in the center opening.

A decked canoe keeps out water in rough conditions. However, it is designed with high ends that catch the wind and a rocker (the curved shape of the bottom) that is inefficient for straight-line movement. The kneeling paddlers sit high and act almost as sails, another drawback, especially in a quartering wind (one blowing obliquely across the path of the boat). The design does provide good maneuverability. In spray covers, the paddlers are warm. For a child in the middle opening, you need a third spray cover tailored to encircle his or her small-sized waist. Loading and access to gear are somewhat awkward, as you must reach in through the cockpits to stuff equipment under the decks.

DOUBLE KAYAKS

A double kayak also is decked, with a storage area that is accessible through the cockpits. The craft is built for two people, and most models require two vigorous paddlers. If your family includes a non-paddling child, cruising doubles are available designed to be powered only from the stern; these doubles feature a stern-operated rudder for more efficient solo steering of the boat. It still provides space for only two; so if one adult and one child ride in this stern-operated model, the other adult must ride in a second craft, such as a single kayak.

BOAT MATERIALS

If you rent from a livery, the canoes almost certainly will be made of aluminum. Aluminum crafts require little maintenance and are highly durable. They can take constant hard use. Aluminum has definite design limitations, however: it can be molded only into certain specific designs and shapes, and the two halves of an aluminum canoe must be joined along the bottom. The more sophisticated and efficient canoe designs cannot be made in aluminum. However, aluminum does become more efficient when employed in longer boats. At 18½ feet, the aluminum canoe enters the realm of easier-to-paddle boats (a smaller open canoe cannot accommodate a family well anyway).

If you have enough to do caring for children, an aluminum canoe's limited-upkeep quality is appealing. No canoe is totally impervious to damage, but the aluminum boat has better-than-average durability. On a wilderness trip, however, on-the-spot repair is relatively difficult.

Double kayaks, decked canoes, and many modern open canoes are made of fiberglass. This material is a boat builder's dream. Fiberglass has excellent design versatility. With it you can easily build boats shaped for maximum paddling efficiency. Fiberglass is not as resistant to damage as aluminum, but when you master the patching techniques, fiberglass boats are simple to repair.

Among other high-quality boat-building materials are various laminates. In the laminates, layers of vinyl, ABS (acrylonitrile–butadiene–styrene), and unicellular foam are sandwiched on top of one another. The result is a durable substance. The material can be molded into fewer shapes than fiberglass, but it has much more versatility than aluminum.

Wood has been the traditional canoe-building material. Wood can be crafted into designs as efficient and sophisticated as you desire (fiberglass molds are made of wood). Building with wood is expensive, both for the material and for the hand-crafting required. Although a wood canoe demands maintenance, to the wood canoe devotee such work is a labor of love.

When you choose a boat, pick what you can afford from among the well-designed offerings. Think of the time you have available for boat care and maintenance and how well the various boat designs are suited to the kinds of trips you want to take.

8

Winter Activities

CROSS-COUNTRY SKIING or snowshoeing can extend your family's backcountry activities into the winter season. When sharing winter sports with children, you must plan outings with child appeal, start slowly and gradually work up to longer trips, and be prepared to motivate, cajole, and encourage your youngsters as you move along.

Winter Weather and Hazards

Winter weather is highly changeable. In a storm at the tag end of an otherwise sunny day, your children may enjoy the novelty of being snowed on. A entire day of stormy skies, biting wind, or relentless snow or rain will be too much for youngsters. On overly cold days, everyone must ski to keep warm, and the fun of stopping and playing is lost. The younger the child, the more important good weather is, but older youngsters are happier, too, when the sun shines.

When planning a full day of skiing or showshoeing, start a little late to give the sun time to warm the air and end your day early too. Once the sun sinks behind the hills, tolerably cool weather can become intolerably frigid. The resulting cold can ruin a child's otherwise pleasant day.

Getting organized at the trailhead takes time. During the long minutes you devote to waxing skis (this must be done at the ski site, because you need to know snow conditions; see later section, "Skis"), your children can become chilled as they stand around or entertain themselves by rolling in or eating the snow. Youngsters do better for the rest of the day if they stay in the warm car until you are ready to strap on their skis and move. When you use no-wax skis, you can more quickly get the whole family out on the trail.

When planning skiing or snowshoeing excursions, remember that the coldest weather hits from early winter through midwinter. Days are short and storms are frequent. Spring, however, is short-sleeve skiing time. For youngsters, spring days provide snow underfoot and blissfully warm air all around. It is an ideal time for the very young to try out their ski legs.

Never go into an area with high avalanche danger. Rangers can alert you to the dangers inherent in particular areas and advise you of avalanche conditions. If you cannot contact a ranger, the ski patrol at an established downhill resort can give you this information. Generally, avoid steep gullies and steep, open slopes. (Even without avalanche danger, such terrain is a poor choice for youngsters.) Immediately following a heavy snow, the danger is high. The avalanche hazard increases with warm, snow-melting weather.

Since children lose body heat more readily than adults, avoid chilling that could lead to hypothermia, the dangerous lowering of the body's temperature (see Chapter 4, "Anticipating the Cold" section and the "Extra Clothes" and "What to Carry in Your Pack" sections in this chapter).

Cross-Country Skiing

One way to enjoy the outdoors in winter is to cross-country ski. You glide over the snow on these skis. With patterned bottoms or waxes on your skis, you can glide uphill as well as downhill. Cross-country skis are loose at the heel and consequently give the skier less control for turning. The loose heel, however, creates a less injury-prone sport. Cross-country skiing is a relaxing, fun activity that is ideal for sharing wintertime in the backcountry with your whole family.

WHEN TO START

A sturdy 3- or 4-year-old can handle cross-country skis as long as you do not expect too much. If you live in a place where snow covers the ground in winter, a young child can practice first in the backyard. To begin, one circle around the house is enough; you can increase the distance later. By skiing at home regularly, your youngster will grow accustomed to the feeling of those long things attached to his or her feet.

In snowless areas or before the snow season arrives, have your child practice on a rug inside (with skis totally devoid of wax and tar). Clear out a room and have the youngster try out boots and skis; save the poles for much later. On a rug a child learns to get used to the feeling of skis before he or she has to cope with the slipperiness of snow. Especially when it is necessary to travel to reach snow, some families confine their young children's practice skiing to inside drills. Youngsters can learn to move without crossing their skis and to get up from a fall alone, and they can begin to buckle and unbuckle their own bindings.

For first trips on snow, even after preliminary at-home preparation, the very young child loses interest and energy fast. A half hour to an hour on skis may be the limit for children 3 and 4 years old. When you join another family with small children, the adults can take turns ski baby-sitting. One adult can work with the young children near the trailhead; the other adults can move out on the trail and return at an appointed time to relieve the baby-sitting adult. If older children capable of sustained skiing are along, divide the youngsters by age and ability into two adult-supervised groups. Similar-aged youngsters from two families make fine ski mates. Seeing another small person on skis will help motivate your youngster to learn, and the outing will be more fun with an after-ski companion for play in the snow (also see Chapter 2, the "Going with Other Families" section). Early trips should be fun and unpressured. Young children should be allowed time to dig and throw and roll in the snow. Between falling and playing, little ones will be at snow level most of the day, so be sure you dress them in doubly warm clothes (see later section, "What Your Family Should Wear," and Chapter 4, the "Dressing for Cold Weather" section). Clothing insulated with fiberfill synthetics or made from fleeces stays warm and comfortable even when damp.

EXTENDING TRIPS

Children 5 and 6 years of age have the coordination and strength for longer family ski tours. For the beginner, your choice of terrain is important. Flat territory is easier, but rolling countryside is more interesting. The ideal location combines trail time with one or more spots for relaxing downhill practice. The beginner may balk at unrelieved trail skiing, but find the child a gently rolling bowl or a series of not-too-steep hillsides, and he or she will climb up and ski down for long periods of time. A trip of this sort may go only a mile into the backcountry, but during the day your child will ski 4 or 5 miles or more.

When youngsters handle shorter trips well, gradually extend the distance covered. Go slightly farther before stopping for play and snacks. Even a child who easily skis a 5-mile day needs time in between the work of touring to have fun. Youngsters' legs tire, but their minds and spirits give out first; so plan your stops to come before children complain or begin to lag behind. For the strong young skier, alternate forty-five minutes to an hour of skiing with ten-minute rests at interesting spots along the trail. Do not be surprised if youngsters play and ski around instead of resting. Stopping provides a change of pace. When you are ready to continue on the trail, that represents an activity change too. Children are happier with stop-and-go touring, and this helps the family cover more miles for the day.

Ski touring takes energy, so children need snacks as they go along. At each stop you may want to insist that youngsters eat and drink. Children lose more body heat than adults, and the cold weather itself causes the body to burn up more calories. As you creep along at a child's speed, do not forget how much energy the youngster is using up.

Experienced youngsters aged 10 through 12 can ski close to an adult's pace. Older children are still children, however. They want breaks and fun and games and snacks like any other youngsters.

NON-SKIING CHILDREN

Before children are old enough to ski themselves, some families take them ski touring in back carriers. When carrying a child on skis, pick your terrain carefully. A fall can be dangerous for carried youngsters. When you pass under snow-laden trees, be careful not to dump snow on your passenger. Do not tour in extremely cold weather. For sun protection, choose a trail that winds through shaded woods. Goggles that attach with an adjustable elastic band sometimes work for even a young child; you may be able to purchase them in downhill ski shops. Apply sunscreen to all skin areas not covered by clothing, but avoid any areas your child likes to suck.

Another way to take non-skiing children is to tow them on a special sled similar to the Fjellpulken popular in Scandinavian countries. The child sits on a curved wooden seat inside a cover similar to a kayak spray cover and behind a windshield. Like a horse pulling a carriage, the adult harnesses him- or herself into belted-on poles. The sled can also double as a gear carrier for extended winter camping trips. The cost of the sled is considerable, however. For the

Figure 65. With the Fjellpulken sled non-skiers can go on winter tours

family who ventures out only once or twice a winter, making do with a year-round child carrier may be the most reasonable solution.

Introducing Ski Techniques

The best way for parents to help children learn good skiing form is to take lessons themselves and improve their own touring abilities. Youngsters imitate; as they follow you along a trail, they will move as you move.

When children first start ski touring, just let them ski. Do not try to explain what their feet and arms should be doing. Go first to prepare a track, and let your youngster

Figure 66. Young beginners do best skiing without poles

follow you. For the very young, hold hands. At the beginning, poleless skiing helps a child concentrate only on feet
and balance.

Help young children to learn early how to get back up
on their skis after a fall. If you stand over your child, strad-
dling his or her skis, you can provide help while the child
goes through the necessary motions to get back up. Since
heels are loose on cross-country skis, a youngster can kneel
on the skis and then stand up, one foot at a time.

For downhill practice some people use the bunny slopes
of established ski areas. As youngsters start learning to
move downhill, poleless skiing is still best. Many families,

even the good skiers, go to experts to learn specific skills, such as turning. Being a fine cross-country skier does not automatically make you the right teacher for your own child. It is often difficult to find the patience necessary to teach a child skills when that child belongs to you. Do not rush into skills instruction, however. First give children plenty of relaxed years of skiing. A youngster who begins touring at 4 may not need additional teaching until 9 or 10 if enjoyable recreational skiing is your primary aim.

Camping on Cross-Country Skis

Unless you are a highly experienced winter camper, do not attempt cross-country ski camping trips with children. Even with the necessary expertise, try out family trips literally around the corner from your car. With winter snow on the ground at home, use your gear first in the backyard. Many families find that day trips on skis give children ample outdoor experiences in winter. They wait until the preteen years, when youngsters are strong skiers and fine summertime campers, before taking them on overnight excursions. Even then, trips should be short, bad weather avoided, and extra care taken to provide adequate in-camp clothing warmth. Springtime, with its longer days and warmer weather, is a good time to test snow camping.

For cold-weather overnights, taking courses, going with highly experienced people, and gaining extensive practical experience yourself are even more important than they are for other outdoor activities. Winter weather can be totally unforgiving of the mistakes you make. Only when you feel that you are an expert should you consider taking your children along.

Snowshoeing

Snowshoeing is more like hiking; you go through the outdoors one step at a time. People who enjoy snowshoeing find it a quiet, relaxing, contemplative activity. In wintertime, families can experience the backcountry on snow-shoes just as they can on touring skis. Snowshoe walking takes more energy, however, than trail hiking or ski touring.

Small-sized snowshoes are available to accommodate the school-age child. For boots, use the same warm combinations appropriate for buckle-on ski touring bindings (see "Bindings" section). Some parents make laced leather bindings to fit a youngster's boots (you can buy materials in a leather shop) or adapt bindings made for small-sized adult's shoes.

What Your Family Should Wear

CLOTHES FOR NON-SKIERS

When you take small children on wintertime jaunts, many layers of warm clothing are necessary for adequate protection. The child on your back generates no activity heat. While one snowsuit warms up a moving child, the equivalent of two is necessary for the non-mover (see also Chapter 4, "Layering" section).

Hands and feet are especially vulnerable. Wool mittens in various sizes can be worn over one another and then covered by lined outer mitts. To prevent losing the mittens, safety-pin the outermost mitt to the child's jacket sleeve.

A youngster's boots must be well insulated. Choose general boots lined especially for winter. Buy them extra large to accommodate several layers of warm socks, but be sure sock thickness does not hamper circulation. You might look for footwear similar to Eskimo mukluk boots. Into large outer boots, fiberfill-insulated booties can be fitted. Devise a way to keep boots on the child's feet. To each snowpants cuff you add a strap of strong elastic or webbed nylon that can be stretched to go under each boot.

To keep the child's head warm, you may need as much as a fiberfill-insulated snowsuit hood over a wool hat. A muffler tied over the head and around the neck can add another layer of warmth. For a cold face, use a ski mask, or wait till the weather warms and then take your child on an outing.

CLOTHES FOR SKIING CHILDREN

Clothes layering is an especially important technique for cross-country skiing. Even a slow-moving child will become warm fast. With clothing worn in layers, the outer layers can be removed before sweat dampens inner clothing (see Chapter 4, "Layering" section). The aim for safe, comfortable touring is to wear enough for warmth but never too much. Children rarely realize they are too hot or too cold until they're extremely uncomfortable. Parents must develop the ability to determine when a youngster needs to wear more or less clothing. Young children cannot be expected to do this for themselves.

When choosing cross-country clothes for children, look for synthetic fills and wool. Both of these fibers retain heat when wet or damp.

Your child needs a wool cap. Tie-under-the-chin types protect the ears. Balaclava-style hats cover chin, ears, and forehead; in most, the lower half rolls up when not needed. You can knit your own out of wool. On warm days a headband can be used, but always carry along a heavier hat too.

For tops, wool shirts and sweaters covered by a windbreaker allow the child to adjust layers. Ready-made wool shirts for youngsters are prohibitively expensive. With thrift shop wools you can make your own shirts at affordable prices (see Chapter 4, "Making Do" section). A rain jacket can double as a windbreaker and will protect other clothes from snow. In dry-snow areas, a wind shirt or wind jacket sheds snow adequately. On especially cold days, young children who move slowly may require a heavy, fiberfill-insulated jacket on top of other clothing layers.

Traditional wool knickers and high wool socks function poorly until youngsters ski at an adult's speed and with an adult's consistency. For the beginner's stop-and-go pace, fiberfill-insulated overpants with a nylon outer shell are more suitable. To be effective, such pants must have two-way, top-to-bottom leg zippers. With increased activity or for warmer temperatures, you open the leg zippers as far as necessary. When your child stops skiing or plays in the snow, you zip up the pants completely. If booted feet slip easily through the pants legs, you can even remove the overpants completely and carry them. Underneath these overpants a youngster should wear regular long pants. In colder climates, wool or fleece pants are best; you can use thrift store woolen materials for making them. You also may need next-to-the-skin long johns. Those made of the various types of polyesters available in long underwear will not itch your child. If you plan to use only long johns with outer pants, you cannot remove a layer unless children ski in their long underwear.

Thin cross-country ski boots may not insulate a child's feet adequately. With these, several extra pairs of wool socks are necessary. (Take these socks with you for fitting purposes when you buy boots.) To prevent itching, use a liner sock next to the skin. Some touring boots for children come with a lining for extra warmth. With buckle-on bindings, you can cover the outside of your youngster's boots with an additional layer. You could make a fiberfill-insulated overboot with an inner sole or use a very thick wool oversock.

Mittens are warmer than gloves, and layers of mittens allow for temperature adjustments. Nylon works well as a windbreaking outer mitt. For snow play, fiberfill-insulated mittens stay warm even if they get damp.

No child should cross-country ski without adequate gaiters, which are basically heavy, coated-nylon spats. Gaiters protect boot tops and pant legs from snow and even

secure low-cut boots on a youngster's feet. A gaiter encircles the ankle and covers the boot top. A back zipper secures the type that is easiest to put on. Elastic at the top
and bottom keeps the material snug around the foot. Elastic under the foot keeps the gaiter from riding up.

For children in long overpants, shorter gaiters are adequate. Low gaiters made for adults often fit even a small
child since the elastic tightens the material around the foot.
Using your own gaiters as a model, you can make a pair
for your youngster fairly simply.

EXTRA CLOTHES

As soon as you stop to rest, put warm layers back on your
child. During an extended break from skiing (for lunch or
play), add a heavy winter jacket with a synthetic fill, which
will remain warm when damp or wet. The jacket should
have an insulated hood. Extra mittens also should be carried. Wool may be warm when wet, but dampness can annoy a tired child at the end of the day. By supplying warm,
dry mittens you provide an extra psychological boost, if
nothing else.

Even in gaiters a child playing in snow can get his or her
socks wet. With extras along, you can give your youngsters
a fresh, dry pair. Wool socks also can double as mittens.

If you ski where rain is a possibility, your raingear
should always be with you (see Chapter 4, "Raingear" section). Carry your child's windbreaker if days are too warm
for wearing it.

CLOTHES FOR ADULTS

On trips with children, adults must reevaluate their
warmth needs. Light cross-country ski clothing keeps you
warm only with physical activity. At a young child's snail-
like pace, you may need to wear almost as many layers as
you would during a lunch stop. Suit your clothing to the
skiing ability of your children.

What to Carry in Your Pack

When cross-country touring, always carry your pack with child and wilderness essentials (see Chapter 3, "Wilderness Essentials" section), and take your ski repair equipment. If your car is out of view, be ready to take care of yourself and your youngsters. Wintertime in the outdoors is beautiful, but for anyone, especially children, the cold is potentially dangerous.

For warmth at stops, each person needs an extra-heavy winter jacket adequate for the climate where you ski (see "Extra Clothes" section). To be prepared for trouble, carry a child's sleeping bag in your pack; it weighs little and ensures warmth. An adult's winter jacket can do the job of a sleeping bag, but then you will not have a heavy jacket to wear yourself.

Closed-cell foam pads for sitting insulate against the cold during lunch breaks. Taking a full-length pad instead of some small squares provides emergency protection too. Do not, by the way, allow youngsters to talk you into using pads for hill sliding; they will disintegrate with such harsh treatment.

A light emergency blanket or large plastic garbage bags can provide bivouac-like shelter. Neither withstands heavy wind, however. A wilderness winter survival course with field experience is the best preparation for the emergency bivouac you hope that you will never make.

For family trips you need large quantities of extra food. Some people carry as much as the equivalent of two full lunches per child. In the cold, youngsters should eat heartily all day long since winter weather increases calorie consumption. Quick-energy snacks are particularly important (see Chapter 3, "Snacks" section). In a small, light daypack a youngster can carry a snack bag and juice. You must judge how much your youngsters can consume, but to be safe, err on the side of overabundance.

On full days of touring, taking along a winter backpacking stove allows for cooking hot food at lunch (see

Chapter 3, "Stoves" section). Hot soup and hot chocolate warm youngsters from the inside out and can give a needed boost for the latter half of the day. You also have your stove in the event of an emergency.

For on-the-trail ski repair, adhesive tape or duct tape and wire allow for some makeshift repairs. Carry your multi-accessoried knife, a small screwdriver, and pliers. You also should carry some replacement parts, such as extra cables (for youngsters in cable bindings), screws, and pole baskets. An emergency ski tip of metal or plastic can temporarily replace a broken tip and enable you to ski out. Be sure the tip fits your children's skis as well as your own. If you check all your equipment carefully before trips, you can avoid many unnecessary repairs on the trail.

Cross-Country Ski Gear for Children

Once children are old enough for cross-country skiing with their parents, appropriate skis, boots, bindings, and poles must be obtained. You will want to match the equipment available with the needs of your age child.

BOOTS

Real cross-country ski boots for children are costly. Because children's feet grow rapidly, all too soon their boots become too small. Especially if your young child skis only occasionally, you can make do with general boots. You must, however, use buckle-on-style child's cross-country bindings (see below). For mild winter weather, flexible hiking boots with layers of wool socks can be used (see Chapter 4, "Socks" and "Soft-Top Boots" sections). You also can use rubber boots with sturdy soles as an outer covering with fiberfill-insulated booties or layers of wool socks inside. For very cold areas, you could make fleece or other synthetic inner booties. Closed-cell foam inner soles also insulate feet against the cold.

When children cross-country ski, their constant movement warms their feet. Nevertheless, heavy wool socks still should be worn with boots. To finagle some extra growth room, buy boots to fit with two pairs of heavy socks and one pair of thin socks. The second year, use one heavy and one thin pair. As long as the boots tie snugly over the instep, stuff a little cotton into excess toe space and let your child grow into the fit. Try out these schemes before you buy; a youngster with very slender feet may slip out of boots that are too large.

A real cross-country boot has a sole that extends out beyond the boot so that it can slip under the toe hold on a cable binding or into the clip closure of a pin binding. Most are just-above-ankle high and are basically flexible. These boots come in leather (very expensive) or with synthetic-coated uppers (more affordable). The fleecy lining in some designs helps keep a youngster's feet warmer. Once children begin developing good cross-country ski technique, the flexibility of a supple boot becomes more important.

For economy, it is worth looking for secondhand children's ski boots. Check into ski swaps, used boot departments in outdoor stores, and trades with other families who cross-country ski. Look for imported leather boots, which are now prohibitively expensive. Inexpensive rubber-topped boots made in Asia once were readily available; these look and perform exactly like more costly touring boots. Good boots are made to last through the hard use of many youngsters.

BINDINGS

Cross-country ski bindings hold the toe secure while the heel lifts and falls freely. Several different binding styles are made for children. A cable binding has a metal toe plate into which the extra-long sole of the cross-country boot is secured. The cable itself goes around the boot heel, where an extra groove holds it in place. For the beginning skier,

Figure 67. Cable bindings used with a cross-country ski boot

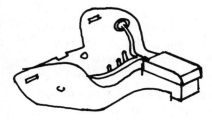

Figure 68. Pin binding

the cable behind the loose heel provides added support; the wobbly foot stays in place on the ski better. Cable bindings adjust to boot length and width. Some children's cable bindings are flimsy, however, and do not hold up under heavy use.

Good-quality cable bindings adjust to fit several boot sizes as your child grows. To adjust, loosen the screws and slide the two sides of each toe plate. Always fit the bindings to the size of new boots. When buying children's cable bindings, find out the maximum boot size they can accommodate. Bindings that are too small may look as if they fit, but they will allow boots to slip out of skis too easily on a fall.

Most adults use pin bindings for cross-country skiing. These consist of metal toe plates to which boot toes are clamped securely. The pins on the front of the plates fit into holes specially positioned in the cross-country boot soles. When youngsters begin skiing confidently and strongly, pin bindings help them develop good cross-country ski form.

Another option for young beginners, the buckle-on

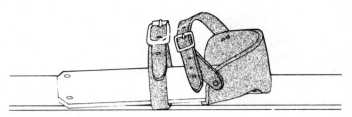

Figure 69. Leather buckle on bindings

binding, may be available only through the used equipment market. Since this binding is ideal for the very small child, it is well worth the effort to find a used set. These bindings are made from a flat piece of relatively stiff leather that screws down onto the ski beneath the child's foot; the attachment spots are positioned at the front part of the child's foot. Two straps keep the youngster's boot in place. The front strap buckles around the boot, approximately at the ball of the foot. The back strap is attached to a curved leather heel-holder and buckles around the boot just below the ankle. The heel itself is loose, just as it would be in any cross-country binding.

Falling rarely disturbs children, but coming out of the bindings on each fall can be more than a youngster and parent can tolerate. Buckle-on leather bindings do not easily slip off a child's boots during a fall, and they are sturdy enough to last through many youngsters. Beginners from 3 or 4 to 7 years old manage well with minimum frustration in leather bindings.

POLES

For the very small beginner, poles are unnecessary. Youngsters do better without poles at first so that they can concentrate on their feet and balance. Although flimsy, the poles that come with packaged sets for small children are adequate for the limited use they will get.

Touring poles should be armpit high. To even the older beginning child, this length may feel excessive. A useful pole has a metal tip, a hand strap large enough for the child's heavily mittened hand to fit through, and a sturdy shaft made of fiberglass. The pole basket is light plastic and breakable, so buy spare baskets for your repair kit when you purchase your youngster's poles.

SKIS

There are two types of cross-country touring skis: skis with waxable bottoms and no-wax skis. The recommended length for children's skis is somewhere between head high and the height from ground to wrist when the hand is extended straight up. Young beginners do better in skis that are shorter and wider than adults require.

If your family has never toured, no-wax skis are the easiest to use. The ski bottoms are molded into patterns that facilitate going uphill as well as downhill. The skis are made of a durable synthetic material.

Until recently, all cross-country touring skis were made of wood. The bottoms of wood skis and the new fiberglass skis that do not have a patterned base need to be waxed. When the correct wax is applied, the skier can glide uphill without slipping backward. The type of wax used depends on snow conditions and air temperature. For temperatures below freezing, hard waxes are suitable. For spring skiing, klisters—which have a softer consistency and must be squeezed out of a tube—are used. Waxing for cold, dry snow is simple. In wet snow or on days with extreme temperature variation, waxing is frustratingly complex. Waxing is a fine art. If you have spent long hours developing your waxing abilities, you may feel compelled to continue practicing your skills. Even so, you might consider waxed skis for yourself and no-wax models for beginning children.

You can purchase waxable skis in wood or fiberglass in children's sizes. Since youngsters' skis originally were made only of wood, look for used pairs to save money.

PACKAGE DEALS

You can buy ski equipment for young children in packaged sets at a substantial savings. In such sets, the skis and boots often are very adequate, but the poles and bindings tend to be flimsy. Although beginners do not need poles, secure bindings are essential. With sets, you often come out ahead financially by purchasing the package and then replacing the bindings. For older, more experienced children you may want to pick particular skis, poles, or bindings that are of a better quality than those available in package deals.

9

In Camp with Children

Finding a Campsite

After a full day of traveling with children into the back-country, you may want to plop down at the first available spot and set up camp fast. Youngsters will be tired from either walking the trail or sitting in the boat. The first site you come across, however, is not necessarily the best place for your family. A good family campsite is safe for children and also provides youngsters with a place for reasonable play.

When you reach the general area in which you want to stay, find a temporary resting spot. Leave the gear there with one adult and the children. Do not take tired, restless youngsters on wanderings to find the ideal site. Within about fifteen minutes' time, an adult who is scouting alone can see and evaluate all the possibilities. To occupy and revive weary youngsters, the parent who stays with the children can start the stove, heat water, and provide soup or hot chocolate. If your stopping place is pleasing to children, the activity change in itself may revitalize youngsters.

With your children resting and content, what do you look for in a site? First of all, safety. If there is a cliff that drops off several hundred feet right behind the site or if poison ivy covers every inch of nearby ground, you are courting trouble. Be sure to find a place that your child's play and activity cannot harm. An established, well-used site (if properly set up to begin with) already has bare ground and no vegetation to destroy. You also need a level area large enough for sleeping, especially if you must arrange bodies in a head-to-foot pattern. Privacy is important. With children along, be particularly careful to keep your family group a good distance from other people. Child noise, even happy sounds, is not what most backcountry travelers have come to the wilderness to enjoy. Other adults can be noisy too. After a tiring day your youngsters may not be able to sleep through the sounds of another party. Even quiet talk can be inordinately loud on an otherwise silent evening. When you move away from the trail and heavily used water sources, you can find lovely private perches. With young children you help avoid accidental dunkings if the lake or stream is less accessible. You protect the shoreline, too, since it is the place most vulnerable to people pressure.

The importance of choosing a campsite that is appropriate for children cannot be overemphasized. You may like the high alpine country where every plant and tree struggles for survival, where panoramic views stretch out in all directions, and where each footstep you take can influence the area's natural balance. A place this fragile is not for young children, however. Taking them to such areas is like pushing them into a shop filled with delicate pieces of china and glass. Instead of having fun, you are going to spend your time saying, "Don't . . . Don't . . ." and "Don't . . ." some more. If you choose a place that is entertaining for children, you will have no trouble figuring out what to do with your time and everyone will have more fun.

Once you find a suitable place, be sure you do no engineering. Do not dig up roots, break down branches, or create moats. Impress on your children that your aim is to disturb the natural environment as little as possible.

Establishing In-Camp Boundaries

Once you have chosen a campsite, set specific boundaries for your children's activities. Before you set up any gear, walk around the area and look for potential hazards. If you are near water, see if there is a sudden drop-off. Check for plants that are poisonous to eat or that induce rashes, such as poison ivy and poison oak.

Then spell out the boundaries you have established for your youngsters. For young grade-schoolers, be very specific; tell them not to go past a certain tree or rock. Older children can understand more general descriptions. Never allow youngsters to explore alone beyond the boundaries you set.

Boundaries are particularly important when you are busy setting up camp. Children can help in this process, but if they are tired, quiet play may be more appropriate. You need to know exactly where your youngsters are while you are completing your chores. For preschoolers too young to be reliable, you can set up a play area near the spot at which you are working. Having youngsters underfoot as you set up the tent or sort gear is better than having them wander off.

As youngsters grow older and more responsible, you may be tempted to ease off and make boundary delineation more casual. This is unwise. Trouble can develop all too easily when an overconfident older child encounters hazards. You owe it to your older child to list the potential dangers in the vicinity of your campsite and to insist that he or she always remain in sight of an adult. You are establishing a kind of buddy system for safety, and the child's buddy must be one of the adults in the party. If your boundary rules are absolutely clear, you keep your children from creating unnecessary problems and dangers for themselves.

WHAT TO EXPECT IN CAMP
AT VARIOUS AGES

A happy, easygoing infant can be relatively easy in camp. The tent is home and provides warmth and protection. For the baby who can sit up, the stand on a child carrier makes a convenient seat if it is used with caution. Many parents carry their young babies on their backs or fronts even in camp.

When babies start to crawl, having them in camp is a major challenge. Crawling children who are restless in the pack and who resist confinement in the tent must be watched constantly. They move about in the dirt, put objects in their mouths, and want to explore everything in sight. They can reach out suddenly for guy lines on tents, hot pans, or the stove.

Toddlers, who are trying to perfect basic walking, move more slowly than fast crawlers. They add the complication of tumbling and stumbling to in-camp life. Obstacles they encounter, such as rocks, branches, roots, and hard ground, are potentially more dangerous than those found at home. If you plan to backpack with a child this age, an extra pair of hands—either a sitter or a willing friend— can help, especially when chores have to be managed. Walking toddlers can find trouble with incredible ease. They are full of unexpected, irrational movements, and their balance is not too great either. I still remember the face-first plunge our daughter took at 2. I let go of her hand for mere seconds, and she lurched right into the lake.

In camp, a toddler requires hand-in-hand supervision. The early walker represents the most difficult age for backpacking or car-camping trips. Although the idea may sound repugnant, a harness and leash is sometimes the only safe solution to protect the toddler from being a menace to him- or herself. (Never, under any circumstances, put a child to sleep in any type of restraining device; the dangers of tangling are too great.)

Children 3 or 4 years old who have developed some sense still must be watched in camp with hawklike intensity. They may listen to verbal instructions fairly well, but they get into trouble quickly and should never be out of sight. At this age, camp boundaries can be established and enforced. You can establish a specific play area. You also can put the fire circle, camp stove, tent, and guy lines out of bounds, and youngsters will, until they forget, manage to follow your carefully explained instructions. Do not be surprised, however, if you have to repeat your rules frequently, since children this young have trouble coping with more than one idea at a time.

Children between 5 and 7 seem easy to have in camp. They know how to take care of themselves and can follow instructions. Always err on the side of caution with older children, however. Their activities should always be supervised, and camp boundaries still need to be enforced. Children this age can be very helpful in camp, but they need your watchfulness and instruction. Especially at the beginning of every camping season, go over all the lessons in outdoor living you thought you taught so well the year before—how to wash dishes and themselves, how to brush teeth away from water sources, how to go far from camp and bury feces, and how to play without destroying the natural environment.

From the middle grade-school years on, experienced youngsters become delightful and easy in-camp companions. They can help with chores and function almost like adults. Do not be fooled, however, into becoming slack on supervision. An experienced child does not have adult judgment and therefore should be with an adult at all times.

In-Camp Fun

Family camping should be fun. Once you arrive at your destination, the hard work of organizing, planning, and getting there is behind you. In camp, adults and youngsters alike can relax and have a good time together in the outdoors.

WATER PLAY

Playing in water is the most entertaining diversion for youngsters. Some children will swim no matter how cold the lake; they will wade even in frigid snow-melt. Be extra careful about children's feet. In any area where there has been mining or logging, where past visitors might have been careless, or where packers have brought horses, there is a good chance of encountering dangerous objects underfoot. A sharp rock or a protruding branch can painfully bruise or cut a small foot. Wearing sneakers or water sandals protects youngsters' feet from injury.

When you are alone, skinny-dipping is fine. In some backcountry areas it is accepted even if others are around. Use your own judgment about carrying bathing suits for children. An extra pair of shorts that dry fast can be used for water play. Very light nylon dries extremely fast.

Bath towels are too heavy for backpacking. Even for the boat they are excessively bulky. A couple of washcloths, half a bath towel, a dish towel, or even paper towels can be used to dry a small child quickly. On sunny days the warm air can dry youngsters. If children suddenly become chilled or shivery, quickly get them into dry clothes and cover them with some extra warm layers.

When you choose a play area at the water's edge, check for hazards. Avoid places with sudden dropoffs and discourage even good swimmers from diving. Very cold water can cause unexpected cramps, so keep youngsters reasonably close to shore and under supervision at all times. If you are boating, children can wear life preservers for swimming.

Lake shores where the forest comes to the water's edge are delicate. Sandy beaches and gravel bars are not so prone to damage, and they are more fun too. In mountainous areas, making dams or changing the water's course should not be allowed. On ocean beaches, tidal rivers that the high tide will cover, and rivers below the winter flood line, children can, within reason, be beavers to their heart's content without harming the environment.

When children build something on a sand or gravel beach, have them dismantle the structure before you leave. It is a simple courtesy for the next people who come along. Rules for playing and building on beaches are much the same as those for setting up a campsite. Be sure not to move or uproot anything living and use only downed, dead wood for play.

DRIFTWOOD BEACHES

The driftwood on ocean beaches has a hundred uses. Older children like to build real shelters if driftwood is abundant and big enough. A driftwood lean-to with a tarp can make a fine I-made-it-myself shelter in which youngsters can spend the night. Tangles of wood, logs, and stumps rival the very best concepts in modern playground equipment; children love climbing and scrambling in these driftwood forests. With flotsam from beaches and the right-sized driftwood branches, a loom for weaving can be fashioned. Children among driftwood can pretend themselves into a thousand and one fantastic adventures.

SNOW

Even when small, a snow patch can delight children. If you camp where snow patches remain, your youngsters will roll, slide, build, and snowball with wild exuberance. Be sure the snow does not drop off dangerously. Also make certain that children do not trample any vegetation on the way to their winter-in-summertime treat.

FISHING

Some children are born fishing people. They have patience beyond comprehension and are ecstatic even when catching nothing. At 4, one of our children once sat an entire morning dangling a safety pin attached to a 6-foot line into the water. She was so still that eventually tiny fish nosed at the pin, and that was enough to keep her thoroughly entertained.

Many streams and lakes are stocked for public fishing. If you find a lake that is rarely fished, your children have a chance to connect with some action. Be sure you are familiar with fishing regulations so that you know which fish are legal keepers, which lures or baits are permitted, and when waters are open. Check the rules governing children's fishing. Youngsters may not need a license, but sometimes you have to count their fish as part of your catch limit.

During these first fishing experiences, teach children the principles of catch-and-release fishing so that streams and lakes will continue to have abundant fish growing in the future. Releasing any fish should be done with care. Teach your children to touch them only with wet hands and to keep the fish in the water while you extract the hook. A barbless hook makes catching harder, but enables you to release fish without harming them. Adults should take out the hooks on any fish to be put back. Keep only legal-sized fish you are going to eat. Either burn the fish guts or pack them out to a place where they can be burned or properly disposed of.

DAY HIKING

When you remain in a single base camp rather than changing locations every night, day hiking can be both pleasant and relaxing for the entire family. Children's packs make excellent daypacks for adults on these excursions. You can take your lunch, warm clothes, raingear in case the weather changes, and wilderness essentials (see Chapter 3, "Wilderness Essentials" section), as well as anything else appropriate for your chosen destination, such as binoculars if you are scrambling to high ridges, fishing gear for a trout lake, or a camera to capture the beauty along the trail. Without packs, children who dragged and complained into the base camp may find new exuberance and energy. When hiking away from your camp, be sure that you allow plenty of time for the trip back so that youngsters do not become too tired or hungry.

On boat trips, a day of hiking provides a good change of pace for the family. Since you probably will not have hiking boots along, pick a destination devoid of rough, ankle-threatening terrain. In the woods surrounding the waters where you are boating you will find a totally different setting than you have experienced at your beach campsites. A boat bag with a shoulder strap makes an adequate carrier for your hiking essentials.

EXPLORING

Exploring around your campsite can provide you and your children with long hours of diversion. The life systems that exist in and around lakes and streams are especially fascinating to observe. You can treat your youngsters to a dawn-to-dusk natural science class. From the beginning of your explorations, stress that you are observers, not disturbers. You are watching, not collecting. Taking a photo when you discover something fascinating is the one and only way to bring home what you have found. (Without a close-up lens, however, many of the tiny lifeforms you see will not show up well on film.)

A nature diary is a good method for keeping track of all your daily finds. Jot down descriptions and draw pictures when you discover a tree, plant, bird, or insect you cannot identify. At home you can add to your family's knowledge by locating the unknown species in a nature book. Paperback field books provide on-the-spot knowledge but are too weighty for backpacking; in the boat, small editions take little room.

Even older children may be only mildly impressed with a view of distant peaks. Youngsters enjoy what is close at hand and what is underfoot. They are fascinated with the small details of the natural world, such as the shiny roundness of agates on a beach and the delicate outlines of fossils in rock. Children can watch tadpoles swim and wiggle for hours and will follow with intense interest the trail of a centipede or the winged wandering of a brightly colored butterfly.

In most areas, chances are you will not see any large animals. In national parks, where animals become quite tame, you may observe some of the larger, more spectacular wildlife. Nevertheless, with your eyes open and your powers of observation sharpened, you can find fascinating evidence of how animals live and function in the area you are visiting. You can discover birds' nests in a variety of sizes and shapes, rotting logs in which chipmunks live and woodpeckers feed, anthills alive with activity, and evidence of tunnel complexes that house rodents.

While exploring nature with children, you are likely to make fascinating discoveries. On one trip our family day hiked from our base camp to a lake that had once housed beavers. The animals themselves had been gone for a long time, but we spent the afternoon discovering all kinds of evidence of their way of life. The lodges were still recognizable, and trees of amazing size lay where the beavers had felled them. We saw, too, how the animals had once raised the level of the lake by damming the outlet streams.

Observing animal tracks can be fun for youngsters too. When your children can see and recognize deer prints, they do not have to see the deer to feel pleased. If you find a track you cannot identify, make a sketch of the print and find out what it is when you get home. Some older children enjoy keeping notebooks in which they sketch the tracks they find and then record the characteristics of the animals that made the tracks.

When you camp with children, you have time to investigate. You are not, as you might be on an adult trip, pushing off on some all-day marathon. Children make wonderful natural scientists. Their powers of observation put most adults to shame. Their fascination and enthusiasm for all they see around them will make your own enjoyment of the out-of-doors grow and blossom.

In-Camp Chores

For some reason chores on camping trips are more entertaining than chores at home, for both adults and children alike. Youngsters should be encouraged to do their share. The real help given by a young child is minimal, but getting a child into the habit of pitching in on jobs is essential if you want the youngster to help out as he or she gets older.

Children like to help pitch a tent or tarp. When you need an extra pair of hands to hold a pole, spread out a tent floor, or pound in stakes, even a small child (if you are in no hurry) can make a contribution. If you want little jobs to grow into big jobs later, lavish praise on any youngster who helps you. Although it is better to let a trail-weary child rest, once you have set up your camp you should assign a number of small tasks to each family member.

At mealtime children should not be right around the stove, especially when you are priming it or when you are boiling a pot of water on it. Most meals require mixing, though, and children can add water and stir as well as anyone. Your child may consider it a treat to make dessert while you work on the main course. Be sure that any special jobs are divided evenly if you have more than one youngster. When children are helping, you can provide a space for them slightly away from the main cooking area to avoid knocked-over pots or dirt kicked into food. We

have a rule that no one walks through the kitchen area during actual cooking time. The child who has a job sits down
on the edge of the cooking area, does the task under adult
supervision, and then moves away from the cooking space
until the meal is served.

Cleaning up should be another shared task. Some families rotate jobs. At each meal a different person is assigned
a particular part of the cleanup. One person washes plates,
cups, and silverware; another washes pots and pans; and
a third person does the drying. Other families work out a
system in which everyone does his or her own washing and
drying while the task of scrubbing pots and pans is rotated.

Preschool children can entertain themselves for hours
playing in dishwater. Give them their cups and spoons, and
they can be happy washing, rewashing, and playing with
bubbles for a long time. Dishwashing is a good first job for
a small child.

Children also can help set up their own beds in your
shelter. They can spread pads on the tent floor and get
sleeping bags out of their stuffsacks. When you break
camp, older youngsters can learn to stuff their own sleeping bags; small children will need an adult's help if the fit
is tight or if an Ensolite pad is to be put inside.

Since gear distribution and list checking are necessary
at home, an adult must load packs before a trip starts. On
the trip, however, children can learn to pack, unpack, and
organize what is in their own backpacks. As children's fingers become more coordinated, they can learn to cinch
their sleeping bags to their packs with straps.

Keeping dirty and wet clothes separated from clean gear
is another responsibility children can handle. In sunny
weather, drying out wet clothes and airing sleeping bags
can be a regular family routine, with each person taking
care of his or her own.

If you are using a fire, children are wonderful wood
gatherers. Always accompany children as they collect,
both for safety reasons and to ensure that they carry back

only downed, dead wood. Youngsters can learn to sort fire-wood into different sizes, from small tinder to larger, long-burning pieces. Older children can learn to light and feed the fire. Care and lighting of the stove, however, should remain the adults' responsibility. Any contact children have with fire should be carefully supervised (see "Children and Help with the Fire" section).

None of these chores is hard work. With all these jobs, though, children need to be encouraged and helped. If you create a positive atmosphere at the outset of your camping trips and if you work side by side with your youngsters, camp chores will seem like fun. Adults always have plenty of job supervising to do in camp, but with each child doing small tasks the amount of work for parents gradually diminishes.

Toileting Children

Once you settle on a campsite and delineate camp boundaries for your children, you must pick an appropriate toilet area. In hot weather and when youngsters have exerted themselves physically, they will drink an abundance of fluids. Children's trips to the toilet area are bound to be frequent. Before you face this need, scout out the region around your camp. You should go no closer than 200 feet from camp; going farther than that is even better. The toilet area should be a spot where no one else would ever set up a campsite and should be far from any water sources. Be sure you have not landed at the back door of another camping site.

When you have found an appropriate toileting spot, figure out how you are going to get your children there fast. Busy children inevitably wait until the last second. If you have to climb and break through brush, your youngsters are never going to make it. A good way to avoid emergency sprints is to take children at regular intervals. Do not wait for them to tell you—you tell them that it is time to go.

Urine is relatively free of disease-spreading organisms. Human feces, however, can pollute the water supply and transmit disease. For some children this distinction is too subtle. Therefore, when you teach youngsters about outdoor toileting, instruct them to urinate and defecate only in the far-from-camp location. That way no child, no matter how young, can get confused.

Always go with your children when they use the toilet area. If it is far enough from camp to be suitable, youngsters will be out of sight, which is something you cannot allow with young children. This way you also can be sure that your children go as far off as they should and that they cover up their waste completely.

The procedure for taking care of feces is fairly simple. You find an appropriate spot away from camp and all water sources and you dig a small hole. Some families carry a small, lightweight, plastic trowel for this purpose, but usually you can scrape out an adequate space with a stick or a flat, hand-sized rock. Show your children, even older youngsters, the proper size and depth needed. A ½-inch scrape will not do, but a hole should never be more than 6 inches deep. It is in the first 6 inches of topsoil that wastes gradually decompose. Tell your children this is the cat hole method. Young children will be intrigued and this may help them remember what to do, especially if they have watched a cat with interest. (When squatting, young children need your help to keep their balance.) Once the wastes are deposited in the hole, take your stick or rock and replace the soil cover.

Toilet paper eventually decomposes if buried in the cat hole. The process is very slow, however, and where backcountry use is heavy you create twice the job when you bury both feces and paper. If you're in snow, you can burn paper where it lies; otherwise, it's best to take the papers back to camp for burning. Parents, alas, are usually left to bring the papers in. When in a no-fires area, carefully encase the used paper in two or three small plastic bags and place them in the litter sack. By wrapping the toilet paper in several layers, odor does not become a problem.

Fires

Campfires are not always appropriate. With children, a cooking fire is slow and inefficient, and a prolonged fire creates a campsite hazard, especially for the very young. All campfires make gear and clothing sooty.

Woodland lakes that can be reached by gentle trails and flat ocean beaches are ideal destinations for family hikes. In many ocean areas, especially in the West, beaches are covered with driftwood. The amount of downed wood in these areas makes a fire no drain on the environment. Rivers and lakes in heavily wooded areas also can support fire use, especially when you gather wood from below the high-water level.

Bare ground away from lake shores and stream banks is the best place for a fire. Never build a fire on a grassy or meadowy spot. Where there are vast banks of driftwood, be sure to keep your fire safely away from dry wood. Use an existing fire circle unless its location is inappropriate.

By explaining to children your reasons for building fires only in certain carefully chosen places you plant the seeds for their eventual understanding of light wilderness use. When you only use a stove, tell why the area will not support fires. In a high alpine area, youngsters can see how tiny and misshapen the trees are and how widely spaced. They do not know about the short growing season or the trees' struggle to survive, but you can explain this. Our children have always been fascinated by the fact that an alpine fir only slightly taller than they are can be well over a hundred years old.

Land managers have closed many popular, heavily used areas to fires. When you go to such a place, tell youngsters the specific reasons no fires are permitted in the region. In heavy woods where sites are stripped of downed wood, explain that rangers are trying to keep people from destroying live trees. In a beautiful but wood-stripped lake region I once saw a misguided visitor climb 30 feet into a Douglas-fir and lop off branches (not necessarily dead ones) for his firewood.

Even when fires are permitted, if you reach a site that looks as if someone meticulously swept away every scrap and chip of wood, use your stove and forget the fire. To have this choice, however, you must always carry along your backcountry stove and an adequate fuel supply. After visiting an area that obviously should be closed to fires, write to the land manager and suggest strongly that a no-fires policy be adopted. Be specific. Give exact locations and describe the damaged state of the sites you observed.

WHEN AND WHERE TO HAVE A FIRE

Family cooking fires are inefficient; they are dangerous, too, since youngsters are on the move before and after meals. To have a safe campfire, wait until your children are just about ready to settle down for the night. Call this your relaxing fire and establish it as a quiet family time. By early evening the temperature drops in many locations, and a fire can provide a circle of warmth for the family. Stories around a campfire are wonderful. If you are a singing family, this is a fine time for quiet songs. There is a certain hypnotic quality to an evening fire that caps off a busy day perfectly.

Fires are appropriate for drying off after a storm too. Although crawling into a sleeping bag in a secure tent can warm you faster, you can dry clothes and raise spirits with a fire. For extended stretches of bad weather, a fire under an extra-high rigged tarp makes a cozy shelter.

Always build a small fire. A roaring conflagration does nothing more than send sparks flying and force the family away from the fire. Sparks can riddle nylon gear with holes

too. For safety, establish strict, well-enforced rules for be-
havior around the fire. A fire circle is no place for roughhousing. It is a good place for storytelling, word games,
and singing. A small fire in a protected spot gives ample
heat if you bundle your children in layers of warm clothing.
A fire takes the damp chill off; it does not replace warm
clothes.

Always use old fire circles if they are in appropriate
places. If someone set up a circle just inches from a lake or
in the grass right next to the campsite, take a few minutes
to dismantle that circle and cover the blackened scar so
that no one will use the spot in the future. Be sure the circle
you choose is not too near your equipment or your tent
and that it is away from overhanging branches that could
be injured by heat or flame. Do not place plastic containers
close to a cooking fire. They melt.

MARSHMALLOWS AND HOT DOGS

Never cut green sticks for hot dog or marshmallow cooking. Instead, find among the dead, downed wood an ap-
propriately long stick. Youngsters can hold the stick high
above the fire, using the heat to roast rather than the
flames. Children rarely like charred food anyway. You
could carry along a few light, long-handled forks for roasting purposes.

CHILDREN AND HELP WITH THE FIRE

Although you must be cautious, children can be allowed
to help with the campfire. They make excellent wood gatherers. Do not, however, send youngsters off to gather wood
on their own; go with them. Tell your youngsters that the
only usable wood is already down on the forest floor. It is
detached from growing things, and it is dead. Explain, too,
that taking stump wood for fuel destroys the homes of
some little creatures and the food sites of others.

The smaller the child, the smaller the wood pieces he or
she can collect. Very little ones can gather tinder. Older

children can be taught about the need for different-sized pieces and can help arrange the wood in progressively larger sizes ready for use by the fire circle.

Fires light best with some form of fire-starter. Candle stubs and solid fuel in tablet form both work well. An older child can help with lighting the fire. At about 10 years of age youngsters are patient enough to start the kindling and gradually add larger pieces of wood. Be sure you supervise the lighting and enforce strict fire safety rules. Never, under any circumstances, should youngsters be allowed to think that fire building is play. It is serious business, and they must be mature enough to accept that fact before you enlist their help.

EXTINGUISHING FIRES

Even young children can help put out a campfire. They love to do it. When you are packing for departure, leave out containers for toting water. Douse the fire area thoroughly. Your children can do this job effectively. The touch test determines whether a fire circle has been adequately doused: if you can put your hand flat on the ground where the fire has burned and on the surrounding rocks, your job has been done correctly. Teach your children that they must carry and apply enough water on the fire to meet the touch test.

LITTERED FIRE CIRCLES

If you arrive at a campsite and find fire circles that are littered with unburnables, orange peels, aluminum foil, and food scraps, you immediately see why you must clean out your own fire circle and pack out the charred trash. Once your fire has been doused, collect any garbage or trash for the litter bag. Better yet, do not try to burn the unburnable. Deposit these items in the litter bag to begin with and save yourself the chore of picking through the ashes.

You help restore the natural setting if you clean up other people's messy fire circles when you find them. Your stay at the site will be more pleasant too; after all, no one wants to camp near someone else's garbage pit. If your children help with this task, they quickly discover why you do not toss unburnables into a fire.

General Trash

Never bury unburnables. Everything, *absolutely everything*, that you cannot burn must be packed out. With youngsters, watch for tiny items that get dropped accidentally.

Establish at the outset of your first trip how important it is to use the litter bag. My youngsters seem to be more careful in the out-of-doors than they are at home, which says something for establishing rules in definite, undisputable terms. Although the litterbug theme wears thin on adults, it catches the fancy of children. Our youngsters have grown to believe that being a litterbug is one of the worst things that can happen, and we have encouraged that attitude.

At a new campsite, have the entire family check the area and pick up after previous visitors who have been careless. Children like to do this, especially when Mom and Dad are involved. If youngsters are slow to enjoy such cleaning up, a special treat may increase their enthusiasm.

Litter bags always should be handy, on the trail and in camp. Some people carry a small bag for trail trash. A small stuffsack with a drawstring can hold the usual non-messy bits and pieces from a day's walk. Tied to a parent's belt or pack frame, it is easy to reach and use. If your family group divides into fast and slow walkers or separates to ride in two boats, make sure both groups have a litter bag.

Plastic fish bags make handy, large litter sacks. Heavier bags last through many trips; you can wash them out and reuse them. Keep the bags in storage with the rest of your gear to avoid leaving them behind.

The litter you pack out is not heavy compared to the

load you carried in. On your way out of a backcountry no-fires area, you might come across a fire circle in an area where fires are permitted. You could burn your trash there. Be sure you soak the ashes and pick out anything not completely burned before you leave.

If your children are wearing disposable diapers, never bury the paper parts of the diapers. Any time you bury something, water can wash away the dirt covering or animals can dig up what you conceal; besides, buried diaper paper decomposes very slowly. To pack out disposable diapers without an unpleasant smell, package wet diapers individually in plastic and then carry them out in a large, durable plastic bag—or even two such bags. Wet diapers are heavy. If carrying out soiled disposable diapers seems like too much trouble, you might use cloth diapers or perhaps your family should wait until children are out of diapers before taking overnight trips (see Chapter 4, "Diapers" section).

No-Waste Cooking

To help leave campsites as you found them, it is essential to cook the right amounts of food, and no more, at each meal. When you cook too much food, you face the problem of what to do with leftovers. If you dump them, you introduce garbage near the camp. Small animals may carry off the waste, but you also invite larger wildlife with this kind of dumping. No animal is helped by being fed people foods. If everyone who comes to a site dumps their extra food, the entire atmosphere can become unsavory.

The first step in avoiding garbage is to plan carefully. With children's unpredictable appetites, cook minimum amounts for first helpings to see how everyone eats. Save the uncooked extras. If children are ravenous, take the extras and cook them on request only. To handle leftover food that has not been rehydrated, carry small plastic sacks or sandwich bags and wire ties or rubber bands to secure the package ends. Cooking in this manner may stretch out the length of your meals, but you avoid unnecessary garbage.

Although not a particularly pleasant alternative, you can pack out garbage the same way that you pack out other litter. If you are in a location where fires are appropriate, some waste food can be burned. The only time that small quantities of garbage can be buried without harm is when you are in a totally out-of-the-way place, and then only far from the campsite. Since the places most parents take youngsters are accessible to others too, no-waste cooking is an especially important camping policy.

Cleaning Up After Meals

Cleaning up after meals is one way children can share the work of family camping. They can learn to wash dishes and pots. With a small child you can instill pride in doing a fair share of the work, and this attitude will grow as the youngster becomes more able to help.

When your children clean up, teach them how to wash dishes without harming the environment. The soap you use should be biodegradable. After you heat some water, take your dishwashing equipment (a small sponge will do for most items; for scrubbing, an abrasive pad with no internal cleanser works well) and your dishes away from any water sources. If you are economizing on pots, pour soapy water into each dish and wipe or scrub. If you carry a pot especially for dishwashing, each person can take a turn washing his or her utensils. When all the dishes are washed, carry some rinse water to your washing area and wash off the soap. Be sure soapy water does not drain into water sources.

When you are done, dump the dirty dishwater away from your campsite and any water sources. Remember that there are tiny food particles in the water, so you do not want the water around camp. For large particles, strain off the water and put the food residue into the litter bag. When you are extra careful with waste food, you do your part to keep campsites wild and natural and you help keep wildlife from becoming camp pests.

Breaking Camp

Teach your children to leave the natural setting as it was when you found it. If a campsite has been carelessly used, your children can help you to clean up after others.

Children like to help break camp. Allow plenty of time to do a good job. Go through the necessary steps slowly, explaining to your youngsters what you are doing and why.

Children do not have to be very old to understand that each person doing a tiny bit of damage eventually can add up to a great deal of damage. Although your tent makes just eight stake holes, after 100 people have camped at the site there will be at least 800 holes. Youngsters can help fill in stake holes and scatter stones, leaves, and twigs back where they were. Children enjoy the challenge of trying to erase evidence of their visit.

Youngsters are attracted to little things. Take advantage of that fact when you check for litter around camp. A child often finds plastic bag wires, tiny corners of candy wrappers, and buried bottle caps that an adult does not notice. With several children along, a pickup contest with treats for all participants and a prize for the child who collects the most trash can help emphasize the importance of tidying the campsite.

Once the family is finished cleaning up, an adult must be responsible for one last look around. Be sure that you leave nothing behind.

Epilogue

EVERY FAMILY TRIP to the backcountry should be enjoyable. You want to enjoy your children, the camping, the unhurried pace, and the natural setting. I once camped with a group of adults near some beautiful alpine lakes. For six days and nights it rained, sleeted, snowed, and then rained some more. On the third day a family of two adults, two children, and a very drippy, long-haired dog wandered up the trail through the fog and set up camp on a knoll just out of sight. They were our distant neighbors for two days, during which time the rains continued unabated. My strongest memory of this family, though, is the laughter that periodically rolled down from their hilltop campsite and punctuated those dreary, rain-sodden days with cheer. These campers were making the best of a situation that was anything but ideal. No family camping trip is perfect—some are less perfect than others—but you can still enjoy.

Carelessness has no place on family trips to the wilderness. Prevention is the best way to cope with potential difficulties. You must know what you are doing and never take any chances with your youngsters' safety. Thoughtful planning requires just a little extra effort. The time spent getting ready and checking gear and wilderness essentials helps guarantee a safe trip for the entire family.

The wilderness is fragile; it will not survive abuse. You must, therefore, learn to use it lightly and gently. When you take children into the backcountry, you become their teacher and must pass on the fundamentals of low-impact camping. The careful steps taken by each person in your family help to preserve the wildlands for future generations of backcountry users.

As you turn your head or sneeze, commercially made outdoor products change or vanish from the market. Do not become frustrated; instead, see what you can devise to make do for your youngsters. You save money this way and have the satisfaction of fashioning gear that really suits your needs, something that ready-made equipment often fails to do.

Finally, no book has all the answers. Consider what you have read a starting point and then go on from there to devise ways of going into the outdoors that suit your particular family. Every camping family develops its own clever ways for making the backcountry experience possible and fun for children. I encountered one parent who had hand-crafted a papoose rack for baby carrying; another family had rigged a frame carrier on top of a regular backpack to haul a toddler. Finding answers for yourself definitely adds to the pleasure derived from sharing the wilderness with your children.

The backcountry is waiting for you. Once you have acquired sufficient wilderness skills and experience, you and your family can begin to enjoy backcountry experiences together.

Appendix

Reading

Books and magazines about the outdoors help to prepare you for trips into the backcountry. These sources also keep you aware of issues relating to the conservation and survival of the remaining wilderness. Reading, however, cannot replace practical experience in the field.

MAGAZINES

Adventure Travel, P.O. Box 7564, Red Oak, Iowa 51591-2564

The Amicus Journal, Natural Resources Defense Council Publication, 40 West 20th Street, New York, New York 10011

Audubon, Membership Center, P.O. Box 52529, Boulder, Colorado 80322, 800-274-4201

Backcountry, P.O. Box 7564, Red Oak, Iowa 51591-2564

Backpacker, P.O. Box 7564, Red Oak, Iowa 51591-2564

Backpacker Footnotes, P.O. Box 7564, Red Oak, Iowa 51591-2564

Bicycle Guide, P.O. Box 52712, Boulder, Colorado 80322, 800-825-0484

Cross Country Skier, 1823 Fremont Avenue South, Minneapolis, Minnesota 55403

Escape, 2525 Beverly Street, Santa Monica, California 90405

Nature Conservancy, 1815 North Lynn Street, Arlington, Virginia 22209, 703-841-5300

Outside Kids, Mariah Media, Outside Plaza, 400 Market Street, Santa Fe, New Mexico 87501

Paddler, 4061 Oceanside Boulevard, Suite M, Oceanside, California 92056, 800-752-7951

Sierra, Sierra Club Magazine, 730 Polk Street, San Francisco, California 94109

Signpost for Northwest Trails, 1305 Fourth Avenue, Suite 512, Seattle, Washington 98101-2401

Summit, 1221 May Street, Hood River, Oregon 97031, 503-307-2200

The Walking Magazine, P.O. Box 56561, Boulder, Colorado 80322

Wilderness Camping, P.O. Box 7564, Red Oak, Iowa 51591-2564

BOOKS

Bennett, Jeff. *Rafting: The Complete Guide to Whitewater Rafting Techniques and Equipment.* Portland, OR: Swiftwater, 1993.

Bennett, Steve, and Bennett, Ruth. *365 Outdoor Activities You Can Do with Your Child.* Holbrook, MA: Bob Adams, 1993.

Brown, Tom. *Tom Brown's Field Guide to Nature and Survival for Children.* New York: Berkley Books, 1989.

Burton, Joan. *Best Hikes with Children in Western Washington and the Cascades.* 2 vols. Seattle: The Mountaineers, 1988.

Cook, Charles. *The Essential Guide to Hiking in the United States.* New York: Michael Kesend, 1992.

Darvill, Fred T., Jr. *Mountaineering Medicine: A Wilderness Medical Guide.* Berkeley, CA: Wilderness Press, 1992.

Dowd, John. *Sea Kayaking.* Seattle: University of Washington Press, 1988.

Fleming, June. *The Well Fed Backpacker.* New York: Vintage Books, 1986.

Fletcher, Colin. *The New Complete Walker.* New York: Knopf, 1993.

Forgey, William, M.D. *Wilderness Medicine, Beyond First Aid.* 4th ed. Merrillville, IN: ICS Books, 1994.

Gillette, Ned, and Dostal, John. *Cross Country Skiing*. Seattle: The Mountaineers, 1988.

Gorman, Stephen. *AMC Guide to Winter Camping*. Boston: Appalachian Mountain Club Books, 1991.

Harrison, David, and Harrison, Judy. *Canoe Tripping with Children*. Merrillville, IN: ICS Books, 1990.

Hart, John. *Walking Softly in the Wilderness*. San Francisco: Sierra Club Books, 1984.

Hodgson, Michael. *Wilderness with Children*. Harrisburg, PA: Stackpole Books, 1992.

Kjellstrom, Bjorn. *Be Expert with Map and Compass*. New York: Scribner's, 1976.

LaChapelle, Edward. *ABC of Avalanche Safety*. Boulder, CO: Highlander Publishing, 1985.

MacManiman, Gen. *Dry It, You'll Like It*. Fall City, WA: MacManiman, 1992.

Manning, Harvey. *Backpacking, One Step at a Time*. New York: Vantage Books, 1985.

McKown, Doug. *Canoeing Safety and Rescue*. Calgary, Alberta: Rocky Mountain Books, 1992.

Prater, Gene. *Snowshoeing*. Seattle: The Mountaineers, 1988.

Prater, Yvonne, and Dyar, Ruth. *Gorp, Glop, and Glue Stew*. Seattle: The Mountaineers, 1991.

Randall, Glen. *The Outward Bound Map and Compass Handbook*. New York: Lyons and Burford, 1989.

Schatz, Curt, and Seemon, Dan. *A Basic Guide to Minimum Impact Camping*. Cambridge, MN: Adventure Publications, 1994.

Schimelpfenig, Tod, and Lindsey, Linda. *NOLS Wilderness First Aid*. Lander, WY: NOLS and Stackpole Books, 1991.

Silverman, Goldie. *Backpacking with Babies and Small Children*. Berkeley, CA: Wilderness Press, 1994.

Sumner, Louise Lindgren. *Sew and Repair Your Outdoor Gear*. Seattle: The Mountaineers, 1988.

van der Plas, Rob. *The Bicycle Touring Manual*. San Francisco: Bicycle Books, 1993.

Waterman, Laura, and Waterman, Guy. *Backwoods Ethics*. Woodstock, VT: The Country Press, 1993.

Topographic Maps

United States, east of the Mississippi:
  US Geological Survey
  1200 South Eads Street
  Arlington, Virginia 22202
United States, west of the Mississippi:
  US Geological Survey
  Federal Center
  Denver, Colorado 80225
Canada:
  Department of Energy, Mines, and Resources
  615 Booth Street
  Ottawa, Ontario, Canada K1A 0E9

Wilderness Travel and Conservation Organizations

National organizations can supply you with a list of their local chapters.

American Hiking Society, P.O. Box 20160, Washington, DC 20041-2160

Appalachian Mountain Club, 5 Joy Street, Boston, Massachusetts 02108

Appalachian Trail Conference, P.O. Box 236, Harpers Ferry, West Virginia 25425

Federation of Western Outdoor Clubs, 4534 University Way NE, Seattle, Washington 98105

The Mountaineers, 300 Third Avenue West, Seattle, Washington 98119, 206-284-6310

Mount Rainier National Park Associates, 15242 SE 48th, Bellevue, Washington 98006

National Audubon Society, 950 Third Avenue, New York, New York 10022

The Nature Conservancy, 1815 North Lynn Street, Arlington, Virginia 22209, 703-841-5300

New England Trail Conference, P.O. Box 145, Weston, Vermont 05161

Pacific Crest Trail Association, P.O. Box 1048, Seattle, Washington 98111

Sierra Club, 730 Polk Street, San Francisco, California 94109
The Washington Trails Association, 1305 Fourth Avenue, Suite
    512, Seattle, Washington 98101-2401, 206-625-1367
Wilderness Society, 1901 Pennsylvania Avenue NW, Washing-
    ton, DC 20006

Land Management Agencies

Land management agencies can supply you with the addresses of
land managers in the areas you want to visit.

Bureau of Land Management
    Office of Information
    Department of the Interior
    Washington, DC 20240
National Park Service
    Department of the Interior
    Washington, DC 20240
US Fish and Wildlife Service
    Department of the Interior
    Washington, DC 20240
US Forest Service
    Department of Agriculture
    Washington, DC 20250

Gear Suppliers

Listed here are the names, addresses, and phone numbers of
many major outdoor gear suppliers. On request they will send
you mail-order catalogues or tell you where to find their products
in or near your community. Keep in mind that suppliers' locations may change; outdoor magazines can provide you with up-
to-date mailing addresses.

•• *Indicates products made for or suitable for children.*

Adidas America, 541 NE 20th Street, Suite 207, Portland, Ore-
    gon 97232, 800-423-4327
Adventure Foods, Route 2, Box 276, Whittier, North Carolina
    28789, 704-497-4113; catalogue available
Adventure Outfitters, RR 2, Box 3452, Elmore Mountain Road,

Morrisville, Vermont 05661, 800-544-7004; catalogue available

Alico Sport, P.O. Box 165, Beebe Plain, Vermont 05823, 514-937-2320; catalogue available

•• Alpina Sports Corporation, P.O. Box 23, Hanover, New Hampshire 03755, 603-448-3101

American Trails, P.O. Drawer G, Haleyville, Alabama 35565, 800-221-7452; catalogue available

Arc Teryx, No. 2 1440 Columbia Street, North Vancouver, British Columbia, Canada V7J 1A2, 604-985-6681; catalogue available

Asolo/Nordica USA, Inc., 139 Harvest Lane, Williston, Vermont 05495, 800-862-2668; catalogue available

Athena/Aervoe-Pacific Company, 1198 Sawmill Road, Gardnerville, Nevada 89410, 800-227-0196; catalogue available

Backpacker's Pantry, 6350 Gunpark Drive, Boulder, Colorado 80301, 800-253-8283; catalogue available

Bibler Tents, 5441-D Western Avenue, Boulder, Colorado 80301, 303-449-7351; catalogue available

•• Bike Nashbar, 4111 Simon Road, Youngstown, Ohio 44512-1343, 800-NASHBAR; catalogue available

•• Burley Design Cooperative, Bicycling, 4080 Stewart Road, Eugene, Oregon 97402, 800-423-8445

•• Campmor, Box 700-T, Saddle River, New Jersey 07458-0700, 800-CAMPOR; catalogue available

•• Camp Trails/Johnson Camping Inc., P.O. Box 966, Binghamton, New York 13902, 800-848-3673; catalogue available

•• Cariboo Mountaineering Inc., P.O. Box 3696, Chico, California 95927, 800-824-4153; catalogue available

•• Cascade Designs, Inc., 4000 First Avenue South, Seattle, Washington 98134, 800-531-9531; catalogue available

Chinook Medical Gear, Inc., 2805 Wilderness Place, Suite 700, Boulder, Colorado 80301, 800-766-1365; catalogue available

Dana Design, 1950 North 19th Street, Bozeman, Montana 59715, 406-587-4188; catalogue available

Danner Shoe Manufacturing Company, P.O. Box 30148, Portland, Oregon 97230, 800-345-0430; catalogue available

Design Salt, P.O. Box 2106, Redway, California 95560, 707-923-4605; catalogue available

Dexter Shoe Company, 1230 Washington Street West, Newton, Massachusetts 02165, 207-924-5444

Diamond Brand Canvas Products, Inc., P.O. Box 249, Naples, North Carolina 28760, 800-258-9811; catalogue available

Early Winters, P.O. Box 4333, Portland, Oregon 97208-4333, 800-458-4438; catalogue available

•• Eastern Mountain Sports, One Vose Farm Road, Peterborough, New Hampshire 03458, 603-924-6154

EpiGas/Taymar Inc., 2755 South 160th Street, New Berlin, Wisconsin 53151, 800-776-7189; catalogue available

•• Equinox Industries Inc., 35722 Ross Lane, Cottage Grove, Oregon 97424, 800-942-7895; bicycling

Eureka! Johnson Camping Inc., P.O. Box 966, Binghamton, New York 13902, 800-848-3673; catalogue available

Explore by Modan, 435 R. Hartford Turnpike, Vernon, Connecticut 06066, 800-755-1797; catalogue available

Feathered Friends, 2013 Fourth Avenue, Seattle, Washington 98107, 206-443-9549; catalogue available

Folbot, Inc., P.O. Box 70877, Charleston, South Carolina 29415, 800-528-9592; catalogue available

Garuda, P.O. Box 24804, Seattle, Washington 98124-0804, 206-763-2989; catalogue available

•• Gerry Baby Products Company, 150 East 128th Avenue, Thornton, Colorado 80220, 800-525-2472; catalogue available

Grade VI, P.O. Box 8, Urbana, Illinois 61801, 217-328-6666; catalogue available

Gregory Mountain Products, 100 Calle Cortez, Temecula, California 92590, 800-477-3420; catalogue available

•• Hi-Tech Sports USA, Inc., 4801 Stoddard Road, Modesto, California 95356, 800-521-1698; catalogue available

Integral Designs Inc., 5516 3rd Street SE, Calgary, Alberta, Canada T2H 1J9, 403-640-1445; catalogue available

•• Jack Wolfskin, 920 Mendocino Avenue, Santa Rosa, California 95401, 607-779-2755; catalogue available

•• JanSport, 10411 Airport Road, Everett, Washington 98204, 800-552-6776

•• Kelty, Inc., 1224 Fern Ridge Parkway, Creve Coeur, Missouri 63141, 800-423-2320; catalogue available

Klepper America, 168 Kinderkamack Road, Park Ridge, New Jersey 07656, 201-476-0700

Lafuma USA, P.O. Box 812, Farmington, Georgia 30638, 706-769-6627; catalogue available

Liberty Mountain Sports/Advanced Base Camp, 9325 S.W. Barber Street, Wilsonville, Oregon 97070, 800-366-2666

•• L. L. Bean, Freeport, Maine 04033, 800-221-4221; catalogue available

Louisiana Data Products Inc., 1101 NW Evangeline Thruway, Lafayette, Louisiana 70501, 800-826-5767; catalogue available

Lowe Alpine, 1062 East Tabernacle, St. George, Utah 84770, 800-726-8106; catalogue available

Madden USA, 2400 Central Avenue, Boulder, Colorado 80301, 303-442-5828; catalogue available

Mad River Canoe, Box 610, Waitsfield, Vermont 05673, 800-843-8985; catalogue available

Markill/Bergsport International, P.O. Box 1519, Nederland, Colorado 80466, 303-258-3796; catalogue available

•• Marmot Mountain Works, 827 Bellevue Way NE, Bellevue, Washington 98004, 206-453-1515; catalogue available

McHale and Company, 29 Dravus Street, Seattle, Washington 98109, 206-281-7861; catalogue available

•• Merrell Footwear, P.O. Box 4249, Burlington, Vermont 05402, 800-869-3348; catalogue available

MontBell America, 940 41st Avenue, Santa Cruz, California 95062, 800-541-2015; catalogue available

•• Moonstone Mountaineering, 5350 Ericson Way, Arcata, California 95521, 707-822-2985; catalogue available

Moss, Inc., P.O. Box 309, Camden, Maine 04843, 207-236-8368; catalogue available

Mountain Equipment, Inc., 4776 East Jensen, Fresno, California 93725, 209-486-8211; catalogue available

Mountain Peak Outfitters, 323 East Gay Street, West Chester, Pennsylvania 19380, 800-251-0138; catalogue available

Mountain Safety Research, P.O. Box 24547, 4225 Second Avenue South, Seattle, Washington 98121, 800-877-9MSR

Mountainsmith, Inc., 18301 West Colfax Avenue, Heritage

Square, Building P, Golden, Colorado 80401, 800-551-5889;
catalogue available

Mountain Tools, 140 Calle Del Oaks, Monterey, California
93940, 408-393-1000; catalogue available

Natural Balance Design, P.O. Box 1573, Fairfield, Iowa 52556,
515-472-7918; catalogue available

Nike, Inc., One Bowerman Drive, Beaverton, Oregon 97005-
6453, 503-671-3939

•• Nordic Track, 104 Peavey Road, Chaska, Minnesota 55318-
2355, 800-445-2606; catalogue available

Northern Lights, Inc., P.O. Box 3413, Mammoth Lakes, California 93546, 619-924-3833; catalogue available

The North Face, 999 Harrison Street, Berkeley, California
94710, 510-527-9700; catalogue available

Northlake Outdoor Footwear, P.O. Box 10, Franklin, Tennessee
37068, 615-794-1556; catalogue available

•• Northwest River Supplies, Inc., 2009 South Main Street, Mos-
cow, Idaho 83843-8948, 800-635-5202; catalogue available

One Sport Inc., 1003 Sixth Avenue South, Seattle, Washington
98134, 206-621-9303; catalogue available

•• One Step Ahead, P.O. Box 517, Lake Bluff, Illinois 60044, 800-
274-8440; catalogue available

•• The Original Bug Shirt Company, 908 Niagara Falls Boulevard, Suite 467, North Tonawanda, New York 14120-2060,
705-729-5602; catalogue available

Osprey Packs, P.O. Box 539, Dolores, Colorado 81323, 303-882-
2221; catalogue available

•• Outbound, 1580 Zephyr Street, Hayward, California 94544,
800-866-9880; catalogue available

Outdoor Outlet, 1062 East Tabernacle, St. George, Utah 84770,
800-726-8106; catalogue available

Overland Equipment, 2145 Park Avenue, Suite 4, Chico, California 95928, 916-894-5605

•• Pacific Water Sports, 16055 Pacific Highway South, Seattle,
Washington 98188, 206-246-9385

•• Paddle and Pack Outfitters, Inc., P.O. Box 50299, Nashville,
Tennessee 37205, 800-786-5565; catalogue available

•• Patagonia, 1609 West Babcock Street, P.O. Box 8900, Bozeman, Montana 59715, 800-638-6464; catalogue available

Peak 1/Coleman Company, Inc., P.O. Box 2931, Wichita, Kansas 67201, 800-835-3278; catalogue available

Premier International Inc., 901 North Stuart Street, Suite 804, Arlington, Virginia 22203, 703-524-6464; catalogue available

Quest, 569 Charcot Avenue, San Jose, California 95131, 800-875-6901; catalogue available

Quest Outfitters, 2590 17th Street, Box B, Sarasota, Florida 34234, 800-359-6931; catalogue available

•• Raichle Molitor USA Inc., Geneva Road, Brewster, New York 10509, 800-431-2204; catalogue available

•• Recreational Equipment Inc., 1700 45th Street East, Sumner, Washington 98390, 800-426-4840; catalogue available

Redfeather, 1280 Ute Avenue, No. 20, Aspen, Colorado 81611, 800-525-0081

Reebok International, 100 Technology Center Drive, Stoughton, Massachusetts 02072, 800-843-4444; catalogue available

•• The Right Start Catalog, 5334 Sterling Center Drive, Westlake Village, California 91361-4627, 800-LITTLE-1; catalogue available

The Rockport Company, 220 Donald Lynch Boulevard, Marlboro, Massachusetts 01752, 800-343-WALK

Safesport Manufacturing Company, 1100 West 45th Avenue, Denver, Colorado 80211, 303-433-6506

Salewa/Bergsport International, P.O. Box 1519, Nederland, Colorado 80466, 303-258-3796; catalogue available

Salomon North America, Inc., 400 East Main Street, Georgetown, Massachusetts 01833, 508-352-7600; catalogue available

Seattle Fabrics, 3876 Bridge Way North, Seattle, Washington 98103, 206-632-6022; catalogue available

Sierra Designs, 2039 Fourth Street, Berkeley, California 94710, 800-SIERRA-2

Sierra Trading Post, 5025 Campstool Road, Cheyenne, Wyoming 82007, 307-775-8000; catalogue available

•• Slumberjack, P.O. Box 7048A, St. Louis, Missouri 63177, 800-233-6283; catalogue available

Stephensons, 22 Hook Road, Gilford, New Hampshire 03246, 603-293-8526; catalogue available

Suunto USA, 2151 Las Palmas Drive, Suite G, Carlsbad, California 92009, 619-931-6788; catalogue available

•• Swallows' Nest, 2308 6th Avenue, Seattle, Washington 98121, 800-676-4041; catalogue available

•• Tecnica USA, 19 Technology Drive, West Lebanon, New Hampshire 03784, 800-258-3897; catalogue available

The Timberland Company, 11 Merrill Industrial Drive, Hampton, New Hampshire 03842, 603-926-1600

•• Tough Traveler, 1012 State Street, Schenectady, New York 12307; 800-GOTOUGH

Trail Foods Company, P.O. Box 9309, North Hollywood, California 91609, 818-897-4370; catalogue available

Ultimate Direction, 1488 North Salem Road, P.O. Box 341, Rexburg, Idaho 83440, 800-426-7229; catalogue available

Uncle John's Foods, P.O. Box 489, Fairplay, Colorado 80440, 719-836-2710; catalogue available

•• Vasque, 314 Main Street, Red Wing, Minnesota 55066, 612-388-8211; catalogue available

Voyageur, P.O. Box 207, Waitsfield, Vermont 05673, 800-843-8985; catalogue available

Walrus, P.O. Box 3875, Seattle, Washington 98124, 800-550-8368; catalogue available

Wenzel, 1224 Fern Ridge Parkway, St. Louis, Missouri 63141, 800-325-4121; catalogue available

Western Mountaineering, 1025 South Fifth Street, San Jose, California 95112, 408-287-8944; catalogue sales

Wiggy's Inc., P.O. Box 2124, Grand Junction, Colorado 81502, 303-241-6465; catalogue available

Wild Country/Journeyman, 624 Main Street, Conway, New Hampshire 03818, 603-447-1961; catalogue available

Wilderness Experience, 20727 Dearborn Street, Chatsworth, California 91311, 818-341-5774; catalogue available

Wild Things, Inc., P.O. Box 400, North Conway, New Hampshire 03860, 603-356-6907; catalogue available

•• Winchester Originals, P.O. Box 3480, LaHabra, California 90632, 800-247-9754; bicycling

Wolverine, 9341 Courtland Drive, Rockford, Michigan 49546, 616-866-5500

ZZ Corporation, 10806 Kaylor Street, Los Alamitos, California 90720, 310-598-3220; catalogue available

Checklist

To help you remember what to take along on family camping trips, keep updated checklists. Lists written on poster board are hard to lose, or you can use a notebook to keep track of your needs. As you become a more experienced camper, eliminate items that prove unworkable and add gear you want to try on future trips.

BASICS FOR FAMILY CAMPING

For shelter:
____ Tent with fly, poles, and stakes or a tarp

For sleeping:
____ Sleeping bags with stuffsacks
____ Pads
____ Extra plastic sack for rain protection

For cooking:
____ Lightweight stove
____ Fuel
____ Matches (waterproof)

____ Fire-starter
____ Pots and pans with lids
____ Pot-lifter
____ Accessoried knife
____ Collapsible water container
____ Juice bottles

For eating:
____ Plates and cups
____ Spoons, forks, and knives

For clean-up:
____ Biodegradable soap

_____ Pan scrubber and sponge

_____ Paper towels or dishtowel

For mending:

_____ Sewing needles

_____ Thread

_____ Safety pins

_____ Adhesive-backed tape

_____ Buttons

_____ Nylon cord

_____ Pack connectors (clevis pins, split rings)

Food:

_____ Basic meals

_____ Emergency extras

_____ Trail snacks

Clothes:

_____ Basic daily clothing

_____ Warm clothes

_____ Raingear

_____ In-camp footwear

Toilet articles:

_____ Hairbrush

_____ Toothbrush

_____ Toothpaste

_____ Soap

_____ Toilet paper

_____ Chapstick

Especially for babies:

_____ Bottles, nipples

_____ Diapers

_____ Rubber pants

_____ Extra basic clothes

_____ Warm clothes

_____ Rain protection

_____ Baby food

_____ Trail snacks

_____ Bottom cleaners

_____ Sun protection

_____ Bug protection

For water purification:

_____ Iodine crystals

_____ Water filter

WILDERNESS ESSENTIALS

_____ Map in waterproof plastic

_____ Compass

_____ First-aid kit

_____ Hats

_____ Sunscreen

_____ Sunglasses

_____ Bug repellent

_____ Flashlight with reversed batteries for carrying, plus extra batteries and bulb

_____ Extra clothes, especially socks

_____ Extra food

_____ Heavy jackets, child's sleeping bag

_____ Accessoried knife with scissors, tweezers, and screwdriver

_____ Matches (waterproof)

_____ Fire-starter

_____ Space blanket or garbage bags

_____ Pads

_____ Stove and fuel

For boating:

_____ Life preservers

_____ Seat cushions

_____ Waterproof bags and gear containers

_____ Extra paddles

_____ Sponges

_____ End lines

For cross-country skiing:

_____ Skis with problem-free bindings

_____ Poles

_____ Boots

_____ Gaiters

_____ Pack with ski tip, repair needs, tape, wire, and accessoried knife, ensolite pads

_____ Warm jackets

_____ Child's sleeping bag

_____ Extra gloves and socks

_____ Windbreaker and/or raingear

_____ First-aid kit

_____ Elastic bandage

_____ Sunscreen, sunglasses, hats

_____ Matches (waterproof)

_____ Fire-starter

_____ Stove and fuel

_____ Map

_____ Compass

_____ Flashlight, batteries, and bulb

_____ Space blanket or garbage bags

_____ Emergency food

_____ Trail snacks

_____ Juice bottles

_____ Waxes (if waxing), blow torch, and fuel

_____ Spray for wax removal

For bike repairs:

_____ Adjustable wrench   _____ Screwdriver

_____ Spoke wrench   _____ Chain tool

_____ Small pliers   _____ Tire patch kit

_____ Tire tools   _____ Pretrip bike check

Index